more
<library
mashups>

more <library mashups>

Exploring New Ways to Deliver Library Data

Edited by
Nicole C. Engard

Information Today, Inc.

Medford, New Jersey

First printing

More Library Mashups: Exploring New Ways to Deliver Library Data

Copyright © 2015 by Nicole C. Engard

Library of Congress Cataloging-in-Publication Data

More library mashups : exploring new ways to deliver library data / [edited by] Nicole C. Engard.
    pages cm
 Includes bibliographical references and index.
 ISBN 978-1-57387-498-4
 1. Mashups (World Wide Web)--Library applications. 2. Libraries and the Internet. 3. Library Web sites--Design. 4. Web site development. I. Engard, Nicole C., 1979-
 Z674.75.W67M67 2014
 020.285'4678--dc23

                                                                    2014033872

President and CEO: Thomas H. Hogan, Sr.
Editor-in-Chief and Publisher: John B. Bryans
Managing Editor: Amy M. Reeve
Production Manager: Norma Neimeister
Book Designer: Kara Mia Jalkowski
Cover Designer: Denise M. Erickson

infotoday.com

To my sisters, Alissa and Kristen,
for being my very first students so many years ago

Contents

Acknowledgments

I would like to thank many people for their support in bringing this second mashup of mashups together. First, I must thank all those of you who read the first edition of this book and kept asking me when we were going to provide you with more great mashup examples. Second, I must thank my colleagues at ByWater Solutions, in particular Brendan and Nate for always supporting me in whatever endeavor I choose to take on.

I'd also like to thank the many authors who contributed to this title, making a wide-reaching view of mashups for libraries. Without all of your contributions, this book wouldn't exist. Lastly, I thank my children (shelties, Coda and Beau) for their understanding while I spent more time with my computer than with them over the last year.

About the Website
mashups.web2learning.net

Each chapter in this book references websites with definitions and examples of mashups. Although links to each of these can be found in Appendix A, the web is not static, and links may move or disappear; even during the editing of this book, several have changed. For that reason, I will be maintaining mashups.web2learning.net, a website that will retain an up-to-date list of links for you to reference whenever you'd like. This website will also save you the trouble of having to type cumbersome links by hand; just visit mashups.web2learning.net and choose either the Links page or the chapter the link appeared in from the table of contents, and you will be able to click through to visit the site.

Should you notice any broken links on the site or in the book, please feel free to email me updates at nengard@gmail.com.

Disclaimer

Neither the publisher nor the editor make any claim as to the results that may be obtained through the use of this webpage or of any of the internet resources it references or links to. Neither publisher nor editor will be held liable for any results, or lack thereof, obtained by the use of this page or any of its links; for any third-party charges; or for any hardware, software, or other problems that may occur as the result of using it. This webpage is subject to change or discontinuation without notice at the discretion of the publisher and editor.

Foreword

Michael P. Sauers

I suspect that most people reading this had the same first encounter with mashups as I did, courtesy of a gentleman by the name of H.B. Reese. His name may not be immediately recognizable to you but the product he invented in 1928 probably is: the Reese's Peanut Butter Cup.

My next encounter with the world of mashups was in 2004 with the release of Danger Mouse's *The Grey Album*. This masterpiece is the result of combining The Beatles' *The White Album* with Jay Z's *The Black Album*. It was with this that I learned of the term *mashup*, defined as the combining of two separate yet distinctive musical sources, to create a third, new musical composition. To this day, I still enjoy listening to musical mashups, especially those containing content that I'm already familiar with and content that I wouldn't normally listen to. Probably the best example of this would be 2008's *American Edit* by Dean Gray, a combination of Green Day's *American Idiot* album with other works, ranging from the *Doctor Who* theme music to Johnny Cash, just to name a couple.

Then, in 2009, mashups dropped into my work life with Nicole Engard's 2009 book *Library Mashups: Exploring New Ways to Deliver Library Data*. With her book, I learned that, beyond food and music, you could mashup data. And, since we're librarians, if we've got nothing else, we've got access to vast amounts of data. What I also learned is that data mashups don't have to be hard; you just need to know where the data is and what tools are available.

However, when it comes to mashups, you also have to have the "idea," and for many of us that's the hard part. Just because you have the tools and the data doesn't mean you automatically know what to do with them. Sure, before 2008, I'd listened to *American Idiot* many times and had previously heard lots of other music too—especially the *Doctor Who* theme. I also had a copy of the audio editing program Audacity. That doesn't mean I realized what I could create with that data and tool.

What I love about *More Library Mashups* is that not only are the contributors giving me more data and more tools to play with, they're giving me ideas and inspiring me to look at the resources at hand a certain way—to ask "If I took this and that, what could I turn it into?"

Keep that question in mind as you read the chapters of this wonderful book. Don't just focus on the exact projects as presented; rather at the end of each one ask yourself, "What can I do with this?" Take that inspiration, along with the tools and data, go forth, and start mashing!

Introduction

Nicole C. Engard

Whenever I give a talk about mashups, I like to start with a picture of s'mores. It's the most delicious type of mashup. The term *mashup* didn't originate with the s'more though; it started in the music industry, as a reference to mixing two or more songs together in various ways. For the purposes of this book, a mashup has to do with taking data from multiple sources and mixing the data together to provide better services for library patrons.

If you read *Library Mashups*, the precursor to this book, then you probably learned a lot of great ways to mash up your data. My favorite mashup from the first book—if an editor is allowed to choose a favorite—is that of Delicious (delicious.com) with a website. I used Delicious to bookmark all of the links found for this book (delicious. com/nengard/mash2nd) and for all the books I've written, so that I can generate easy-to-access pages of links for your reference. All it took was a consistent taxonomy and a little snippet of JavaScript provided by Delicious. For example, to get the links from Chapter 1, I just pasted

```
<script type="text/javascript" src="http://
feeds.delicious.com/v2/js/nengard/mash2ndch1?
title=&count=200&sort=alpha"></script>
```

onto the links page. To learn about how you can use Delicious in this way, check out Chapter 5 by Brian Herzog in *Library Mashups*.

In *More Library Mashups*, I bring together some familiar names and many new ones to share all new tips, tutorials, and stories of how libraries are using mashups. Some are as simple as copying a snippet of code while others are a bit more complex, but all are fascinating reads and will kickstart your creativity for mashing up your own library resources.

Part I begins with a few introductory chapters—some basic mashups that anyone can do with just the knowledge of a few simple web applications. These will introduce you to IFTTT (ifttt.com), a tool that allows you to pull in data from many sources to make content delivery and publication easy; ArcGIS (arcgis.com), a mapping application that makes map mashups easy; OpenRefine (openrefine.org), a tool for working with messy data; and Umlaut (github.com/team-umlaut/umlaut), a just-in-time aggregator of "last mile" specific-citation services (you'll have to read more to learn what that means).

Part II introduces you to various ways to enhance your library website with outside data. The authors in this section will help you integrate outside tools such as cover images, event calendars, subject guides, and social networks into your library website to give your patrons a one-stop shop for information. Some of these mashups require a bit of programming knowledge, while for others, it's just a matter of finding the right widgets for the job. Whatever the case, the authors give you all the tools you need to get the job done.

In Part III, experts will walk you through ways to create mashups with your library catalog data. Five years ago, the hardest mashup to achieve was the catalog data mashup, and things have not really changed much, but that doesn't stop us from trying. Learn how to answer reference questions on Twitter with a bot and present library information on a map. Explore an interactive physical device that lets users do anything from looking up and exploring library books to finding top stories on Wikipedia and delivering them alongside library holdings information.

Part IV takes you from the textual to the visual, through creating timelines and maps, and sharing pictures from your library. Visualizations are some of the most obvious types of mashups; in fact, the most common type of mashup listed on ProgrammableWeb (programmableweb.com) is the map mashup (Figure I.1).

Finally, Part V will cover general ways to add value to library services, including BookMeUp (lib.montana.edu/beta/bookme) and Serendip-o-matic (serendipomatic.org), two tools that help you find library resources; SearchWorks at Stanford (searchworks.stanford.edu) for finding information in any library collection; Yahoo! Pipes (pipes.yahoo.com) for mashing news sources together; and Libki (libki.org) and MarcEdit (marcedit.reeset.net), each with Koha (koha-community.org), for providing better data and services

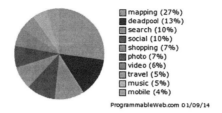

mapping (27%)
deadpool (13%)
search (10%)
social (10%)
shopping (7%)
photo (7%)
video (6%)
travel (5%)
music (5%)
mobile (4%)

ProgrammableWeb.com 01/09/14

Figure I.1 Top mashup tags on ProgrammableWeb

for your patrons. It also shows you how to use various data sources to generate a current awareness service.

Besides directing you to online tools to help you mash up data at your library, I hope *More Library Mashups* sparks your imagination. The contributors and I would love to hear from you after you've read the book, so contact information is provided in the About the Contributors and About the Editor sections at the end of the book. A website with links to resources in the book and stories from our readers will also be maintained at mashups.web2learning.net.

Part I

The Basics

## CHAPTER 1

IFTTT Makes Data Play Easy

Gary Green
Surrey County Council Public Library Service

IFTTT (If This Then That; ifttt.com) is a free online service that can be used to automate the collection, manipulation, mashing, and sharing of data and information across a range of online sites and services without any knowledge of APIs or computer programming. The only thing you need to make use of the service is an IFTTT account. In addition to explaining how IFTTT works, this chapter will provide practical examples of how it can be used.

How IFTTT Works

IFTTT can be used to share data across more than 90 sites and services (referred to as channels). IFTTT channels (ifttt.com/channels) make the discovery and sharing of data easier and less time consuming, since users do not have to visit each site individually and log in to either pull out or share the data.

The types of services available in IFTTT include:

- Social networks

- Bookmarking sites

- Image, video, and audio sharing sites

- Blogging services

- Document storage and collaboration

- Email and messaging services
- Date, time, weather, and stock alerts

Using these channels, you can coordinate your data sharing from a single place, with options to: (1) perform the same or similar tasks in a variety of locations, (2) perform the same tasks in the same place on a regular basis, and (3) re-use information in different places.

Many of the channels offered by IFTTT are used by libraries, including Blogger, Delicious, Diigo, Dropbox, Evernote, Facebook, Flickr, Gmail, Google Calendar, Google Drive, HootSuite, Instagram, LinkedIn, Pinboard, Pocket, Tumblr, Twitter, Vimeo, WordPress, and YouTube. IFTTT can connect with SMS messaging, weather, date alerts, and remote controlled services. There is also a dedicated RSS channel, so users can access any service with an RSS output, even if it doesn't have a dedicated channel on IFTTT.

The main purpose of IFTTT is to allow users to push data from one channel to another. It gives the user some control over how that data is pushed to the receiving service. Users can tweak the data by defining which fields are shared, can leave out unwanted information, and can add their own data as part of the collection process.

In most cases, you will be required to authorize IFTTT to access your accounts on any channels you are using. This enables IFTTT to do things like identify when you've posted an update to your social networks and post information to your accounts based upon the actions you ask it to perform.

IFTTT uses some unique terminology, which is worth highlighting before getting into the intricacies of using the service:

- *Channels*: The services you connect together
- *Trigger channel*: The channel you are sharing the data from
- *Action channel*: The channel you are sending the data to
- *Recipe*: Any connection (process) you set up between two channels to share data
- *Ingredients:* The pieces of data you want to share from the trigger channel to the action channel

To create an IFTTT recipe you need to decide:

- The source of data, or the trigger channel (e.g., Flickr)
- The criteria for selecting specific data from the trigger channel (e.g., any public photo uploaded by you to Flickr)

- The action channel where you want the data to appear (e.g., Facebook)

- Which data from the trigger channel will appear in the action channel (e.g., the URL of the photo and its text description from Flickr)

IFTTT's unabbreviated name "If This Then That," describes this process: "IF the trigger channel does THIS, THEN the action channel does THAT."

Each channel has a unique range of triggers and actions. For example, when you use Facebook as the trigger channel, you can use any one of five triggers (Figure 1.1). Alternatively, if you use the social bookmarking service Diigo as the trigger channel, you only have two triggers to choose from (Figure 1.2).

However, when a service is used as an action channel, the options change. For example, as an action channel, Facebook only has three actions available (Figure 1.3), while Diigo still has two options (Figure 1.4).

In addition, some channels can only be used as a trigger channel or action channel, not as both. For example, the HootSuite channel has no trigger options (meaning that you can't get data directly out of HootSuite using IFTTT) and the RSS channel has no action options. The available triggers and actions for all of the channels can be viewed by visiting the Channels page on the IFTTT site and clicking on the appropriate channel icon.

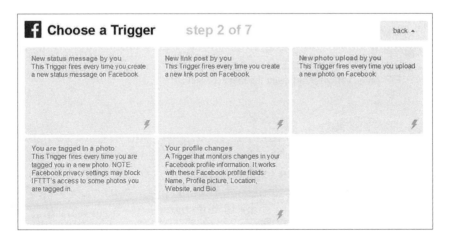

Figure 1.1   Trigger options for use with the Facebook channel

Figure 1.2   Trigger options for use with the Diigo channel

Figure 1.3   Action options for use with the Facebook channel

Figure 1.4   Action options for use with the Diigo channel

As well as having control over the triggers and actions, you also have some control over the data that is passed between them. For example, you might want to share a bookmark on Facebook, but not your own private description. Each channel offers you access to fields specific to that channel to share or not share.

Once you've set up a recipe, it is regularly checked by IFTTT and is automatically run whenever the criteria has been met by the trigger channel. You can go back and edit or delete your recipes, and you can also turn them on or off as needed.

IFTTT also allows users to share recipes they have created with others. Shared recipes appear in the IFTTT public area (ifttt.com/recipes) as templates, which include the basic ingredients of the recipe, such as the trigger and action channels used, the specific triggers and actions, and a description. Other users can copy a shared recipe, modify it for their own purpose, and save it as a recipe in their own account.

IFTTT in Action

This section provides practical examples for using IFTTT, illustrating how recipes can be set up to perform various tasks. The first example provides the most detail, and the subsequent examples highlight the channels, triggers, and actions used as well as the purpose of the recipe and how that specific recipe works.

Collecting Library News and Sharing Individual Items on Various Social Networks

This example uses IFTTT to pull news articles from various RSS feeds into a Pocket account (getpocket.com), where the user can assess each article, tag the articles worth sharing with any social networks, and then automatically send the tagged articles to specified social networks or save to read later. In this instance, I am using Pocket as an RSS feed reader—my chosen method of aggregating and sharing information. This example requires two sets of IFTTT recipes to be set up. The first set pulls RSS news feeds into Pocket, and the second set sends tagged news articles from Pocket to the social networks.

Feeding the RSS Feeds into Pocket

This recipe uses the following triggers and actions:

- Trigger channel: RSS feed

- Trigger: New feed item

- Action channel: Pocket

- Action: Save for later

First you decide on the RSS feed you are going to use as the source of information. In this instance, I'm going to use a Google news alert I have set up specifically for library news (news.google.co.uk/news/feeds?hl= en&gl=uk&q=library+OR+libraries&um=1&ie=UTF-8&output=rss).

Once you have logged into your IFTTT account, click the Create button at the top of the screen. Next, click on the word *this* to choose a trigger action (Figure 1.5). When the list of available trigger channels appears, click on the RSS feed symbol (Figure 1.6).

Figure 1.5   Click *this* to make your trigger selection

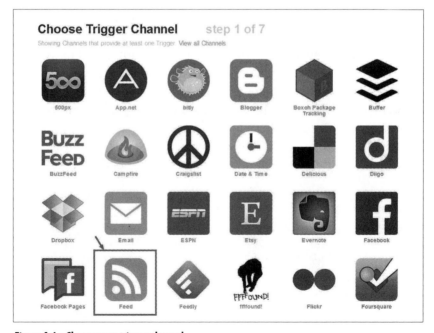

Figure 1.6   Choose your trigger channel

Figure 1.7   Choose the New Feed Item trigger

Figure 1.8   Enter the URL for your RSS feed and create your trigger channel

With RSS feeds, you have two options for triggers: New Feed Item (Figure 1.7) pulls any new items that are added to the RSS feed; New Feed Item Matches allows you to specify a keyword so that only matching items are pulled from the feed.

In Figure 1.7, notice that there is a small Back button on the top right side. If at any stage during the creation of a recipe you need to make a change, you can return to a previous stage by clicking this button. You can also scroll up the page and look for the link to Restart From Here.

Figure 1.8 shows the New Feed Item page, where you will add the URL for your RSS feed [1] and create your trigger channel [2].

Once you have created your trigger channel, the screen shown in Figure 1.9 will open. In the phrase "if this then that," *this* is replaced by the trigger icon and feed URL information. Click on the word *that* to move to the list of available action channels. Click on the Pocket symbol, as shown in Figure 1.10.

The first time you use Pocket (and many of the other channels on IFTTT) you will be asked to activate the channel. This activation process authorizes IFTTT to access specific data from your account on this channel, as detailed on the authorization screen. At this point, log in with your Pocket username and password and click on Authorize and then Done.

Figure 1.9 Click *that* to make your action selection

Figure 1.10 Choose your action channel

Now that you have authorized IFTTT to access your Pocket account, you will not need to go through this process again when you create further recipes using the Pocket channel. When the next screen appears, click on Continue to choose the desired action.

In this case, Pocket has only one action available: Save for Later (Figure 1.11). This action automatically posts any item published in the trigger RSS feed to Pocket.

You now have the option to specify what data will be pulled through and how you want it to be presented or manipulated (Figure 1.12). In the case of Pocket, there are two data fields you can access: the URL of the item that is to be saved, and the keyword tags you associate with that item. (Different action channels will allow you

Figure 1.11   Choose the Save for Later action

Figure 1.12   Choose your data presentation

to access different data fields, as you will see in later examples.) The text in both of the fields appears with or without a grey background (e.g., IFTTT and FeedTitle in the Tags field). Any text with a grey background indicates that it is a data field taken from the trigger feed, whereas data without a background is data you are adding via IFTTT (e.g., enter the keyword *IFTTT* and the feed's title in the Tags field). You can remove any field by clicking in the field and pressing the Delete key. When you are editing, the data fields from the trigger feed appear in {{ }} brackets. Additional data fields from the RSS trigger feed can be added via the plus sign next to an action field.

Once you click on a plus sign, you will be presented with a list of the data fields available within the RSS trigger channel: EntryTitle (title of news story in the feed), EntryUrl (the URL for that particular news story), EntryAuthor (the author of the article), EntryContent (the text of the entry; either a summary or full text of the news article), EntryImageUrl (the URL for an image used in this story), EntryPublished (the date the news story was published), FeedTitle (the title of the RSS feed used as the trigger), and FeedUrl (the URL of the RSS feed used as the trigger). To add a data field from the trigger channel, click on the field name in the list displayed and click Add Ingredient. (Pocket will automatically pull EntryTitle or EntryContent through when it pulls through the URL.)

In this example, I decided to delete the existing information in the Tags field and replace it with my own text to indicate the topic and source: LibraryNews and GoogleNews (Figure 1.13). I didn't pull through any other data fields apart from the EntryUrl. Once the action fields have been edited, click on Create Action.

The next screen provides an overview of the recipe you have created, which in this example is *if* a new item is added to this RSS feed *then* automatically post it to my Pocket account (Figure 1.14). To remind yourself of its purpose at a later date, add a summary of this recipe to the Description box (Figure 1.15). You can add hashtags to the description, which can be useful for organizing your recipes at a later date. Finally, click on Create Recipe.

You have now created your first recipe using IFTTT. To view your new recipe, click My Recipes at the top of the screen.

From your list of recipes (Figure 1.16), you are able to do the following:

- Switch the recipe on and off [1]; it is automatically set to "on"

- Delete the recipe [2]

- Share your recipe with others [3]

- View the recipe in more detail and edit it [4]

A summary of when the recipe was created, how many times it has been triggered, and when it was last triggered appears below these buttons.

Click on the view/edit button [4] to make any changes to the recipe. You can now see the recipe in more detail (Figure 1.17) and can

Figure 1.13   Customize RSS data fields

Figure 1.14   Recipe summary

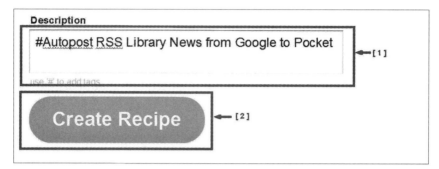

Figure 1.15 Recipe description

Figure 1.16 List of recipes

edit the Description [1], the RSS feed URL used for the trigger channel [2], and the data to be passed from the trigger channel to Pocket [3]. To save any changes you make to the recipe, scroll to the bottom of the page and click on Update [4].

When this recipe runs, it will pick up any new items from the specified Google news search (items that mention *library* or *libraries*) and save them to Pocket along with the tags you specified in Figure 1.13 so that they can be read there and subsequently shared.

If you have a number of sources of information you want to feed into Pocket in the same way, you can create more recipes like this example and just change the RSS feed you use as the trigger.

Feeding the News Items from Pocket to LinkedIn

This recipe uses the following triggers and actions:

- Trigger channel: Pocket
- Trigger: New item tagged

- Action channel: LinkedIn

- Action: Share a link

Once you have set up your recipes to pull news information feeds into Pocket, you will need to set up the second stage recipes that

Figure 1.17   Recipe detail

enable you to share the individual news items from your Pocket account to your social networks. This stage of the process relies on Pocket's tagging feature. You can add tags manually to specific items, and the tags you add will trigger the items to be posted to various sites and services (e.g., add the tag *tolinkedin* to an item to share it on LinkedIn [linkedin.com] or add the tag *totwitter* to send it to Twitter). If you use Feedly (feedly.com) instead of Pocket, you can set up similar recipes using the same principals in this example, as Feedly also provides similar trigger functionality. Figure 1.18 shows the process of sharing a link from a news article in a Pocket account to a LinkedIn account [1]. The recipe is triggered when the tag *gglinkedin* [2] (a tag I defined for this purpose) is added to an article in Pocket. IFTTT looks for any article with that tag and pulls through the article's URL, a brief excerpt of the article, and an image from Pocket if the article contains one. This information then appears as a post on LinkedIn [3].

The previous example is focused on LinkedIn, but similar recipes can be set up to send items from Pocket to channels such as Twitter, Facebook, Buffer, or indeed anywhere you want to share those links. To share information from Pocket to these other channels, you will need to set up a new recipe for each one, indicating the tag you want to use as the trigger. Remember when setting up your recipes that different social networks have different conventions and etiquette for sharing information. For example, if you are sharing a link from Pocket to Twitter, you may want to set up a recipe that includes an appropriate hashtag.

Creating a Continuing Professional Development Log From Your Social Networks, Web Presences, and Google Calendar

The purpose of the following recipes is to pull together information about your work- or study-related activities from a variety of sources into a single place to build up a continuing professional development (CPD) log, which can be referred back to for formal qualifications (e.g., chartership) or annual work appraisals. If you already share information about your work activities via social networks, blog about your work activities, and add work-related meetings and events to an online calendar, then you are already recording this information in a variety of places. However, it will be much easier to refer back to all of this information if you are also compiling it in a single place.

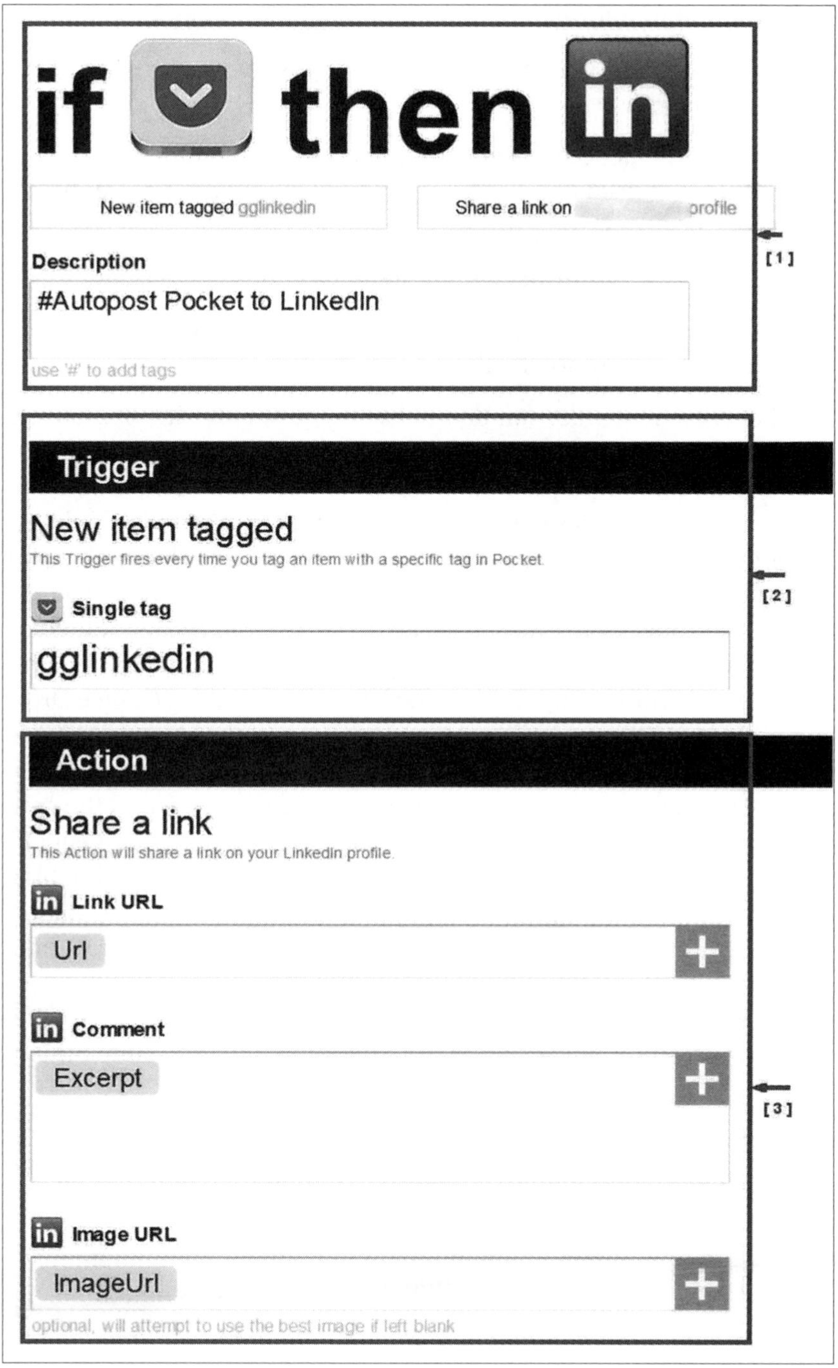

if ▼ then in

New item tagged gglinkedin   Share a link on ████ ████ profile

Description   [1]

#Autopost Pocket to LinkedIn

use '#' to add tags

Trigger

New item tagged
This Trigger fires every time you tag an item with a specific tag in Pocket.

▼ **Single tag**   [2]

gglinkedin

Action

Share a link
This Action will share a link on your LinkedIn profile.

in **Link URL**

Url   +

in **Comment**

Excerpt   +
                                                                   [3]

in **Image URL**

ImageUrl   +

optional, will attempt to use the best image if left blank

Figure 1.18   Feed news from Pocket to LinkedIn

As sources of information, the following services can be useful:

- LinkedIn: A social network used for posting work-related status updates

- Google Calendar (calendar.google.com): An online calendar used to record work-related meetings and events

- SlideShare (slideshare.net): A place to share your presentations from training sessions and conferences

- Blogs: Somewhere you write about your work or training activities in more detail

All of these resources can be used as triggers. LinkedIn and Google Calendar have dedicated channels on IFTTT. SlideShare and blogs provide RSS feed as output, so RSS channels can be used for both of them.

To turn these various feeds into a continuing professional development log, we need to use an IFTTT channel that will enable us to generate either a text file or spreadsheet of information in a single place. A number of IFTTT channels can be used in this way, including Google Drive (drive.google.com), Dropbox (dropbox.com), and Evernote (evernote.com). In this example, I will be using Google Drive to build up a CPD spreadsheet. Whenever one of the channel triggers is activated, a new row is added to the spreadsheet indicating the activity that was undertaken, any links to relevant URLs, and the date on which the activity happened (e.g., "July 23, 2013, attended equalities in public libraries training" with a link to a reflective writing blog post about the training). I've aimed to standardize the information that is recorded from the different triggers, although date formats may not always be the same.

To automate the process of building a CPD log on Google Drive, it's necessary to set up a recipe for each source of data to be fed into the log.

Pulling Through a LinkedIn Status Update to Google Drive

This recipe uses the following triggers and actions:

- Trigger channel: LinkedIn

- Trigger: Any new shared update

- Action channel: Google Drive

- Action: Add row to spreadsheet

This recipe pulls through any updates publicly posted to LinkedIn [1] (Figure 1.19). It records the LinkedIn CreatedDate (when the update was posted to LinkedIn) and StatusText (text of the update) in data fields on a new row in the Google Drive spreadsheet. The two data fields are saved in separate cells. In the Formatted Row box [2], " ||| " appears between the names of the two data fields. This is used to indicate that the data fields pulled through should be saved in adjacent spreadsheet cells. As well as indicating how the data should be recorded in the spreadsheet, the recipe specifies the Spreadsheet Name (where the data should be saved), in this instance, Personal

Figure 1.19 Post LinkedIn updates to spreadsheet

Log. You are also required to specify the file path in the Drive Folder Path field, in this instance, IFTTT/Personal Log. Any status update posted to LinkedIn would then be pulled through to the Google Drive spreadsheet.

Pulling Through Events From Google Calendar to Google Drive

This recipe uses the following triggers and actions:

- Trigger channel: Google Calendar
- Trigger: Event from search starts
- Action channel: Google Drive
- Action: Add row to spreadsheet

This recipe pulls through any events on my Google Calendar attended for work purposes (Figure 1.20) into the same spreadsheet in Google Drive that we used in the previous LinkedIn example. I have used the trigger Event From Search Starts as this allows me to filter out any events that are not work related [1]. To do this, I need to tell it that I only want events to activate the recipe if I have included the tag *sccwork* in the description (my own personal tag for work-related events in the calendar) [2]. It records the Starts date (when the event is happening), the Title (event name as it appears in the calendar), and the EventURL (link to the event in my calendar). You can see in Figure 1.20 in the Formatted Row box [3] that I have placed the data fields in order of Starts, Title, and EventURL, so that the date and event text appear in the same columns as the LinkedIn date and status text information indicated in the previous example. You will also see that it uses the same file path and file name as the previous example.

Uploading Presentations From SlideShare to Google Drive

This recipe uses the following triggers and actions:

- Trigger channel: RSS
- Trigger: New feed item
- Action channel: Google Drive
- Action: Add row to spreadsheet

This recipe records any presentations uploaded to SlideShare (Figure 1.21) in the same spreadsheet as the two previous examples [1]. It uses an RSS feed that is available from my SlideShare account [2]. All of my

Figure 1.20 Add Google Calendar event to Google Drive

presentations on SlideShare are work-related and so are all relevant. Again, the recipe records the information in the Google spreadsheet, using EntryPublished (date the presentation was uploaded), EntryTitle (name of presentation), and EntryURL (link to the presentation on

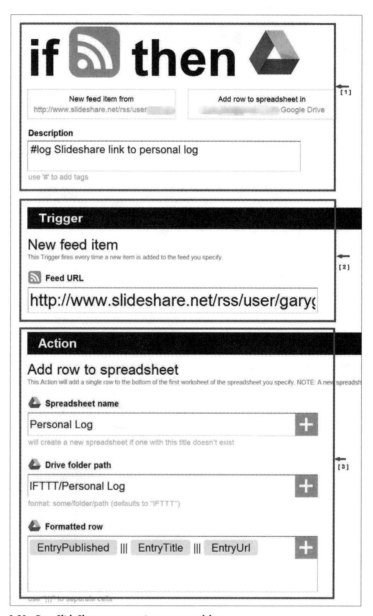

Figure 1.21   Post SlideShare presentations to spreadsheet

SlideShare) [3]. Again, I provide a standard order that the information is recorded in—date, title, link—so that the information appears in the correct columns in the spreadsheet.

If you want to record links to blog posts about work activities or reflective CPD writing, you can create another recipe using your blog's RSS feed. Some of the fields in your RSS feed may be different than the fields in the SlideShare feed, so make sure to include the fields that pull through the date the blog post was written, its title, and a link to the blog post itself in the Formatted Row box.

These are just a few examples of how I built my own CPD log. You may use other services and channels that suit your needs better.

Forewarning People of Possible Library Closures Due to Snow via Twitter

This recipe uses the following triggers and actions:

- Trigger channel: Weather

- Trigger: Tomorrow's forecast calls for

- Action channel: Twitter

- Action: Post a tweet

With the IFTTT Weather channel, users are able to enter a location and create an action based on the current weather or tomorrow's forecast in that location (Figure 1.22). Using this channel, the following recipe [1] automatically sends out a tweet to forewarn library users of possible heavy snowfall the following day. This is one way of alerting library users to possible closures due to bad weather, with the weather channel trigger set to look for a condition of snow [2]. Even though this recipe makes use of the Weather channel, it does not pull through any data fields into the Twitter channel, as you will see in the Formatted Row text box in Figure 1.22 [3]. We added the text for the tweet ourselves ("Possible snow in Surrey tomorrow. Please check website for library closures if heavy snowfall occurs."). This is a useful illustration of how you can make use of valuable data from the trigger channel in the recipe without passing any of the actual data fields into the action channel.

The Weather channel also provides triggers based on other weather conditions (e.g., clear, rain, cloudy, high and low temperature ranges). Using some of these other triggers, you could set up more recipes to

Figure 1.22 Send weather alerts to Twitter

creatively promote library stock (e.g., *if* the temperature tomorrow is forecast to reach at least 23C *then* send out a tweet promoting our walking guides for the county.)

Building an Archive of Shared Links From a Number of Resources

This recipe uses the following triggers and actions:

- Trigger channel: Pocket
- Trigger: New item tagged

- Action channel: Diigo

- Action: Add a public bookmark

Expanding on the idea of sharing links to a range of networks, library news articles could also be pooled into a single social bookmarking service to build an archive of useful links for all to access. The idea is not only to share the information, but to keep an organized record of those links for future use. Many social networks experience a flood of information, and a link you shared months ago might be lost in that flood no matter how hard you try to track it down. I like to make sure I can find those old links I've shared elsewhere and provide a way for others to find them too. With IFTTT, it is easy to organise these shared links into a useful resource. In this instance, the recipe connects Pocket to the social bookmarking service Diigo (diigo.com) (Figure 1.23). Again, we would use the same Pocket New Item Tagged trigger [1], but this time we Add a Public Bookmark to Diigo [2].

When setting up the recipes, any tags you have added to the item in Pocket can be exported to the bookmarking site and are stored along with the link itself. In the following example, I use the tag *librarynews* to save the news article to the social bookmarking account along with a number of standard tags (including *library news* and *libraries*) and subject-specific tags (for example, *technology in libraries*) that I have added in Pocket. In addition to the URL of the original article and the tags, the recipe pulls through a description of the article to be stored as part of the process. Once the item has been bookmarked, users of the Diigo site will be able to find the item via a tag search.

Building a Source of Data for Mashups

A number of the examples I have provided use channels that not only share data, but store it too. For example, the CPD log information is stored as a spreadsheet and the shared link resource stores the information as bookmarks. With this in mind, it is easy to see how data could be collected to be used as a source in a data mashup. For example, instead of collecting details of your CPD activities via Google Drive, you could pull in mentions of the library from a variety of resources, either with a dedicated channel on IFTTT or with an RSS feed as output (e.g., news articles, social network updates, photographs, videos). You've then got a source of data you can make use of.

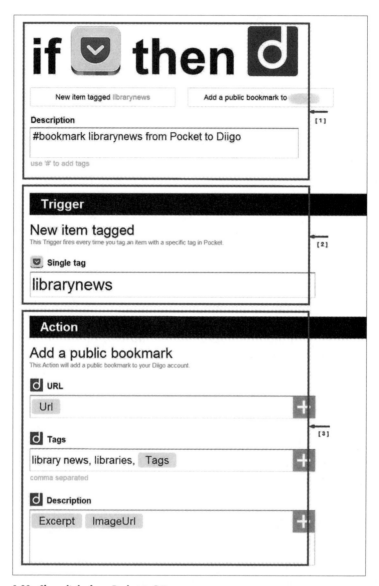

Figure 1.23 Share links from Pocket to Diigo

Google Drive spreadsheets provide users with the capability to easily publish the documents in various formats, including RSS and CSV output, and it provides a unique URL that can be accessed by data mashup tools. Diigo provides a RSS, which is also a useful output method. Again, this can be used as a data feed for a mashup.

The Human Touch

While IFTTT does most of the work for us, it is still important to include human input in the process when setting up the recipes and also once they have been set up. When setting up recipes, we need to be aware of how data is structured in the trigger channel as its structure will impact what data is pulled through into the action channel. Once the recipes are up and running, you will need to regularly check that they are still active and that the data being pulled through is correct. Changes to a channel's authentication procedure may require you to re-activate that channel in IFTTT. As well, changes to a channel's data structure could affect how that data is passed through to IFTTT. Such changes may be particularly relevant if you are using RSS feeds rather than dedicated channels.

Other Services

Throughout this chapter I have talked about using IFTTT to automate information sharing, as it is the service I'm most familiar with. However, there are other services available that work along very similar lines that you may want to try. If IFTTT doesn't quite suit your circumstances, information needs, or the way you work, it's worth taking a look at one of these other services:

- CloudWork (cloudwork.com)
- elasti.io (elastic.io)
- We Wired Web (wewiredweb.com)
- Zapier (zapier.com)

Like IFTTT, each of these services shares the common aim of passing data easily between different channels. However, the way they do this varies, as does the range of channels they work with. Of the services on this list, We Wired Web and Zapier are most similar to IFTTT.

Summary

IFTTT is a way to connect different internet and communication services together, to move and share data and information between them. The examples in this chapter show just a small number of ways you could use IFTTT. With over 90 channels, numerous triggers and actions within each channel, and access to untold numbers of RSS feeds and data sources, IFTTT offers countless opportunities for library and information services and anyone working in these sectors. If you are looking for more inspiration, browse through the thousands of the recipes IFTTT users have shared on the site (ifttt.com/recipes).

IFTTT can be a great time saver, especially if you are trying to cope with data sharing between a number of networks. If you are looking for a tool that will help you manipulate and share data across popular online services without the need to write code or understand APIs, it is worth investigating IFTTT.

## CHAPTER 2

The Non-Developer's Guide to Creating Map Mashups

Eva Dodsworth
University of Waterloo

Recent developments in both open source and proprietary software have not only moved applications to the web, but they have made application building—something that used to be only possible for web developers—a social, educational, and informational novelty. With the availability of widgets and easily edited code, more and more web users are turning to a variety of online mapping applications to deliver their thoughts, findings, and stories. In addition to the true online mapping applications, like Google (maps.google. com), ArcGIS Online (arcgis.com), and OpenStreetMap (open streetmap.org), there are now several more applications available, most often using Google Maps API (developers.google.com/maps) to host their own mapping program, that can help you create your own customized map. Regardless of which program users turn to, there are now hundreds of thousands of map mashups online that have been created using various mapping services to host their basemaps and spatial information. Some require a little JavaScript knowledge and coding; others do not. Since many library staff members are not developers or coders, but rather liaisons for information distribution, I will focus on introducing the readers to creating map mashups in a non-developer's environment.

There are many applications that can be used to build a map mashup. Scribble Maps (scribblemaps.com), for example, runs on Google Maps and offers a nice selection of features like dynamic symbols and GIS file importation. MangoMap (mangomap.com) is a newer application that manages, edits, and stores your data, and also offers interactive features for creating dynamic online maps. ZeeMaps (zeemaps.com) uses the Google Maps API and operates similarly to Google Maps, but it does offer more layer customization. GeoCommons (geocommons.com) offers advanced visualizations and is quite similar to ArcGIS Online. There are of course many more that are being used on a daily basis, but this chapter will specifically focus on ArcGIS Online, Google Earth (earth.google.com), and SIMILE Exhibit (simile-widgets.org/exhibit). All three are excellent candidates for organizing, storing, editing, manipulating, and delivering information.

Mashups With ArcGIS Online

ArcGIS Online is a public cloud-based, collaborative content management system created by Esri (esri.com) for creating and sharing interactive maps and other types of geographic information. Using the built-in ArcGIS.com map viewer, you can create a variety of maps using points, lines, polygons, links, images, and external files such as tables, GeoRSS feeds, Keyhole Markup Language (KML), and Shapefiles. The latest addition to ArcGIS Online enables you to also select from a number of templates to create dynamic story maps. Once maps have been created, they can be shared with individuals, groups, and the public via the ArcGIS Online web server.

Working With Built-in Features

Like many other online mapping programs, ArcGIS Online offers free basic map-making capabilities. Users can create points (placemarks) and embed text, links, and photographs into those points. Lines (paths) and polygons can also be drawn, and text can be added to the map as well. The built-in viewer also provides a selection of base maps to choose from such as OpenStreetMap, topographic, and a variety of satellite and aerial images.

To begin working with these basic tools, you will first need to create a free account with ArcGIS Online. Once registered and logged in, you are ready to begin. Start by adding Map Notes, available from the main horizontal menu.

This opens up the tools menu, which includes a handful of symbols (points, triangles, squares, arrows, etc). You can select any of the symbols to begin adding features to the map. Each feature added can be embellished with additional information such as links to websites, images, and text. You can also add additional layers available from the Esri community database directly into the map. Over 10,000 layers are available, added by Esri or other map users, including data such as political boundaries, transportation lines, census data, soil classifications, and property parcels, to just name a few. These files can be searched by keyword, or they can be browsed, and more than one dataset can be added to the map at a time.

Working With External Files

If the built-in layers don't meet your needs, you can import external files to fully customize the map. From simple points, to dynamic polygons, there are several file types that are supported. Simple points can be added and mapped based on the latitude and longitude coordinates listed on spreadsheets. In lieu of manually adding individual placemarks to the map, users can add lists of records populated with information. Google Drive (drive.google.com) does a nice job converting Excel files into Comma Separated Value (CSV) files, and since the files are stored online they can be imported into the mapping program fairly seamlessly by Adding Layer From Web. Besides tabular data, popular KML files can be added as well. Often used with Google Earth, KML files are popular with online mappers and have become a more standardized spatial format in mapping. KML files need to be added to your ArcGIS Online account before you can map them. To add the files, access My Contents from the main menu on your Profile page (the page you started with after you registered).

Once you have uploaded the desired KML files, you can go back to your map and Search for Layers In: My Content. ArcGIS places some restrictions on KML files however, typically in terms of file size and number of features, so you may wish to work with smaller files to start.

Unlike many other online mapping programs, ArcGIS Online supports the importation of Shapefiles. Shapefiles are GIS datasets that are typically used in desktop GIS programs and are much more commonly used than KML files. These files can be downloaded from many data portals and libraries, and they typically offer rich attribute information. Shapefiles do have size and feature limitations as well, so it's best to import a Shapefile for a small geographical area. Shapefiles can be imported directly into your map by Adding Layer From File, again from the Add menu.

Saving and Sharing your Map

With so many supported data types, both new and experienced users can work with GIS files within this simple lightweight application. The final map created can be easily shared as a web application with others by email, Facebook (facebook.com), or Twitter (twitter.com) by providing a link to your online map. The map can also be embedded into your website by copying the HTML code that is provided.

To share your map with others, you will need to save it first. Saving and Sharing tools are available on the horizontal menu at the top of the map. Once the map is saved, click on the Share tool; if you wish the public to be able to view your map, be sure to select that setting. You will be provided with a direct link that allows others to see your map the way you see it. You can go a step further and turn your map into a web application, which will very quickly make your map look more professional (Figure 2.1).

Clicking on Make a Web Application will bring you to a page that offers dozens of different templates you can choose from, depending on your map's purpose. For now, select a basic template to see what your map looks like (another option, storytelling templates, will be

Figure 2.1 Sharing your map

discussed more in the next section). Once you have selected your template, you will be given a URL for your final map.

Using Story Maps

Story maps enable individuals and communities to become story-tellers by creating, collaborating, and sharing information on topics that have a spatial and temporal component. Story maps provide templates that can incorporate text, multimedia, and interactive functions to inform, educate, entertain, and inspire people about a vast array of topics (storymaps.arcgis.com). Story map templates are an easy solution for creating map mashups as no written code is required. The Story Maps site provides web files for download as well as instructions for customizing the web map. There are 10 templates available (storymaps.arcgis.com/en/app-list) that offer features such as ranked lists, side panels, drop-down legends, thumbnail image carousel, text panel, and map swipes that enable users to swipe between two maps, just to name a few.

As dynamic and complex as a story map may look, it's actually just as easy to create as any other map in ArcGIS Online, as you follow the same map-making steps. Once you have added your data and features and you are ready to share your map, you simply select the storymapping template of your choice. For example, if you are interested in creating a map that compares two census variables for a specific geographic location, it may be best to use the Story Map Swipe template. This map will enable the user to swipe between the two maps in order to compare census variances between them. Each map will first need to be created of course, which is as simple as adding the individual census variables to each map. When you are ready to share, select the Story Map Swipe template. A wizard will walk you through customizing your final map's look and feel. Again, no coding required, but the final map looks complete professional.

Google Earth Mashups

Google Earth is a free, powerful yet simple tool for displaying information spatially, whether your purpose is to view climate information, analyze change over time, review sights seen, or remember routes taken. Google Earth can also integrate with powerful GIS tools if or when advanced analysis is needed. Google Earth provides users with the ability to create customized maps using dynamic placemarks that support images, videos, links, and customized descriptions and layouts, using a combination of HTML code and KML code. Image overlays can be added to enhance the map as well as external KML files to create a true mapping experience. Resources are available online to assist users with the creation of KML code that allows additional features such as screen overlays, animation, and time-lapse analysis.

Maps created in Google Earth are saved in KML format and then can be shared with the world. A simple method of sharing KML files is making them available for download from a website. A more sophisticated way is to embed the Google Earth API into the webpage so that Google Earth is available from the internet browser and the KML file can be viewed seamlessly. This section will cover the most popular features available in Google Earth that can be used to create Google Earth mashups.

Creating Dynamic Placemarks

Almost every Google Earth user has created at least one placemark using the "pushpin" tool. Many Google Maps mashups display yellow pushpins that can be clicked to gain more information about the location marked. What many users don't know is that the pushpin does not need to be yellow, nor does it need to be a pushpin. A point can be represented in myriad ways in this application, as it welcomes customized symbols, even photographs. Points can be created manually, one by one, or they can be imported from a table that was converted into a KML file. Any table that has geographic coordinates provided with each place of interest can be converted into a KML file (the only geographic file that Google Earth supports). Once the placemark has been created or imported, details can be added via the description box, which will be available to map users when they click on the placemark. The map creator can add simple text to the description box, without formatting. There is also a button that allows for adding an image or an online link. For more advanced users, the description box supports HTML and KML coding to control the look of the text (font type, style, size, color, tables, columns) as well as the look of the pop-up window (color, frame) and images (frames, size).

An HTML tag is a command used to control how the text or image is displayed. HTML tags are surrounded by brackets [< >]. For example, <strong> is a bold tag and is used to make the text display in bold font. Most tags require an accompanying end tag, in this case </strong>. For more information on how to use HTML code and for a list of HTML tags, visit Web-Source (web-source.net/html_codes_ chart.htm).

A popular resource to link to maps via the pop-up window is video. A YouTube video can be added in the pop-up window by copying the video's embed source or URL and pasting it into the description box. In YouTube, there is also a Share button that provides users with the code needed to embed the video directly into Google Earth.

Creating a Dynamic Map

Google Earth offers more than just placemark creation. You can add text, images, and KML files to a map to make it a much more interactive experience. Using KML code, you can also add a number of features to the map that are not standard within the Google Earth application. One example often seen on professional maps is screen overlays, which are commonly used for static legends or logos. If you wish to have an image on your map that doesn't travel with you as you zoom in and out, create a screen overlay KML file. Such a file may consist of the following code:

```
<?xml version="1.0" encoding="UTF-8"?>
<kml xmlns="http://www.opengis.net/kml/2.2">
  <ScreenOverlay>
    <name>Absolute Positioning: Top left</name>
    <visibility>1</visibility>
    <Icon>
      <href>http://kml-samples.googlecode.com/
svn/trunk/resources/top_left.jpg</href>
    </Icon>
    <overlayXY x="0" y="1" xunits="fraction"
yunits="fraction"/>
    <screenXY x="0" y="1" xunits="fraction"
yunits="fraction"/>
    <rotationXY x="0" y="0" xunits="fraction"
yunits="fraction"/>
```

```
    <size x="0" y="0" xunits="fraction"
yunits="fraction"/>
  </ScreenOverlay>
</kml>
```

overlayXY and screenXY indicate the positioning of the image, in this case on the top left of the screen. The <Icon> tag indicates the URL where the image is hosted. The rest of the lines will remain the same, so you can customize this code to your own image.

Since many people are not developers and don't write code, this code and many others are available to be copied, used, shared, and changed from the KML Interactive Sampler Website (kml-samples. googlecode.com/svn/trunk/interactive/index.html), a fantastic website that offers a large number of mapping possibilities not included in Google's standard features. The site is best viewed in Firefox or Chrome. You can preview what each feature will look like in Google Earth, along with the code needed for that feature. The code needs to be copied and pasted into a basic text program such as Notepad, the user needs to make appropriate changes (i.e., changing the URL to point to their own map, logo, etc.), and then the text needs to be saved as a KML file. Once saved, this KML file can then be opened in Google Earth.

Other KML codes available include non-standard placemarks, such as a floating or extruded placemark, which appears to hover in the air and does not cover any of the features seen on the ground. Some popular polygon placemark files include textured colors and roll-overs, which change color when the viewer mouses over the polygon. For non-standard pop-up windows, or balloons as they are sometimes called, the KML Interactive Sampler offers code that adds a background color to the balloon. The code may look something like this:

```
<?xml version="1.0" encoding="utf-8"?>
<kml xmlns="http://www.opengis.net/kml/2.2">
  <Placemark>
    <name>My office</name>
    <description>This is the location of my
office.</description>
    <Style>
      <BalloonStyle>
        <bgColor>ff7f1020</bgColor>
```

```
    </BalloonStyle>
    </Style>
    <Point>
        <coordinates>-122.0821604290386,
  37.42041505714916</coordinates>
        </Point>
    </Placemark>
  </kml>
```

The color choice can be entered in the <bgColor> tag.

For the complete selection of dynamic tools, please visit the KML Interactive Sampler website. Figure 2.2 shows a screen image of the application.

Completing and Sharing Maps

When your map is finalized, and depending on the extent of your project, you can either offer your KML file directly to online users, allowing them to view your project on their local Google Earth application, or you can embed the map into your webpage and allow viewers to access your map seamlessly with a Google Earth plug-in on their supported browser. The Google Earth API (developers.google. com/earth) will display your map features in the web browser, just like the standalone versions of Google Earth. To embed your map into your webpage, you will need to obtain a Google Maps key and write the necessary JavaScript code. Your viewers will be able to view

Figure 2.2   KML Interactive Sampler: A screen overlay

your map with their Google Earth plug-in (google.com/earth/explore/ products/plugin.html) on most modern browsers. Instructions on how to modify your HTML code to support the Google Earth plug-in is available from Google Earth's website (developers.google.com/earth/ documentation).

Mashups With SIMILE Exhibit

Developed by the Massachusetts Institute of Technology (MIT), the SIMILE (Semantic Interoperability of Metadata and Information in unLike Environments) Exhibit project (simile-widgets.org/exhibit) is an open source web toolkit that organizes, filters, and dynamically visualizes data without the need for complex databases and server-side technologies (simile-widgets.org/wiki/Getting_Started). Only basic familiarity with HTML code (and optionally JavaScript code) is needed. It is an ideal open source application for building webpages with advanced text searching and filtering functionalities using Google Maps.

SIMILE Exhibit has become popular with libraries as more and more collections are being searched and retrieved using a mapping application. This dynamic and easy-to-use application provides the tools needed for libraries to offer their collections online. An example of how the Exhibit toolkit can be used to map historical information is the Sonoma State University Library's Sonoma County Timeline (library.sonoma.edu/regional/timeline.php), which offers geospatial mapping of historic places, notable people, and key events. Although the end product looks as though a lot of work and programming went into building the applications, in reality, only two pages need to be built: an HTML page that acts as the application's framework, and the database file that fuels the visualization. There are three other components that work in the background, called Views, Lenses and Facets.

Views are used to explore the entire collection of records in a number of different views: tile, table, calendar, map, timeline, runaway, or a combination of these views (e.g., map and table views, map and timeline views, etc.). Facets are properties of items that allow users to select and filter the data. Lenses allow the application builder to manipulate the presentation of an individual item, selecting which parts of the record to display and how to display them.

HTML Page

The HTML page consists of a file that connects all the necessary pieces of your SIMILE Exhibit map together. Once uploaded, the HTML page connects to the MIT server that hosts the APIs as well as the widgets that can display your data in a variety of formats. The HTML code does not need to be written from scratch, as SIMILE Exhibit offers a number of templates so the user can simply use the source code from the selected template to begin. The code can be copied into a simple text editor like Notepad or TextEdit and then customized to ensure that all connections work properly. A sample HTML file taken from the SIMILE Exhibit website looks like:

```
<html>
    <head>
        <title>My Exhibit's Title</title>

        <link href="my-data.js" type=
"application/json" rel="exhibit/data" />

        <script src="http://static.simile.mit.
edu/exhibit/api-2.0/exhibit-api.js"
            type="text/JavaScript"></script>

        <style>
            /* Override styles here */
        </style>
    </head>
    <body>
    <table width="100%">
        <tr valign="top">
            <td width="25%">
                <!-- facets:

                    <div ex:role="facet"
ex:expression=".property"></div>
                    -->
            </td>
            <td>
                <div ex:role="view"></div>
            </td>
```

```
        </tr>
    </table>
    </body>
    </html>
```

Essentially this text is simply the connection string to the MIT APIs, style formatting in the form CSS, instructions for formatting data from the data file, and a link to the data file itself (seen in the line starting with <link href="my-data"). From your simple text editor, you will make any necessary modifications. You will wish to give your page an appropriate title and have your data appropriately linked. You will also want to add your facets and the view panel into the code.

For further customization and to learn more about SIMILE Exhibit's code, refer to their step-by-step guide (simile-widgets.org/wiki/Getting_Started).

The Data File

The data file is the meat of the project and will populate the information made available through the map application. So if for example, your library is interested in offering digitized historical maps to the public, then a number of fields are mandatory: titles, description of the collection, links to the digitized maps, and the geographic locations of the maps (this geographic field representing latitude and longitude, "latlng," must be included). It's up to you how much information you would like your spreadsheet to contain, but each row must correspond to a particular map record, and each column describes one of the features of the map, as listed above. The table needs to be saved in the JSON format as SIMILE Exhibit doesn't recognize .xlsx. Fortunately there is a SIMILE widget called Babel that easily converts .xlsx into JSON format and gives your data file a .js extension. Once your data file is converted, save it into the same folder as your HTML file and then open your HTML file in a web browser to view your map. If you find that your map isn't doing what you want it to, there are many online resources that offer hints and tips for creating a successful online application using SIMILE Exhibit. Figure 2.3 is an example of one of the freely available map mashup templates.

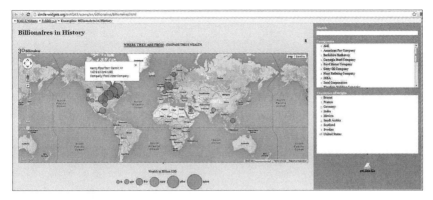

Figure 2.3   Example of a map mashup template

Conclusion

Map mashups have come a long way since they first appeared in 2004. What used to require expertise in both cartography and computer coding now involves a simple web interface. With today's technology, anybody can easily create customized markers, images, and descriptions to share information. Recently, many libraries have taken advantage of map mashup technology to create finding aids for library material. Libraries are linking their digital collections to maps, geocoding locational data, and offering easier access to library catalogues and the collection themselves. Map mashups are joining a variety of subject matters, such as the sciences and the humanities, to mapping tools. Story mapping has taken off, and students and instructors at all levels are using these mashups in classrooms. Learning about all kinds of spaces is more effective when those spaces can be visualized.

Various applications are available for online map making, and many social media sites support geoweb features such as geotagging and GeoRSS feeds. With these geo tools, users can link data from applications to an online map such as Google Maps or Esri Maps. This chapter reviewed several applications that do not require programming or coding expertise. Products such as ArcGIS Online offer easy- and fun-to-use templates that aid in dynamic map creation. Whether designed for personal or professional purposes, today's map mashups have revolutionized the way information is discovered, presented, and used.

## CHAPTER 3

OpenRefine(ing) and Visualizing Library Data

Martin Hawksey
Association for Learning Technology

Even with the best of intentions library data can be messy. Whilst we can apply structural frameworks like cataloging rules, subject classifications, and controlled vocabularies, at some point the machine world is interfaced by humans. *Messy data* was the challenge faced by Metaweb Technologies, which in 2007 announced the launch of Freebase (freebase.com), described as "an open shared database of the world's knowledge" and "a massive, collaboratively edited database of cross-linked data." Freebase created a community space where messy data harvested from a range of sources including Wikipedia could be refined into structured data. To support the creation of structured data, Metaweb developed a number of tools that could be used by community members. One of these tools was Gridworks, an open source desktop application for Windows, Mac, and Linux, which let users import datasets from a variety of formats, and explore and refine data before exporting in other formats. Following the purchase of Metaweb by Google in 2010, Gridworks remained open source and was renamed Google Refine, before being entirely gifted by Google to the community in 2012 and becoming OpenRefine (openrefine.org).

Google's interest in Freebase stems from its desire to enhance search results with semantic data, or as Google terms it, the *knowledge graph*. The word *graph* here isn't referring to a visual diagram or chart, but rather the computing science concept of a graph as an abstract data structure. One of the reasons Freebase adopted a community approach was the concept of having many eyes looking over the data to spot mistakes and patterns. In this chapter, we will draw on reading and refining library data using OpenRefine, and visualizing that data in a stimulating way.

To start, we need a data source. So that you can play along (if you haven't already, download and install OpenRefine at this point), we'll use data from an open access repository. The OpenDOAR site (opendoar.org) has a directory of over 2,000 such repositories; for this project, I will use the Jorum repository (jorum.ac.uk). Jorum is a national repository for Open Educational Resources (OERs), which anyone with an affiliation to a U.K. college or university (as well as anyone else with a "trusted depositor" account) can deposit to. The public nature of submissions makes this data extra messy. One of the other reasons for choosing Jorum is because it implements the Open Archives Initiative Protocol for Metadata Harvesting (OAI-PMH). OAI-PMH is designed to make it easy to harvest repository metadata. Repositories rarely advertise the existence of OAI-PMH but fortunately this is something recorded in OpenDOAR. Visiting the OpenDOAR record for Jorum (opendoar.org/id/1834/) we can see there is an OAI-PMH endpoint at open.jorum.ac.uk/oai/request? verb=Identify. At this point, it's probably worth familiarizing ourselves with the OAI-PMH specification documentation (open archives.org/OAI/openarchivesprotocol.html). The protocol uses six verbs, or services:

- Identify: To retrieve information about the repository (e.g., base URL, protocol version)

- GetRecord: To retrieve an individual metadata record

- ListRecords: To harvest batches of full records

- ListSets: To retrieve the identifiers of record sets

- ListIdentifiers: To get record headers (the header only includes the record identifier, datestamp, and the sets the record is in)

- ListMetadataFormats: To retrieve the metadata formats available from the repository

These services plus any required or optional parameters are requested from the repository, which returns any successful response. In our scenario, you may assume that the ListRecords verb is ideal for our purposes as it returns a full record. The issue in our case is that ListRecords results are usually paginated, requiring a resumption token to get the next batch (like hitting the next page on your search results). Because OpenRefine isn't designed to handle this process, we have to find an alternative route. In the case of Jorum the repository is configured to return all ListIdentifiers without pagination, giving us an entry point.

Getting Repository Records Into OpenRefine

To get repository records into OpenRefine, having started the application, you can choose to Create Project From Web Addresses (URLs) (Figure 3.1).

For the web address use the OAI-PMH endpoint previously identified, but with verb=ListIdentifiers and also not forgetting the required metadataPrefix (openarchives.org/OAI/openarchives protocol.html#ListIdentifiers). This gives the following URL to enter as the web address:

```
open.jorum.ac.uk/oai/request?verb=
ListIdentifiers&metadataPrefix=oai_dc
```

After you click Next, OpenRefine will fetch the records and give you some parsing options. First, you want to make sure in the Parse Data as option that you are using XML files. When you hover the mouse pointer over the data preview area, you can then highlight the first element that contains a complete record, in this case capturing the entire <header> element as shown in Figure 3.2.

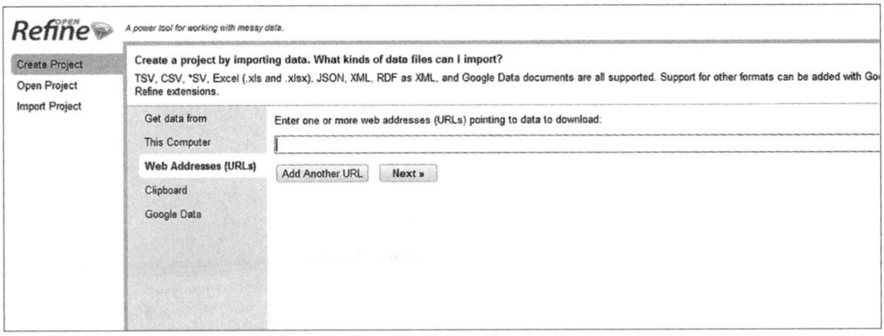

Figure 3.1   Creating a project in OpenRefine

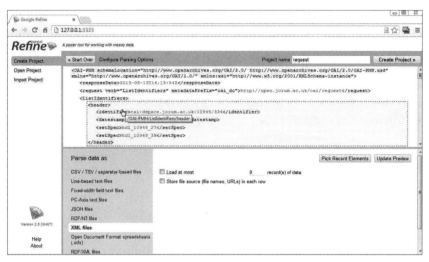

Figure 3.2 Highlighting the entire <header> element in OpenRefine

At this point the preview should switch to showing three columns: Header – setSpec, Header – datestamp, and Header – identifier. If you don't get this, you can click the Pick Record Elements button to adjust your selection. When you have the desired elements, enter a project name in the box toward the top right and click Create Project.

Once you've created the project you may notice an extra column appears: Header – status. This is because the preview is shown using a subset of the data; the extra column is introduced when it processes the entire XML document. At this point, you may want to explore some of the interface features yourself or watch the video at youtube.com/watch?v=B70J_H_zAWM for a summary. You'll also pick up tips from the remainder of this walkthrough.

To make things a little easier let's remove the Header – setSpec column. Click on the down array icon next to its heading name and select Edit Column > Remove This Column. This leaves us some blank rows. We can select these for removal by clicking on the Header – identifier menu button and then select Facet > Customized Facets > Facet by Blank (Figure 3.3).

In the Facet/Filter panel on the left hand side, you can click on the True choice to include only blank rows. Before deleting these rows, make sure you are viewing the data as rows rather than records by clicking the Rows link next to Show as: located at the top of the page just beneath the record count. To finally remove the blank rows, use

Figure 3.3 Finding all blank rows

the drop-down menu under All to select Edit Rows > Remove All Matching Rows (Figure 3.4).

At this point you may be panicking because you got 0 matching rows. This is because the Facet by Blank is still on. You can switch it off by clicking Exclude in the facet options, or remove the facet altogether by clicking the "X" close window button in the top corner of the facet. At this point, you might want to also delete all the rows with deleted records. To do this, we can use a similar technique: faceting the Header – status column by blank, this time choosing to facet where the condition is false (i.e., contains the "deleted" cell value, and then again removing all matching rows.)

Right now all we have is the record set, datestamp, and identifier. How do we get the full record? OpenRefine has a powerful feature to fetch additional data based on cell values. In this instance, we can use

Figure 3.4 Removing blank rows

the OAI-PMH GetRecord verb to fetch the full record for each item. To do this from the Header – identifier column, open the drop-down menu and select Edit Column > Add Column by Fetching URLs. In the dialog box that opens, use the following settings (Figure 3.5):

- New column name: record

- Throttle delay: 500

- On error: store error

- Language: GREL

- Expression: "http://open.jorum.ac.uk/oai/request?? verb=GetRecord&metadataPrefix=oai_dc& identifier="+value

Click OK and sit back. OpenRefine is now using the identifier value to fetch the full record from Jorum and then pausing 500 milliseconds (the throttle delay to prevent the target server from crashing) before getting the next record. Given that there are over 15,000 records, it's going to take a couple of hours to get all the data. If you would prefer not to wait and don't mind using stale data, an export of the project is available from goo.gl/wCpYok.

At this point you should have something similar to Figure 3.6, with each row having a cell with a raw XML markup of the record. To help us visualize this data, let us extract What, Who, and When.

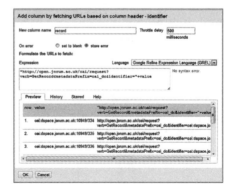

Figure 3.5   Fetching the full record

Figure 3.6   Full record as raw XML

Refining the Data

Before refining the data it's always worth defining the What. First we can immediately see that Dublin Core is being used to mark up the record elements (e.g., <dc:creator> identifies author etc.). A basic trick is to use is the web browser's Find feature (Ctrl+F on Windows). This will however only highlight results in the records that you can see in your browser window. To survey the entire dataset we can use custom facets. Within the record column menu select Facet > Custom Text Facet. In the dialog window that opens, we are prompted for an expression. You can write this using one of three programming languages: Clojure, Jython, or Google Refine Expression Language (GREL) (github.com/OpenRefine/OpenRefine/wiki/Google-refine-expression-language). For this project, we are going to use GREL. One of the GREL functions is *contains*, which tests if a string contains a substring. In the expression box make sure the language is set to GREL and enter:

```
value.contains("dc:publisher")
```

In the Facet/Filter tab, we can see that around 12,000 records contain dc:publisher and that 3,000 do not. Again from the record column menu, we can add another custom text facet, this time for dc:creator using:

```
value.contains("dc:creator")
```

This time over 15,000 records include dc:creator and less than 200 do not. Trying value.contains("dc:title"), we can see all the rows contain this substring, so let's make this our starting point. Similarly to Add Column by Fetching URL, we can add columns based on other columns. As part of GREL, there is a dedicated HTML parsing function (github.com/OpenRefine/OpenRefine/wiki/GREL-Other-Functions#jsoup-html-parsing-functions) that actually lets you extract parts of any well-formed XML document. To extract the item title, click on the record cell column menu and select Edit Column > Add Column Based on This Column. In the dialog box that opens, set the new column name to dc:title and enter the following expression:

```
value.parseHtml().select("dc|title")[0].
htmlText()
```

It is important to remember that when adding new columns or doing any other cell transformations, these changes will only be applied to the faceted results. Make sure your data isn't being faceted before applying this expression.

What this expression does is *parseHtml* the source cell, *select* all elements marked with <dc:title>, and put them into a temporary array before emitting the first value (*[0]*) as *htmlText*. Our assumption here is that if there is more than one <dc:title>, the first is the one we use.

Next let's extract the Who. From the record column menu, again select Edit Column > Add Column Based on This Column and enter the new column name dc:publisher and the expression:

```
forEach(value.parseHtml().select("dc|
publisher"),v, v.htmlText()).join("||")
```

This expression is similar to the title extraction, but this time instead of getting the htmlText for the first element item in the array, we use *forEach* to apply the *htmlText* operation on all <dc:publisher>. The last part of the expression, *.join("||")*, converts the array of elements into a string joining each item with '||'. If you'd like to get a sense of the number of records with multiple publishers, you can use a custom numeric facet. To apply this from the new dc:publisher column menu, select Facets > Customized numeric facet. You are again presented with the expression dialog where you can enter:

```
value.split("||").length()
```

With this we are using our *join* in reverse, performing a *split* on the string converting it into an array before then using *length* to return the number of items in the array. This gives us a histogram facet with adjustable handles to filter the number of publishers. Adjusting these to filter the 0.00–1.00 range (Figure 3.7), we get the 3,000 records without dc:publisher.

With this facet on, you can now edit the dc:publisher cells without a value. From the dc:publisher column menu, select Edit Cells > Transform and enter the following expression:

```
cells['record'].value.parseHtml().select
("dc|creator")[0].htmlText()
```

This is similar to the way we extracted the dc:title column, but you'll notice we are using *cells['record']* to use a value from a different column. To get a sense of the values you now have in the dc:publisher column, you can use a text facet. To turn this on from the dc:publisher column menu, select Facet > Text Facet. Switching this facet to sort by count, you can see in Figure 3.8 that over 4,000 repository items have been published by Staffordshire University and so on.

There is an opportunity here to do some manual refinement of the data by, for example, faceting on a single publisher and then editing the cell values en mass (e.g., changing *Core-Materials||University of Cambridge* to just *University of Cambridge*). OpenRefine has some useful tools to also help us do this. From the dc:publisher facet,

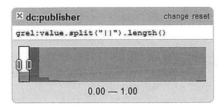

Figure 3.7   Filtering to find items without a publisher

Figure 3.8 Facet with count of items per publisher

click Cluster (or from dc:publisher column menu, click Edit Cells > Cluster and Edit) (Figure 3.9). With this feature, you have a number of methods to edit cells that might be referring to the same thing (e.g., Nottingham University and University of Nottingham). With the cluster, you can run repeated merges until you are happy with the shape of the data. How much time to spend on this is usually dependent on what you are going to use the data for.

We now have What and Who; let us now turn our attention to When. Within each record, you have multiple <dc:date>. Using a similar technique, you can extract this as a date by selecting the column menu from record and choosing Edit Column > Add Column Based in This Column and entering the column name dc:date and the expression:

```
forEach(value.parseHtml().select("dc|date"),
v, if(length(v.htmlText())>11, v.htmlText(),
"null")).sort()[0]
```

Again you are selecting the <dc:date> elements but this time only storing the *htmlText* value *if* its string *length* is greater than 11 (i.e., in yyyy-MM-ddTHH:mm:ssZ format). You then *sort* the array and get the first (*[0]*) value, which should be the earliest date. Currently the new dc:date column is stored as a string but you can make sure

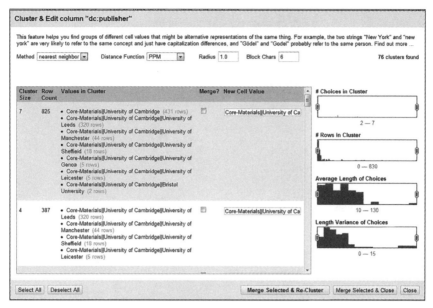

Figure 3.9   Clustering and editing the publisher field data

OpenRefine interprets this as a date by selecting the dc:date column menu and Edit cells > Common transforms > To date. To see if this has worked from the same column menu, you can add Facet > Timeline facet. This gives you a histogram of record dates shown in Figure 3.10.

By making sure the Non-Time box is only selected in the facet, we can see what went wrong with these rows: The dc:date has become malformed with an extra month name and year. At this point, we have a couple of choices:

- From the Undo/Redo tab, roll back a couple of steps and modify the expression (e.g., only permitting strings greater than 11 and less than 21)

- Hover in the dc:date cell and click Edit, remove the malformed part (e.g., March2009), switch the data type to date, and apply (see Figure 3.11)

- Ignore three records from over 15,000

For the last OpenRefine trick, we will replace the setSpec identifier (e.g., hdl_10949_4) with its corresponding human readable name

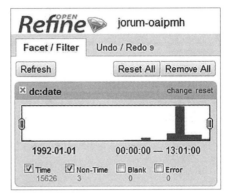

Figure 3.10 Histogram of records by date

Figure 3.11 Updating date types to be consistent

(e.g., FE - Arts & Crafts). To do this, you need to go back to the Jorum OAI-PMH and request the verb ListSets. In your current OpenRefine project, click Open (top right) and then Create Project. As before, we want to use Web Addresses (URLs) to make our project, this time requesting:

```
http://open.jorum.ac.uk/oai/request?verb=
ListSets
```

Switch the preview to XML Files and select the <set> element as the first element to load and use jorum-setSpecs as the project name. You have essentially now made a lookup table. Back in your original project, in the column menu for record, select Edit Column > Add Column Based in This Column and enter the column name setSpec and the expression:

```
forEach(value.parseHtml().select("setSpec"),v,
v.htmlText()).join("||")
```

Because some of the records have multiple setSpecs, we want to separate these out on one per row. To do this from the new setSpec column, select Edit Cells > Split Multi-Valued Cells (Figure 3.12).

You can now finally replace the setSpec with a name by opening the setSpec column menu and choosing Edit Cells > Transform With the Expression:

```
cell.cross("jorum-setSpecs","set - setSpec")
[0].cells["set - setName"].value
```

Using the cell *cross* function, this looks up our other OpenRefine project (jorum-setSpecs) and returns the row with the matching set – setSpec value. Because this function can return multiple rows in an array, the expression indicates that you want the first returned row (*[0]*) and gets the corresponding cell value.

You may have noticed that the Split Multi-Valued Cells operation used earlier has introduced some blank rows. You can fill these from the menus for the columns we've added by selecting Edit Cells > Fill Down.

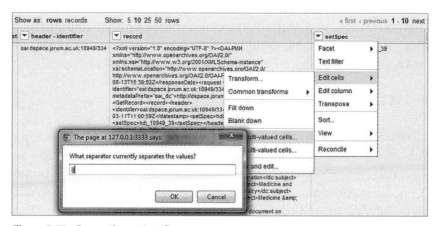

Figure 3.12   Separating out setSpecs

Visualizing the Data

There are a number of ways this data could be visualized and a growing number of tools to help with visualization. As well as some standard export options to formats like Excel/Comma Separated Values (CSV), OpenRefine has a powerful Templating feature that lets you shape any text-based export. This is particularly useful for applications with custom import/export formats. For our project we are going to use Gource (code.google.com/p/gource), which is a Software Version Control visualization tool for Windows developed by Andrew Caudwell.

This software has the option of using a custom log format, which uses the following pipe- ('|') delimited syntax *timestamp|username| type|file|colour*:

- *Timestamp*: A UNIX timestamp of when the update occurred

- *Username*: The name of the user who made the update

- *Type*: Initial for the update type - (**A**)dded, (**M**)odified or (**D**)eleted

- *File*: Path of the file updated

- *Colour (Optional)*: A colour for the file in hex (FFFFFF) format

Because our extracted dc:dates aren't in UNIX timestamp format, we need to make one last tweak to our dataset. From the dc:date column select Edit Column > Add Column Based on This Column and enter the column name as timestamp and the expression (for this to work, you need to change the Language option to Jython):

```
return value.getTime()/1000
```

One final thing to do is sort the timestamp column by selecting this option from its column menu. You can now build your log by selecting the Export menu (top right) and select Templating. In the Template Export dialog (Figure 3.13) remove all values in the Prefix and Suffix boxes and remove the comma in the Row Separator, but keep the carriage return. For the Row Template use:

```
{{ cells["timestamp"].value
}}|{{cells["dc:publisher"].value}}|A|
{{replace(cells["setSpec"].value," / ","
\\")}}/{{if(length(cells["dc:title"].value)
>60,cells["dc:title"].value.slice(0,60)
+"...",cells["dc:title"].value)}}
```

Using the '{{ }}' you can specify the row values to include. For the *timestamp* and *dc:publisher* you can just include the value. For the *setSpec* you are using a GREL string function to replace slashes in the name, which might be confused as new directories in Gource. Finally for *dc:title* you are trimming any long titles. Hitting the Export button will generate the custom log in .txt format. Placing this file in the same directory where you have installed Gource, opening your command line, and running the following command should render a nice interactive visualization similar to the one at youtube.com/ watch?v=v4HQM6qk6kM:

```
Gource jorum-oai-pmh.txt
```

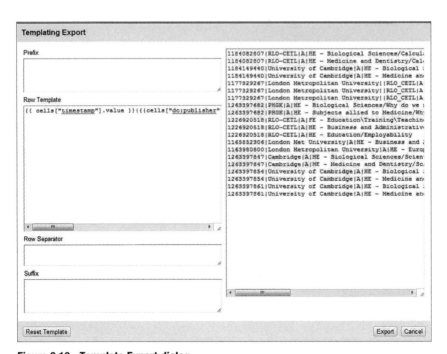

Figure 3.13 Template Export dialog

Summary

While the Gource visualization is limited in usefulness, I hope this chapter has shown the power of using OpenRefine to clean, explore, and extract useful datasets. Having a clean dataset is often the critical first step before conducting explanatory or exploratory visual analytics. This was the case in the UK Open Educational Resources Visualization Project (mashe.hawksey.info/2012/02/oer-visualisation-project-fin-day-40-5) in which a number of different visualizations were developed based on a similar refinement of the Jorum repository.

If you would like to learn more about OpenRefine, the project has an extensive wiki of resources (github.com/OpenRefine/OpenRefine/wiki) and a very active community around its mailing list (groups.google.com/forum/?fromgroups#!forum/openrefine).

## CHAPTER 4

Umlaut: Mashing Up Delivery and Access

Jonathan Rochkind
Johns Hopkins University

Umlaut (github.com/team-umlaut/umlaut) is software originally written by Ross Singer, then at the Georgia Institute of Technology, as an open source front-end user interface to the SFX link resolver. SFX, one of several library link resolver products in the field, is mainly thought of as software that tracks a library's article full text licenses and gets users to licensed copies of articles they are interested in.

I started adapting and adopting Umlaut for use at Johns Hopkins Libraries in 2005, and we went live in 2006. (Shortly after that, Georgia Tech stopped using Umlaut, and I became the lead developer for the project.)

Through my experience developing and using Umlaut, I have to come to understand that Umlaut is far more than a "link resolver front end." Rather, it's a platform for presenting unified delivery and access services to users.

Discovery to Delivery

Libraries have collectively paid much attention in the last five to 10 years to improving our discovery services. By *discovery*, we mean "Discover that a resource exists,"[1] and in actual practice, we usually specifically mean by a search or browse process. Users may want articles, books, or other information resources on a given topic or by a given author, or they may even know the name of a specific item that they want. They enter a query into a discovery system of some kind and get a list of citations back. That's discovery, and libraries have spent a lot of attention on trying to improve the discovery systems we can offer our patrons, both with open source solutions and with purchased discovery products.

Our users have a lot of alternatives for discovery of information resources, including free search engines like Google (google.com) or Google Scholar (scholar.google.com), online product catalogs like Amazon (amazon.com), the multitudinous variety of specialized research databases we license on their behalf, and a host of other services. Of course, researchers can also discover citations of interest from bibliographies and reference lists, colleagues, blog posts, and many other places.

Alternatives are good. Our job is to help our users, and whatever helps them discover what they need is great for our users. But many information resources are not available online for free. After discovery, our users will actually need to obtain the resources discovered, via some kind of fulfillment, access, request, or *delivery* process. Discovery without delivery is incomplete.

In 2008, Steve Shadle of the University of Washington wrote:

> Historically, libraries have had the (mistaken) belief that they were all about discovery. Research by OCLC and others provides evidence that libraries are rarely the first place students go when looking for information and our usability testing anecdotally confirms that. Libraries must recognize the fact that they are all about *fulfillment* and not necessarily about discovery.[2]

Does it make sense for us to spend so much effort on discovery? Have we been neglecting delivery as we focus on discovery? The Utrecht University Library has taken an unusually strong position on this. Recognizing that users had a variety of suitable options for discovery, but still relied on the library for delivery and access, the library decided to focus almost entirely on delivery instead of discovery in their work to improve services:

> The Library should not invest in a new library discovery tool. The benefit for our users will be marginal. Instead, we should concentrate on improving delivery of the materials purchased and licensed for Utrecht University users or

produced by Utrecht scholars. We should phase out Omega
[a custom local article search service]. For discovery of electronic articles there are sufficient alternatives available. [3]

Way back in 2005, Lorcan Dempsey of OCLC recognized that discovery and delivery were bifurcating:

> We will increasingly see the discovery process separated
> from the location/request/delivery process. So, for exam-
> ple, a user may discover that something exists in a search
> engine or Amazon and then want to be connected through
> to library services. This is different than the current com-
> mon presumption, where the user's discovery experience
> is in the catalog. ... The end-to-end process articulation
> required to give a user a smooth or "well-seamed" discovery-
> to-delivery experience is still not quite in place.[4]

Eight years later, the variety of different discovery tools available
to and used by our users continues to increase, but the tools to provide a smooth path from discover to delivery are still rare. To be sure,
many libraries have increased their investment in delivery and access
options—from increased licensed ebooks to increased investment
in consortial and pseudo-consortial borrowing. But our users' experience in finding and utilizing this increasing variety of access and
delivery options is still disjointed and challenging, with many poorly
stitched seams.

Umlaut is software focused on smoothing out the delivery end of
the process and the jump from discovery to delivery. Umlaut is not
about discovery or search. It's about delivery, fulfillment, access, and
other library services for specific items already discovered. Umlaut
takes over when a citation has already been identified and tries to
unify the presentation of diverse services a library can provide for the
identified known item.

From the Link Resolver to
the Unified Delivery Platform

There is one product in the typical software stack for academic
libraries that specializes in delivery/access, independent of any one
particular discovery system: the OpenURL Link Resolver.[5] Most

academic libraries have one, commonly known as "that thing that gets you to article full text." Commercial products include Ex Libris SFX, Serials Solutions 360Link, and OCLC WorldCat Link Manager; such link resolver products are increasingly bundled as components of larger web-scale library management systems.

Link resolvers were invented to get the user from a citation in a licensed database that does not include full text to an appropriate full text copy licensed by the institution on a different vendor platform. They are the one piece of software most academic libraries deploy that can be entered from multiple discovery starting points—any system that can "hand off" the user via a link formatted in the OpenURL standard, which includes most library licensed databases as well as Google Scholar.

In fact even for typical commercially purchased link resolvers, article full text isn't all they handle. Your link resolver probably provides Inter-Library Loan (ILL) links for a given item when not available in full text and maybe some kind of attempt to link you to a search in the catalog for the specified item.

However, most commercial link resolvers don't do things very well outside of their core competency of article full text—and sometimes are challenged even inside these bounds.

Umlaut is an answer to the question: What if your link resolver took its role as gateway to library delivery and access services seriously, and tried to do it as well as possible, including all relevant library services?

What if these services included not just full text, but ILL, other document delivery options, other things you can do with the citation (search inside the book, search inside the journal title, various kinds of export, show me similar articles), and more?

Services Rendered

Our first motivation in using Umlaut was to improve presentation of book and catalog information. A user may find a citation in a non-full text database like Scopus, and click on an OpenURL to wind up looking at the link resolver delivery options page. And she may find out that there is no full text licensed copy available and even be presented with an ILL link.

If there's no licensed online copy, we wanted to tell the user about our print copies, including our local document delivery options. And if a user clicks on a link for a book and winds up at our link resolver—out of the original use case, but quite possible—we wanted the page to include not only possible ebook links, but a listing of our physical copies in our stacks, with location, call number, availability, and local hold/request/delivery options.

So the first thing we did was create a function in Umlaut that would consult our local catalog for the item of interest. It starts out trying to do a lookup by ISBN or ISSN, but then resorts to title/author keyword—putting the results directly on the link resolver page. Only when heuristics suggest a low level of confidence in any possible matches does the screen include a link to execute a search in the alternate catalog, which is the best option you'll get in most standard link resolvers.

One of the core principles in Umlaut's user experience is saving the time of the user by including relevant information directly on the page. Save the user from multiple clicks, but also do as much pre-checking as possible of what's on the other side of those links (e.g., never include a link that says "Click here to see if there's a match in the catalog," if you can include a link that says "Six matches in the catalog"—or best of all, put the six matches directly on the original page). If you are providing a list of physical items in the stacks, and the user has access to a request function, provide the button for that function directly on the initial page; don't make them first click through to a catalog page to see a Request button. Our users don't care how our internal software systems divide functionality between them, and they shouldn't have to.

Once we had Umlaut providing this "last mile" service, consulting both the catalog and our SFX link resolver knowledge base, I soon realized there were other services that could be integrated onto the page: The page could serve as a unified entry point to any services we could provide on a specific known item. For books, this included checking Google Books (books.google.com), Internet Archive (archive.org), and HathiTrust (hathitrust.org) for free online full text (Figure 4.1).

Useful services can include more than actual full text delivery, too. In 2009, Eric Lease Morgan noted that our users were well served with discovery options, but in addition to delivery, we could help them do more things with what they discovered:

I then made an attempt to describe how our "next generation" library catalogs could go so much further by providing services against the texts as well as services against the index. "Discovery is not the problem that needs to be solved."[6]

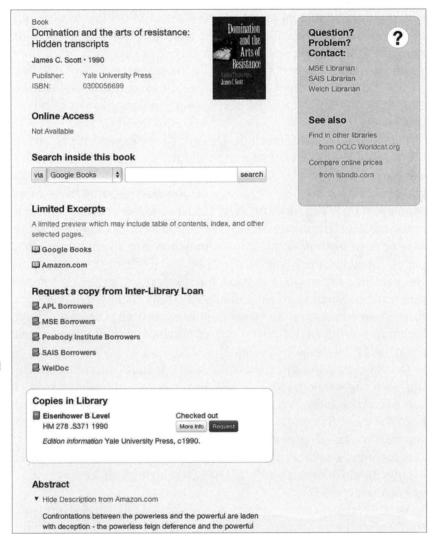

Figure 4.1   Umlaut's service offerings for a book, as configured at Johns Hopkins Libraries

By providing pre-checked links to limited excerpts or "search inside the book" on Amazon, Google, and HathiTrust, we could help users determine if they needed a full copy of the book (digital or physical) after all.

For articles, I realized the Umlaut "last mile" known item services page could advertise and provide smoother access to our licensed citation chaining services (Figure 4.2). We license both Scopus and Web of Knowledge, both of which provide functions to go from an article citation to other articles that cited your original article. But ordinarily a user needs to know this service exists, manually navigate to the service, manually enter their citation details, and make several clicks to access results. An Umlaut page already knows citation details for a citation of interest, so it could use Scopus and Web of

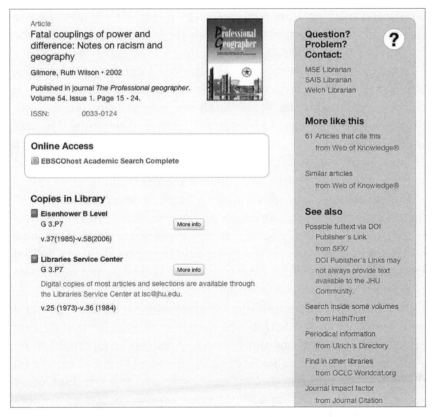

Figure 4.2   Umlaut's service offerings for an article, as configured at Johns Hopkins Libraries

Knowledge API's to pre-check for known "cited by" information and link the user directly there. This function is not about delivery, but is still about smoothing the path from multiple discovery starting points to "last mile" services we can offer for items discovered.

As You Mash, So May You Be Mashed

Umlaut was able to insert itself into the discovery-to-delivery process by taking advantage of the existing OpenURL infrastructure, where database providers are set up to hand off the user to a particular institution's delivery service using an OpenURL.

But we may want the assemblage of known item services that Umlaut provides to be available in other circumstances too, including one or more library-managed discovery services. For instance, if we are displaying a book in our local catalog, we will also want to display all the same known-item services we're displaying when the user arrives through the OpenURL path.

Umlaut provides a suite of APIs meant to support embedding Umlaut-assembled services in other discovery systems. There is a fairly typical API that provides all the information necessary to display an Umlaut page, in individual delineated semantic data elements in XML or JSON. But I found that this still left too much work on the client side, to construct HTML from this API response that more or less duplicated what Umlaut was already doing.

So Umlaut also provides a jQuery-based JavaScript API that can be used in a discovery service, to take pre-rendered HTML snippets from Umlaut and easily specify where to embed each Umlaut page section on a discovery service webpage. We've used this to embed Umlaut-provided services on our catalog (Figure 4.3) and in the past to embed them in a local federated search product.

If you have a web application where you have the ability to add your own custom JavaScript, and there's some way for that custom JavaScript to get citation information to construct an OpenURL, then you can use the Umlaut jQuery helper to embed Umlaut content on the page—the content Umlaut has aggregated from various other sources already. This capability lets us expose consistent services across our applications, while maintaining the logic centrally inside Umlaut.

Figure 4.3   Umlaut content embedded in our catalog

Once we had Umlaut as a flexible component providing "last mile" services, new ways of using it sometimes occurred to us as we developed new local features. We were developing a local article search discovery feature, based on underlying search provided by a vendor article database API. It made sense for a click on the title of an article result to take the user directly to full text *if* we had full text, otherwise to our Umlaut link resolver screen providing other delivery and access options. Of course, our Umlaut installation was already the piece of infrastructure that knew whether we had full text access and, if so, how to link to it. It was easy to add a feature to Umlaut so a URL could be pointed at Umlaut that would result in a redirect to the first listed full text source if available, and otherwise to the Umlaut services page for the known item.

Increasing Our Control, Reducing Vendor Lock-in

Umlaut is a central hub, combining service information derived "just in time" from multiple sources and delivering that information to multiple platforms, as the result of multiple discovery-to-delivery paths.

Umlaut's aims are bigger than its current capabilities, but its current capabilities aren't too shabby and are so far beyond commercial link resolvers that I've come to consider it a qualitative jump to new sort of library online services infrastructure.

Eventually I realized that Umlaut was not a front-end to a link resolver anymore; adding Umlaut to your link resolver gives you an entirely new kind of service. It's such an unusual thing in library technological infrastructure that we have trouble knowing how to talk about it, but we could call it a unified delivery platform.

One thing Umlaut gives you is a layer of insulation between those sources providing service information on the one end, and the consuming end-users and next-level services on the other (Figure 4.4).

We first implemented Umlaut service integration into our public catalog when we were using the standard public catalog from our Integrated Library System (ILS). Later, we switched away from the vendor's OPAC to a Blacklight/Solr-based open source discovery system.

To maintain the embedded Umlaut capability, I had to write functionality in this new open source discovery system to use Umlaut's JavaScript services to import Umlaut-delivered HTML sections onto the page. But once I had written this one piece of joining functionality, *all* of the selected services delivered by Umlaut were now embedded on the specific item pages of our new discovery service. I did not

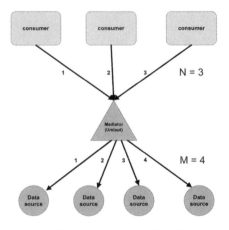

Total connections: N+M = 7

Figure 4.4 System interconnections using Umlaut

have to rewrite logic for putting Google Books results in the discovery interface and for putting Amazon results in the discovery interface and so on—just one function to put Umlaut's aggregated results on the discovery page.

Likewise, if a producing data source changes its API—say Amazon deprecates one API and introduces another—I would need to rewrite the Umlaut connector for that one data source, and the functionality would be fixed in Umlaut's own user-facing services pages, as well as my discovery tool, and anything else using the Umlaut API.

This flexibility can extend to fairly major changes in infrastructure. Ordinarily, switching commercial link resolver products would be a very disruptive change, affecting staff workflow, the interface end-users see, and any software you have that uses the link resolver's API. With Umlaut, we aren't even using our link resolver's end user UI; Umlaut provides the UI. And the only thing using the link resolver API is Umlaut itself; other consumers use Umlaut's own API.

This means we can evaluate a switch of link resolver product—so long as it has an API suitable for Umlaut's use—based solely on the quality of its knowledge base and on behind-the-scenes staff work-flow with the product. If we decide to switch, we'll have to write a single Umlaut connector to the new link resolver product's API. Any software consuming Umlaut's own API services will keep working uninterrupted; all user-facing interfaces will remain substantially the same. We have significantly increased our ability to switch vendors with minimized disruption.

Umlaut's Technology Architecture

Umlaut has been designed as reusable shareable code, not custom fit for just my own library's needs. In addition to Johns Hopkins Libraries, New York University (NYU) and Vanderbilt University both use Umlaut. In fact, Scot Dalton at NYU is a co-developer. Other library developers have contributed bits and pieces. By combining our efforts, based on Singer's initial work, we've managed to achieve more than any of us could have done alone.

Umlaut is written using Ruby on Rails and is delivered as a Rails "engine gem" that allows you to build a local Rails application on top of Umlaut functionality. This allows you to keep your local configuration and any local extensions separate from the shared Umlaut code.

The code for querying each source (library catalog, Google books, etc.) is in a separate adapter or plug-in. There is a plug-in architecture allowing more of these adapters to be added.

In order to handle querying multiple external sources at once while still maintaining relatively quick responses for the users, Umlaut also has an internal multi-threaded concurrency architecture that runs different plug-ins in different threads. If it takes 1 second to get a response back from Amazon, and 1.5 seconds to get a response back from the local catalog, a multi-threaded concurrent architecture allows the total time to query both to be the longest service time (1.5 seconds), instead of the sum of both (2.5 seconds). When configuring which plug-ins will be used in a particular Umlaut installation, the developer can specify what order the plug-ins should be run in, which ones should be run simultaneously, and which should be delayed to run after initial delivery of the Umlaut screen to increase initial responsiveness. The concurrency architecture involves both back-end threading components and front-end JavaScript components to update the Umlaut end-user interface progressively as more results come in. And Umlaut's API is also constructed to make it easy for client applications to take account of the asynchronous execution.

The concurrency architecture has been one of the trickiest parts of Umlaut to get right, especially because Ruby and Rails have historically had somewhat uneven reliability when it comes to multi-threaded concurrency. However, at this point it has become relatively solid. With Umlaut's internal framework taking account of concurrency in a flexible way, developers authoring a new adapter plug-in to query a source can take advantage of Umlaut's underlying concurrency framework without having to account for concurrency themselves explicitly.

While Umlaut comes with a variety of general-purpose plug-ins for querying sources, I expect local installations will often have to customize or write their own plug-ins to query custom local sources in locally appropriate ways. The Umlaut framework tries to make this as straightforward as possible, allowing the developer to focus on unique aspects of the local problem, and not have to write boilerplate code or solve generic problems common across Umlaut's problem domain. Umlaut can be considered a platform for building a unified delivery and access service provider customized to the local context, rather than a complete out-of-the-box solution.

Between Bespoke Designs and One-Size-Fits-All Commodities

The abstract, flexible framework nature of Umlaut's design can have both positive and negative consequences.

Programmers know that the more tightly focused a piece of software is, the greater chance you have of making it maintainable, efficient, bug-free, and generally high quality.

Software that tries to be flexible and generic runs the risk of being over-complicated and over-engineered, and yet it still makes certain assumptions that can get in the way of meeting certain specific needs. On top of this, Umlaut is over 8 years old, which is quite old when it comes to library open source software. This means that it has stood the test of time and had many bugs found and fixed. But it also means it has certain legacy architectural features that I would do differently today, and that sometimes get in the way of what I want to accomplish today—an experience that any programmer looking at code they wrote years ago will sympathize with.

For all the risks of trying to make shareable reusable software, it's still common because we simply can't afford to write custom solutions for every context. Shareable software can help developers stand on the shoulders of giants, and get further than if they had to start from scratch themselves.

I know of one nearby university that considered using Umlaut, but decided instead to create their own bespoke software focused on delivery and access needs specific to their own environment and context. This is not necessarily a mistake; like all software architecture decisions, it involves a trade-off.

On the other side, some institutions that lack the resources to create their own bespoke software from scratch may also be scared even of running Umlaut themselves. Running Umlaut can require more local technology resources than simply buying a vendor's product. There is a trend right now to move as much of our technology as possible to vendor-hosted software-as-a-service offerings. I think that decision can make a lot of sense, especially when a tool has become commoditized and standardized.

But a unified delivery platform like Umlaut is definitely not commoditized or standardized software. No vendors currently offer such a thing. As library vendors continue to try to integrate their library management offerings into unified web-scale platforms, I have no doubt they will try to make their delivery endpoints more complete and smoother for users. But I think the need to localize our delivery and access provisions—and maintain control and some vendor-neutral independence—is probably not going away soon.

It is my opinion that control of the delivery and access experience and workflow is too important to libraries' futures to simply hand over to out-of-the-box vendor software, and the need for a platform like Umlaut will continue for some time. I think the choice Umlaut makes for an architectural middle ground make a lot of sense: neither a one-size-fits-all solution delivered complete by a vendor, nor a bespoke solution custom developed just for our university, but instead a flexible platform trying to solve common problems, while supporting locally developed pieces where necessary. However, Umlaut's adoption has been less widespread than I would have expected and hoped, and I suspect that is because most libraries have not made improving delivery and access workflow a sufficiently high priority to justify the technological investment.

Future of Umlaut

I consider Umlaut as it currently stands to be just at the beginning of its possibilities to smooth the seams on the discovery-to-delivery process. There are a number of missing features and clear directions for further development.

The real goal in online discovery-to-delivery service provision is to streamline the user's path to library fulfillment and access options *wherever* they do their discovery, including the open internet. Umlaut right now works well with the existing OpenURL infrastructure, and it provides hooks to integrate into your local discovery options, but there still isn't a clear path from any arbitrary webpage to Umlaut.

You've got to have some place to arrive before you can provide a path to that destination. Umlaut does provide that front door to library services for a specific discovered item. Providing that path from third-party web services that may have no interest in cooperating with libraries requires some technological creativity and iterative experimental research. There are some avenues worth exploring, including using a customized LibX (libx.org) or a LibX-style browser plug-in, or a JavaScript bookmarklet. Or the solution might simply involve better free-text entry points for known-item entry, based on machine learning algorithms. I think that aggressively pursuing these directions has the potential for huge improvements to our users' research processes starting from diverse discovery points, but it also involves some exploratory experimentation, and we haven't been able to prioritize such work at my library thus far.

There's also room for substantial innovation in the user interface of Umlaut's services page. I think it's quite a bit better designed than the typical out-of-the-box link resolver interface—and quite a bit more customizable for local needs. But Umlaut's user experience is still essentially similar to most link resolver menu pages: a list of links. I think there are opportunities for a more radical rethinking of how simple and easy we can make the user experience of delivery and access services—within the very real constraints of our existing infrastructures. One of the biggest problems our users still encounter is when full text links we provide do not work, due to failures in licensed knowledge bases or platforms. I think there might be some creative ways for Umlaut to work around these failings, pre-checking links in a just-in-time fashion before delivering them to users. Investigating these directions would also require some time for exploratory research and creative experimentation.

Umlaut is far from complete. As the libraries' role in our users' research processes continues to evolve, I would expect Umlaut to continue to evolve too. But I agree with the writers cited at the beginning of this chapter that it is to our strategic benefit to start reallocating some of our attention from *discovery* to *delivery*, and I see Umlaut as work in this direction. The importance of streamlining our online provision of delivery, fulfillment, and access services is only going to continue to grow, and we can't rely on simply waiting for our software vendors to provide an all-in-one one-size-fits-all magic bullet solution. Umlaut provides a solid platform for continued experimentation, innovation, and production of improved online delivery and access workflow for our users. My hope is that additional libraries will find Umlaut useful as interest grows in improving the delivery and access experience, the part that happens after discovery.

Endnotes

1. Lorcan Dempsey, "Discover, locate, ... vertical and horizontal integration," Lorcan Dempsey's Weblog, November 20, 2005, orweblog.oclc.org/archives/000865.html.

2. Steve Shadle, "The local catalog is dead! Long live the local catalog! *Serials Librarian* 34, no. 2 (June 2008): 85–87.

3. Simone Kortekaas, "Thinking the unthinkable: A library without a catalogue—Reconsidering the future of discovery tools for Utrecht University library," LIBER Blog, September 4, 2012, www.libereurope.eu/blog/thinking-the-unthinkable-a-library-without-a-catalogue-reconsidering-the-future-of-discovery-to.

4. Lorcan Dempsey, "Systemwide discovery and delivery," Lorcan Dempsey's Weblog, December 22, 2005, orweblog.oclc.org/archives/000903.html.

5. "OpenURL is a standardized format of Uniform Resource Locator (URL) intended to enable Internet users to more easily find a copy of a resource that they are allowed to access. Although OpenURL can be used with any kind of resource on the Internet, it is most heavily used by libraries to help connect patrons to subscription content." en.wikipedia.org/wiki/OpenURL.

6. Eric Lease Morgan, "Quick trip to Purdue," Infomotions.com, April 1, 2009, infomotions.com/blog/2009/04/quick-trip-to-purdue.

## Part II

Mashing Up
Library Websites

## CHAPTER 5

Building a Better Library Calendar With Drupal and Evanced Events

Kara Reuter and Stefan Langer
Worthington Libraries

The Challenge of the Library Calendar

Along with borrowing books and other materials, programs and events are among the top services people expect from public libraries. According to a 2013 survey on library services from the Pew Research Center's Internet & American Life Project, the vast majority of respondents (93 percent) say it is somewhat or very important that public libraries provide free events for people of all ages.[1] Of the people who said they visited a public library in the past year, 41 percent did so to bring a young person to a library event and 21 percent visited to attend an event for adults.[2]

Since library events are a major part of the public library experience, it should come as no surprise that people turn to library websites to find out about upcoming events. In the Pew study, nearly half (48 percent) of the people who said they had visited a library website in the past year were looking for information about library events.[3] Unfortunately for us, library patrons aren't always finding what they're looking for. The Pew researchers found that patrons were unlikely to visit library websites to find events "unless they already knew that the library had those events."[4] More specifically, participants in the study described "stumbling across a list of activities at their library only by accident, when they were on the website for another purpose."[5]

When it comes to promoting library events on our websites, the challenge libraries face, as we see it, is producing an online calendar that allows patrons to discover library events "accidentally on purpose," by distributing event listings across our websites in the places they're otherwise visiting as they go about their online library business. With a crowded market for online calendars, including many products geared directly toward libraries, you might expect to easily find a product to help meet this challenge. Unfortunately, in our own survey of the market, we didn't find this to be true. To build a better library calendar, we ended up developing—and releasing—the mashup you'll read about in this chapter.

Who We Are

We are the two-person web team at Worthington Libraries, a public library in the suburbs of Columbus, Ohio. We have three locations and belong to the Central Library Consortium, with 10 other library systems.

In the years since we have worked together, we have slowly migrated away from being a ColdFusion shop, responsible for dozens of homegrown systems, such as online calendars, reference statistics tracking, summer reading program registration, and more. Over the years, as more features and functionality were tacked on, our various systems began to exhibit the tendencies of Rube Goldberg machines. These systems became difficult to maintain and support, and ultimately error-prone and unreliable. We learned the hard way that our expertise does not lie in large-scale software engineering.

Five years ago we used a comprehensive, user-centered approach to completely redesign our website (worthingtonlibraries.org). At the same time, we took steps to cease developing our own software systems and to instead deploy and integrate third-party solutions whenever possible. As a team, we have shifted our focus from software development to system integration—from "rolling our own" to "mashing things up."

What We Did

The mashup we're discussing in this chapter combines a purpose-built event management system—Events from Evanced Solutions, Inc.—with a general-purpose content management system (CMS)—Drupal—to produce a full-featured, flexible online calendar.

Drupal

Our shift in approach from software development to system integration was made possible largely due to the migration of our website to Drupal (drupal.org), the PHP-based open-source CMS. One of Drupal's greatest strengths is the ability to add functionality to websites via "modules," which are like plug-ins. Modules developed by the Drupal community are available to download on its website and, used individually and in combination, can solve a variety of problems from small to large. You can also create your own custom modules to develop specific functionality for in-house use. The extensible nature of Drupal has made it an excellent platform for our system integration efforts.

Drupal, like most CMSs, offers powerful tools to dynamically display content, a key feature for creating a calendar and distributing event listings across our website for patrons to stumble upon. Drupal offers existing modules—most notably Date (drupal.org/project/date) and Calendar (drupal.org/project/calendar)—for creating an online calendar with daily, monthly, and annual views, and a variety of other display options. In addition to providing a public-facing online calendar, our library wants to track program attendance statistics and manage registrations for events, adding a layer of complexity to the online calendar project. We also need our events calendar to integrate with room scheduling and resource management, making the project more complex still. The question of an all-in-one calendar, event registration, and room reservation solution comes up periodically on the Drupal4Lib listserv (listserv.uic.edu/archives/drupal4lib.html), but we are not aware of any library that has put all the pieces together for a Drupal-only event and room management solution.

Evanced Events

When it comes to event management, Events from Evanced (evanced solutions.com/support/events) is a popular product geared toward the library market, with hundreds of installations across more than 4,000 locations.[6] The Events software offers a robust online calendar with useful event management tools, including attendance tracking as well as registration (see a demo at demo.evanced.info/events/lib/eventcalendar.asp). Events also integrates nicely with a sister product, Room Reserve (evancedsolutions.com/support/roomreserve), to schedule and manage rooms and equipment across internal library events and public room reservations.

While Events includes many options to configure the software, few customizations are available for the user interface. If you've seen one Events calendar, it's easy to spot them on other websites (Figure 5.1). While you can add a custom header graphic and specify custom colors, you can't add in additional HTML code to include your site's overall navigation, for instance. And while Events offers widgets that allow you to embed event listings and mini calendars on a webpage, your library's event listings are not truly integrated into your website and the options for distributing the listings across your website are limited. With a typical deployment, the library website and the online calendar exist in separate silos: The library website must link out to the standard Events calendar interface, which then passes patrons back to the library homepage.

Evanced Events Importer Drupal Module

While vetting event management products, we learned from Evanced that the Events software offers a built-in XML feed for event data (Figure 5.2), introducing the possibility of integration with Drupal. Evanced refers to their data feed as extended XML, or EXML, feed

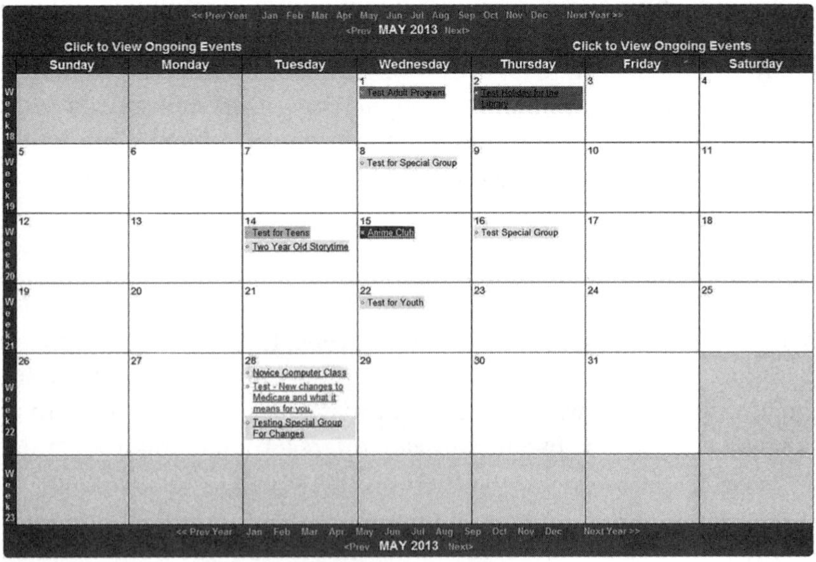

Figure 5.1 The standard Events calendar interface

since it includes so much data. The feed can even be customized by means of URL parameters that modify the range of data displayed, such as adjusting how many days the feed should include or the types of events that should be listed. The rich data feed available in the Events software seemed a perfect match for a CMS as extensible as Drupal.

After signing up with Evanced, we expected to easily find existing Drupal modules we could use to import the Events data to our website via XML. Indeed, a search of Drupal.org identified several modules that read and process RSS feeds. However, we found that these modules handle only simple XML documents consisting of the fields typically associated with a blog post, such as title, author, description, link, publication date, and possibly a few general categories. The Events software's EXML document includes much more

```xml
1  <xml version="1.0" encoding="ISO-8859-1">
2  <event>
3      <item>
4          <title>Novice Computer Class</title>
5          <date>Tuesday, May 28, 2013</date>
6          <time>10:00 AM</time>
7          <enddate/>
8          <description>'Novice' computer class being held. Learn something "new" today. </description>
9          <location>Brown Study Room</location>
10         <library>My County Public Library</library>
11         <link>http://demo.evanced.info/events/lib/eventsignup.asp?ID=5843</link>
12         <id>5843</id> <recordtype>0</recordtype>
13         <RCID>0</RCID>
14         <date1>2013/05/28</date1>
15         <date2>20130528100Novice Computer Class</date2>
16         <enddate1/>
17         <length>60</length>
18         <status/>
19         <endtime>11:00 AM</endtime>
20         <prieventtype>Adult Program</prieventtype>
21         <eventtypes>Adult Program, Computer Classes, </eventtypes>
22         <eventtype1>Adult Program</eventtype1>
23         <eventtype2>Computer Classes</eventtype2>
24         <eventtype3/>
25         <agegroups>Adults</agegroups>
26         <agegroup1>Adults</agegroup1>
27         <agegroup2/>
28         <agegroup3/>
29         <otherinfo/>
30         <featuredevent>0</featuredevent>
31         <presenter>Michael Hunter</presenter>
32         <signup>1</signup>
33         <signupstarts/>
34         <signupends/>
35         <contactname/>
36         <contactphone/>
37         <contactemail/>
38         <linktext>URL</linktext>
39         <linkaddress>http://google.com</linkaddress>
40         <imagepath/>
41         <imagetext/>
42         <imageheight/>
43         <imagewidth/>
44         <lastupdated>2013-05-23T10:45:39Z</lastupdated>
45         <extratag/>
46     </item>
47  </event>
```

Figure 5.2   A sample from the Events EXML document

data that is, in turn, much more complex, including dates with start and end times, multiple category terms for type of event and target audience, compound locations consisting of library branch and room, and more.

In order to import the data from Events, each element in the EXML document must be mapped to a corresponding field in Drupal optimized to handle it, such as connecting dates to specially formatted date fields or event type and age group categories to what Drupal calls *taxonomy terms*. Unfortunately, none of the existing Drupal modules we identified were up to the task, so we concluded that the only way to successfully import Events data into Drupal would be to create a custom module of our own.

How It Works

The premise of the Evanced Events Importer module (drupal.org/ project/evanced_events_importer) is simple: It reads the Events software's EXML document and creates new events in Drupal, mapping specific pieces of data from the Events feed to corresponding fields in Drupal. The module also keeps the imported data in sync, updating and deleting existing events in Drupal whenever changes are made in Events. The syncing process repeats at regularly scheduled intervals, based on maintenance tasks that already happen in Drupal.

The Events software provides a standard form for creating an event, consisting of dozens of fields (Figure 5.3). Along with basic fields related to event name, description, date, and location, the event form includes a sophisticated interface for setting up recurring events and offers a range of registration settings, such as maximum attendees, start and end times for registration, and more. Additional optional fields are offered for including links and graphics. While you can customize the form by specifying lists of branches and locations, event types (e.g., Storytimes, Author Visits, and Book Discussions) and age groups (e.g., Babies, Teens, or Adults), Events does not offer the ability to add, remove, rename, or otherwise customize the fields on the form.

In contrast, Drupal requires you to start from scratch in defining custom data fields that are bundled together as "content types." In this case, we set up an Event content type with fields such as Event Name, Event Description, Start Date, Start Time, End Time, and others to correspond with the fields we use in Events (Figure 5.4).

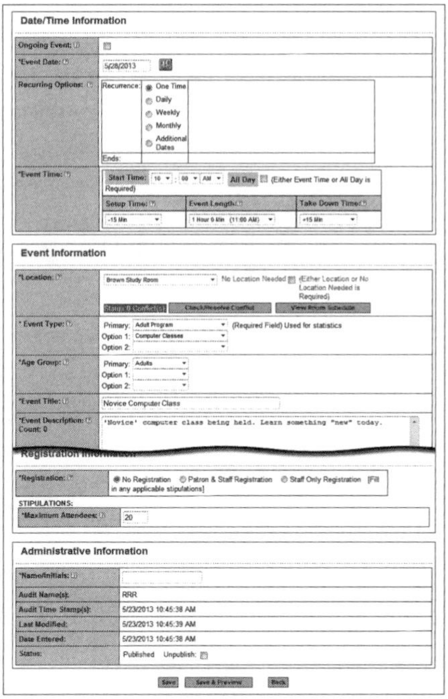

Figure 5.3 Event form in Events

Drupal includes a core module called Taxonomy that offers the ability to create vocabularies consisting of hierarchically arranged taxonomy terms. To match the categories we set up in Events, we set up vocabularies for locations, age groups, and event types in Drupal.

To configure the module, you must supply the URL to the Events EXML feed and select the Drupal content type you're using for your events. Using these settings, a separate configuration screen we call the XML Mapper acts as the bridge between Events and Drupal (Figure 5.5). On the left side of the screen is a list of the elements found in the Events EXML document and on the right side is the name of each field from your Drupal event content type. To connect the fields, you simply select the name of an XML element on the left and click the arrow next to its corresponding form field on the right. For example, selecting the element "title" and clicking the arrow next to the Event Name field associates those fields. The EXML document for each event also includes a unique ID number, which is required to connect the Drupal version of an event with its Evanced counterpart and keep them in sync.

Figure 5.4   Event form in Drupal

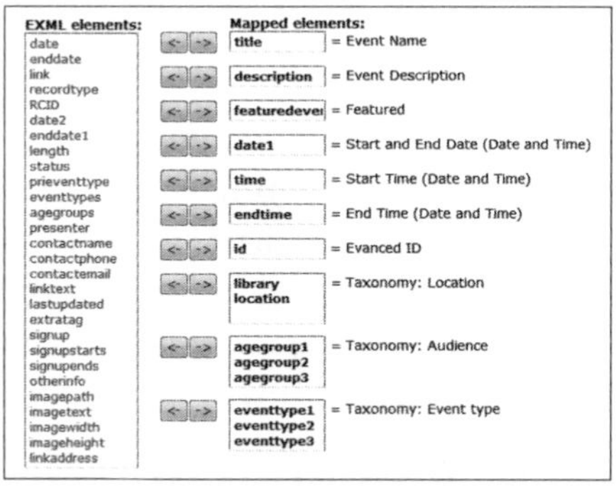

Figure 5.5   The XML Mapper

With Events and Drupal configured properly and the mapping in place, the module is ready to do its thing. Initially, a library staff member uses the Events software to create a new event listing. Once saved and published, an associated listing automatically appears in the EXML document. The module is activated whenever Drupal's cron job is scheduled to run—in our case, once each hour. The Evanced Events Importer module reads the EXML feed and automatically updates the Drupal website, adding new events and editing and deleting existing events as necessary. Once the data has been imported and an event has been created in Drupal, the content is indistinguishable from any other content in Drupal.

How We Did It

The earliest version of the Evanced Events Importer module was developed solely to meet our own needs. Since many libraries use Evanced's products and many libraries use Drupal, we assumed that there would be at least a small cross-section of libraries using both who would be interested in the functionality our module offers. We followed an iterative process, transforming the module from an in-house solution to a full-fledged Drupal module, but not without some trial and error.

Writing (and Rewriting) the Code

For anyone who has at least a passing familiarity with PHP, getting started with Drupal module development is fairly straightforward, thanks to numerous online and print tutorials and how-to guides[7] and Drupal's well-documented API (api.drupal.org). The source code of other Drupal modules can also be rich territory for ideas and approaches. Luckily, existing knowledge of other programming, scripting, and markup languages still applies, too.

Starting with several how-to guides helped us to get a bird's-eye view of the overall structure of a Drupal module, including the functions and files required in every module and the necessary naming conventions as well as best practices. For example, every module needs both a .info file describing what the module does and any requirements it may have, and a .module file where the bulk of the custom PHP code is stored. In addition, files and functions should almost always begin with a machine-friendly name for your module, in our case, "evanced_events_importer." You can quickly create a bare-bones module that Drupal is able to recognize and install by copying code from how-to guides resources, even without completely understanding what you're doing. Of course, fleshing out the unique functionality of a custom module is more complicated and requires deeper understanding of Drupal's inner workings.

Referring to Drupal's API is essential to getting a custom module to work properly. Drupal modules require specific "hooks," or access points to core software functionality that developers can implement in their own modules. Hooks are available for sending email [hook_mail()], customizing forms [hook_form_alter()], and connecting to the navigation menu system [hook_menu()]—in fact, for almost any feature built into Drupal. In our case, the Evanced Events Importer creates two tables in the Drupal database, which are used to store configuration information. The structure of these tables is defined by hook_schema() working in conjunction with hook_install(), which automatically creates the database tables the first time the module is enabled in Drupal. To ensure that the module syncs up with the Events software on a regular basis, hook_cron() adds the process to a list of maintenance tasks Drupal performs whenever its cron job runs. We learned about each of these hooks via the Drupal API, which offers detailed information about each available hook, including any return values or parameters as well as example functions we could modify.

We began developing our module's main functionality starting with the hooks described previously and working outward. For example, to kick off the data import process, hook_cron() needed to call a master PHP function that would then activate other functions, including parsing the feed, determining whether an event was new or just needed updating, and saving the event data in Drupal. We also developed more discrete functions for retrieving configuration information, processing data to make it more database-friendly, and so on. Functions began to branch out from each Drupal hook like a family tree.

At first, we took many shortcuts to get the module up and running, such as hardcoding references specific to our Drupal installation. Before we could share our module with anyone, we needed to make the code "agnostic," or not specific to our development environment. To do that, we had to make the module more configurable. Primarily, we needed to create an administration panel for our module. The Drupal administration section includes a sub-section called Site Configuration where most modules house their administration panels. Some are quite simple with only one or two options on a single screen, while others are more complex, spanning multiple screens and dozens of options. To figure out how to get a similar panel for our module, we examined the source code of some of our other installed modules to see how they did it. We were particularly curious about how other modules created multi-screen admin panels, and we ended up copying their approaches.

After figuring out how to create our module's administration panel, we quickly realized we needed to beef it up. In the earliest versions of our module, the elements from the Events software's EXML feed were mapped to specific Drupal fields through hard-coded PHP. Although the EXML element names are standard for all Events users, Drupal field names are totally customizable. The names we happened to choose were unlikely to match those used in other installations. Furthermore, many of the fields from Events are optional. Although we may have chosen not to use some fields and could ignore portions of the EXML feed, we couldn't assume that would be true for other libraries. The XML Mapper we developed allows you to pick and choose which fields you'd like to map, regardless of the naming convention you've used, without having to modify the code. The XML Mapper functionality we outlined earlier was built without any special Drupal tools, just standard PHP and jQuery.

Releasing the Module

Distributing a Drupal module can be as simple as zipping together all the program files and sharing them via email or the web. To reach the widest audience—and to achieve official status—we wanted to see our module available for download from Drupal.org. A home on Drupal.org comes with certain amenities, including an issue queue where users can report bugs, make feature requests, and generally ask for help, as well as a mechanism for pushing out notices for users when a new version of the module is released. As it turns out, creating the module was simple compared to prepping the module for release on Drupal.org.

Seeking Approval

Officially sharing our module was much more involved than creating an account on Drupal.org and posting the code for others to download. To ensure code comes from trusted contributors, the Drupal community uses a multi-step application process.[8]

The first step is obtaining access to Drupal's version control system, currently Git (git-scm.com) and, at the time we released our module, CVS (cvs.nongnu.org). The second—more involved—step is submitting a project application, including a description of your module highlighting what it does and what sets it apart from any existing Drupal modules, as well as the full module code. Volunteers in the Drupal community then review the code to ensure it conforms to Drupal standards.[9] Every aspect of the code was scrutinized, right down to how subsections of code were indented. If a function wasn't taking advantage of some efficiency already built into Drupal, we were required to rewrite it.

After several rounds of review and modification (and several months), our module was approved. We were able to create a project page on Drupal.org and release our first version of the Evanced Events Importer.

Maintaining the Module

After officially releasing the module, we began a new chapter as official contributors to the Drupal community. Along the way, we've faced challenges in learning Drupal's version control system and have taken responsibility for responding to bug reports and providing support.

After persevering through the code review process, we found that the CVS version control system had a learning curve all its own. We needed to figure out how to generate different branches of code when releasing new versions of the module, and learn how to create and apply patches to provide code updates between major releases. Because new releases trigger an alert for users with our module installed, a simple mistake with CVS in packaging a release of our module meant that all our users were alerted. Since Drupal has transitioned from CVS to Git, we've gotten to learn yet another version control system.

We also had to learn to manage the issue queue for our module, respond to bug reports, feature requests, and other questions. We worried about being inundated by feature requests, but in 3 years we've averaged just one issue reported each month. We faced one real stumper that turned out to be related to an incompatibility with another contributed module, but most have been fairly straightforward support requests. A few genuine bug reports have come in that have offered us opportunities to improve the module. More recently, one user reported a bug and submitted a patch that another user vetted. That code and their exchange got the ball rolling for us to produce our own patch that we will eventually incorporate into the next release of the module.

Although we initially created the module to solve our own problem, we had hoped that releasing the module would address a need for other libraries, and we are delighted to find that other libraries are now contributing back. In the true open source spirit, we're learning from each other and benefiting from each other's experience.

The Rewards of a Better Library Calendar

Since the module was officially released in September 2010, at the time of press, reported installs has hovered around 100 and there have been more than 1,000 downloads.[10] The response to the module has been positive. Evanced featured our module on its blog[11] upon its release, and we regularly receive inquiries from other libraries about our calendar.

Aside from the rewards of participating in the open source community, the major advantage of using the Evanced Events Importer module has been providing our library patrons with access to a library calendar that is seamlessly integrated into our website (Figure 5.6). By bringing the Events data into Drupal, we can offer a monthly

Figure 5.6   Via the Evanced Events Importer, event listings as they appear on our website and a mobile device

calendar and a webpage for each library event, but we're also able to scatter event listings across our website where our patrons can stumble upon them. Using basic Drupal tools, we're able to display the day's upcoming events on our homepage, list upcoming closures on the page listing our hours, display a list of featured events on our library catalog, and more. Our site search turns up hits against individual event listings. We can display events on our mobile website, producing an entirely separate calendar optimized for mobile devices. We can repackage event data to produce iCal feeds that people can subscribe to. We also repackage event feeds to auto-populate our enewsletter with content. After the Evanced Events Importer brings the data in to Drupal, the possibilities are virtually endless.[12]

Endnotes

1. Kathryn Zickuhr, Lee Rainie and Kristen Purcell, "Library Services in the Digital Age," Pew Internet & American Life Project, January 22, 2013, libraries.pew internet.org/2013/01/22/Library-services, 46.
2. Ibid, 24.
3. Ibid, 28.
4. Ibid, 38.
5. Ibid, 46.
6. "Sales," Evanced Solutions, evancedsolutions.com/Sales.
7. Our favorites include "Module developer's guide," Drupal, accessed September 17, 2014, drupal.org/developing/modules; "Best practices for creating and maintaining projects," Drupal, accessed September 17, 2014, drupal.org/node/7765; and, Todd Tomlinson, *Pro Drupal 7 Development* (New York: Apress, 2010).
8. "Apply for permission to create full projects," Drupal, drupal.org/node/1011698.
9. "Project application checklist," Drupal, drupal.org/node/1587704.
10. "Evanced Events Importer," Drupal, drupal.org/project/evanced_events_importer.
11. "Evanced Events Importer Drupal Module is Ready!" Evanced Solutions, evanced solutions.com/evanced-events-importer-drupal-module-is-ready.
12. The Evanced Events Importer module is limited in the level of integration it provides. Because Evanced does not offer an API for its products, there are cases—namely event registration and room reservation—when we must hand off our patrons to the default Evanced interfaces. Events only offers a mechanism for feeding data out via its EXML feed; this one-way communication doesn't permit us to submit data back to Events from Drupal, as would be required for online registration. Furthermore, our module is limited to handling the data Events is configured to feed out. For instance, the feed includes three elements related to registration—type of registration, registration open date and registration close date. We can use this data to flag events that permit online registration and display relevant content when registration is open, but we are unable to display

detailed information about how many slots are available for an event, whether registration is full, and so on. Instead, on individual event listings that offer online registration, we open the default Events registration form in a JavaScript Lightbox. Similarly, since Room Reserve lacks even an XML feed, we use frames to embed the standard room reservation form in our overall site layout.

## CHAPTER 6

An API of APIs: A Content Silo Mashup for Library Websites

Sean Hannan
Johns Hopkins University

At Johns Hopkins University, we were waging a web content battle from many fronts. Like other institutions, our content was siloed in designated systems based on the type of content. Databases are managed in our "database-of-databases." Blog content is created, edited, and published within WordPress (wordpress.org). Our subject-oriented instructional material is maintained in LibGuides (springshare.com/libguides). Tweets reside with Twitter (twitter.com). As a result, our website functioned as an oft-confusing signpost to direct users to the various silos depending on the content they were after. On top of that, we had an increasing number of venues where our users could possibly be: Facebook (facebook.com), the university's portal, the various courseware systems in use across the university.

Our philosophy about library content has been to put our content where our users already are. Users have different research behaviors for different reasons and all of them are valid. We understand that some undergraduates may not visit the library website in their entire time with us. We're okay with that. By the time most of our users reach us, they have a way of using the internet that already works for them. We need to catch them where we can.

Unfortunately, having these multiple outlets of information means that when we update contact information in the library website, it needs to be updated in LibGuides where our subject and topic guides are maintained. It also needs to be updated on the university-managed student and staff portal, and on the websites of branch libraries. Minor content updates became a full-day workload of managing multiple content management systems and custom applications. The approach was unsustainable.

Once we identified this issue, our goal became to decouple website content from the platforms in which it was displayed. What if we were able to create a central repository of our content that was devoid of any kind of presentation mechanics? We could then have an authoritative record of staff contact information, building and service hours, and blog posts and tweets that could be displayed on any platform. This would drastically reduce staff time dedicated to updating content and reduce the amount of conflicting and outdated information permeating the whole web presence.

Now, creating centralized repositories is actually something that libraries are getting quite good at. A small database application could certainly handle the task. As we fleshed out this idea, though, the project began to look a lot like a traditional content management system like Drupal (drupal.org). This is not what we were after. It would involve duplicating a lot of content that is already stored in separate systems. As much as we would love to consolidate systems, many of our silos are purpose-built and are the right tool for the job. A lot of these silos also have their own APIs for delivering content.

What we actually needed was our own API that could bundle all of these external services together under one umbrella. Where we had gaps in our content silos, we could offload to cloud providers. Small, tabular data (such as contact information) is at home within a Google Spreadsheet (drive.google.com), as much as it is in a MySQL database. With Google's professional Google Drive API (developers. google.com/drive), we can query that information as powerfully as SQL. RSS feeds from blogs can be parsed and act as a content API for longer-form content. In the end, what we would need was an API wrapper around these existing APIs.

Silly though it sounds, an API of APIs actually solves many technical problems with existing APIs. What if the vendor's API response is in XML when you need it to be in JSON? What if your API use is rate-limited? What if you need to switch content vendors without breaking implementations across multiple websites and platforms? All of this can be handled by rolling your own API wrapper.

Enter Rapier

Rapier is what we call our API of APIs. It provides contact information, service and building hours, lists of subject guides, lists of licensed databases, tweets, and blog content across our platforms.

If there is an existing API for the content store we are accessing (such as the Google Drive API), we can modify and proxy the response before it goes out. If there is no existing API, we can screen scrape websites and create our own response from scratch.

We currently run our own blog on a locally hosted WordPress installation. If we were to move the blog to Tumblr (tumblr.com), we need only modify Rapier's blog response to parse Tumblr's RSS, and all of the places that we publish this blog content would seamlessly follow suit. This type of modularity and ease of swapping services is highly desirable as vendors come and go and technology marches forward.

With many APIs, there is a limit to the amount that you can query. Once you hit this limit, you are out of content until the limit resets. Sometimes that's an hour, sometimes that's a day, and sometimes it's even longer. Any content drought as a result of API rate limits is rather unacceptable. By passing our API requests through our own API, we have many options to mitigate rate limiting. We can save the API response locally. We can run a reverse proxy server (such as Varnish, varnish-cache.org) in front of Rapier to cache and load API responses as needed, and generally speed up API responses.

In addition to these very functional concerns, Rapier offers us greater flexibility with our content and services. We can now make use of systems that are specifically designed to handle the type of data we are storing. It makes sense to keep track of building hours within Google Calendar. It does not make sense to keep that information in, say, WordPress. We no longer have to shuffle our users off to a separate site that maintains our list of databases because we can now display that content directly on the library home page. While our data may still be as siloed as it was previously, we are making smarter use of the silos and our users are less likely to be aware that they are interacting with six different systems at once.

Forging the Rapier

Rapier is written in Ruby as a Rack application. Rack acts as a simple interface between your web server and your web application. Rack on its own is very capable for API applications. For example, here's a very basic Rack application:

```
app = lambda do |env|
  body = "Hello, World!"
  [200, {"Content-Type" => "text/plain",
"Content-Length" => body.length.to_s}, [body]]
end
run app
```

When you go to the web server, you will see the text "Hello, World!"

To simplify the development process, we make use of a gem called grape (intridea.github.io/grape). Grape is a domain-specific language (DSL) for creating APIs. Whereas coding directly for Rack requires you to send proper HTTP statuses and HTTP headers for your app to work, Grape sits a layer above Rack and handles those gritty details for you. If you want to get fancy with your API, you can do all kinds of high-end things like versioning, parameter validation, namespacing, authentication, and data templating with Grape. It's powerful stuff. For our sleek, internal implementation, Grape allows us to keep it simple, too.

This is what the basic Grape API definition looks like:

```
class SimpleAPI < Grape::API
  namespace 'api' do
    get 'hello' do
      { hello: "world" }
    end
  end
end
```

Requesting /api/hello.json will return:

```
{"hello":"world"}
```

A JSON object with the "hello world" data. Simple. Let's build on this. Let's grab the list of guides from the LibGuides API and put them in a more useful format.

LibGuides' API returns results as a list of HTML anchors. That's wonderful if you are going to display the list as-is, but not so wonderful if you'd like to process the list in any way, or display the content in a drop-down menu, for example.

Because the list returned is in HTML, we'll use Nokogiri (nokogiri. org) to manipulate the list of guides. Nokogiri is a very handy library for manipulating both HTML and XML data. You can pull out document elements using either XPath or CSS selectors. Keep it in mind if you are trying to create an API response by screenscraping a webpage.

The LibGuides API definition will look something like this:

```
class SimpleAPI < Grape::API
    namespace 'api' do
        get 'libguides' do
            # Open the URL for reading and create
a Nokogiri object from that content
            list = Nokogiri::HTML(open("http://
api.libguides.com/api_search.php?iid=...").
read)

            # Create an array for output
            output = Array.new

            # Grab each anchor tag and...
            list.css('a').each do |guide|
                # Add the URL and title of the
guide as hashes to the output array
                output.push( { url: guide.
attr('href'), title: guide.text } )
            end

            # Send the output
            output
        end
    end
end
```

This returns a JSON object that is much more programmatically useful. You could split the object by letter of the alphabet to create an A to Z list of guides or filter the guide names to display only the Special Collections guides, for example.

Cleaning up questionable API responses is one reason to use this approach; another would be to slim down obese API responses. Let's take Google Calendar. We use it to manage the opening and closing times of multiple locations and services across multiple libraries. It has a nice scheduling interface that non-technical staff can use to create and modify these schedules. The Google Calendar API response is hefty to say the least. It includes creator information, timestamps for the last update, time zones, and internal Google identifiers, amongst many other things. All useful information for someone, I'm sure, but it's a bit of overkill here. Getting a list of opening and closing times for a single week gives a 9k response for a single location. Add in nine more locations and you have almost 100k of plaintext JSON that the user must download on each page request. Taking a similar approach as above, we take the JSON from Google and parse it into native Ruby data structures using Ruby's JSON.parse. We then convert the date and time information into user-presentable strings and return only the necessary information in 600 bytes. It provides a snappier interface for the end user at the expense of some flexibility, but since we maintain the API response, we can always add back in whatever we need.

Show Off

Okay, all of your data is being retrieved and manipulated through an API. How do you get it out to the end user? We make use of AJAX calls to retrieve and query the content, which is returned as JSON objects.

Using jQuery, the request looks something like this:

```
$.getJSON("http://www.library.jhu.edu/api/...",
function(data) {
    // Do something with data here
});
```

Now, we just need to transform the JSON object into HTML that can be injected into the page. For this we use Mustache (mustache.

github.io). Mustache is a minimal templating engine that has implementations in many different languages. This is of particular interest to us, as we are trying to keep our content platform agnostic. Need to display library content within Central IT's Java environment? No problem, just use the Java implementation of Mustache.

For most website purposes, we use the very convenient JavaScript implementation:

```
Mustache.js.
```

Let's say your API returns a JSON object that looks like this:

```
{
    "header": "Staff Contact List"
    "members": [
        {"first-name": "Sean", "last-name":
"Hannan", "phone": "555-555-1212", "e-mail":
"shannan@jhu.edu"},

        . . .

    ]
}
```

A Mustache template to display the data could look like this:

```
<h1>{{header}}</h1>
<ul>
{{#members}}
    <li><a href="mailto:{{e-mail}}"><strong>
{{first-name}} {{last-name}}</strong></a>
{{phone}}</li>
{{/members}}
</ul>
```

Mashing the data and the template together, the HTML would look like this:

```
<h1>Staff Contact List</h1>
<ul>
```

```
<li><a href="mailto:shannan@jhu.edu">
<strong>Sean Hannan</strong></a> 555-555-1212
</li>
    ...
</ul>
```

It displays the header in an H1 tag, creates an unordered list of staff members, lists the contact details, and links the users' names as a mailto: link.

To put all of this together in JavaScript (using jQuery), it would look something like:

```
$.getJSON("http://www.library.jhu.edu/api/...",
function(data) {
    var template = "<h1>{{header}}</h1>
    <ul>
    {{#members}}
        <li><a href="mail
to:{{e-mail}}"><strong>{{first-name}} {{last-
name}}</strong></a>   {{phone}}</li>
    {{/members}}
    </ul>";
    var html = Mustache.to_html(template, data);
    $('#contact-list').html(html);
});
```

Very simple.

Mustache, by design, has very few options for applying logic to templates (e.g., "If this user's name is Sam, then make it red"). However, what you are processing is a block of JSON. Do whatever you want with this JSON as you would in JavaScript prior to applying your Mustache template. Run Array.filters on it to whittle down the response on the client side. Use regular expressions and substrings to manipulate the data. If you can do it to a variable in JavaScript, you can do it to your API response.

The benefit of keeping logic out of the template is that it keeps your templates clean and reusable. In addition to serving up content from the API, you could centrally maintain your templates and serve them up from the API as well.

Let's take a look at manipulating response data on the client side for display purposes. We have a Twitter feed that returns tweets in the form of:

```
{
"twitter": [
    {"tweet":"Public Library of Science
not immune to impact factor http://t.co/
UYpAdWW2j3"},
    {"tweet":"Detlev Bronk, JHU president
1949-1953, a founder of biophysics, wrote
about unity of the sciences &amp; humanities.
http://t.co/bLoyYYSPkP"},
    {"tweet":"Trivia moment: What began as a
poem, written by a lawyer, called the Defense
of Fort M'Henry?  http://t.co/KOd8uEulCg"}
    ]
}
```

Our Mustache template looks like this:

```
{{#twitter}}
    <li>{{tweet}}</li>
{{/twitter}}
```

Everything works as it should—except for the fact that you can't actually click on the links embedded in the tweets. One regular expression and JavaScript String.replace function later, and the links are now clickable:

```
$.getJSON("http://www.library.jhu.edu/api/
website/twitter.json?num=3", function(data) {
    // Define the Mustache template
    var template = "{{#twitter}}<li>{{tweet}}</
li>{{/twitter}}";

    // Define a regular expression that pulls
out strings that look like URIs
    var exp = /(\b(https?|ftp|file):\/\/[-A-Z0-
9+&@#\/%?=~_|!:,.;]*[-A-Z0-9+&@#\/%=~_|])/ig;
```

```
// Replace the URIs in the Twitter content
with HTML linking to those URIs
  $.each(data['twitter'], function (key, value)
{
    value['tweet'] = value['tweet'].replace
(exp, "<a href='$1'>$1</a>");
  });

// Use the Mustache template to convert the
JSON to HTML
  var html = Mustache.to_html(template, data);

// Add the content to the page
  $('#twitter').html(html);
});
```

Payoff

Rapier is around 300 lines of Ruby code. Just 300 little lines allow us to pull the bulk of our content from six different content silos. For the library website, it takes about 25 lines of JavaScript to query, process, and display the content as HTML (Figure 6.1). The actual development cost in creating and implementing the centralized API is rather minimal.

This rather small amount of code gives us immense freedom. Staff would rather maintain long-form content in a wiki rather than

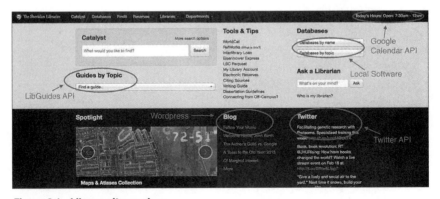

Figure 6.1   Library site mashup

in WordPress? Not a problem, just swap them out. So long as we keep the same API response, we can move from one content silo to another with no development on end-user interfaces.

We can also more nimbly add our content into whatever popular social media site, library technology, or institutional web presence crops up. By leveraging Mustache and its many implementations for display, it doesn't even matter what the underlying technology of these new ventures is or what coding language they are written in. Unlike our previous approach, in this environment adding additional outlets for our content does not compound the time it takes to maintain all of those locations, either.

We can now more smartly choose our vendors knowing that the content aimed at our users is going to be completely divorced from internal staff workflows and the vendor's possibly questionable design decisions.

Our new freedom also manifests itself as what we no longer have to do. We no longer have to run multiple MySQL databases connected to custom applications. That alone cuts down on maintenance time and support costs. Leveraging free accounts on cloud services can also save costs. Basic tabular data is at home as a Google Spreadsheet. Google Calendar can take care of all of your scheduling needs. Need a document store? Dropbox (dropbox.com) offers free two gigabyte accounts and a wonderful API. We only run locally what we choose to run locally.

From this just little bit of Ruby and a smidgen of JavaScript, we have the freedom to manage our library content and web systems more efficiently, and be more responsive to our users' needs.

## CHAPTER 7

Curating API Feeds to Display Open Library Book Covers in Subject Guides

Rowena McKernan
Whatcom Community College

Whatcom is a small community college that chose to build its homegrown subject guides on a self-hosted install of WordPress (wordpress.org). This application has a wonderful and very active community supporting it, and its design and configuration options give us tremendous control over our subject guide presentation; however, it lacks some of the easy tools found in proprietary products like LibGuides (springshare.com/libguides). Specifically, there was no WordPress plug-in we could use to easily add book cover images to the subject guides, with links back to our OPAC. We decided to look for a mashup solution.

We knew that uploading cover images individually to our web server would be neither a sustainable option nor a good use of our time; an outside image source needed to be secured that would populate our system and allow our subject guide authors to easily manage their digital book displays moving forward. "Using the Google Spreadsheets Data API to Build a Recommended Reading List" written for the ALA Code Words blog by Jason Clark (alatech source.org/blog/2012/05/using-the-google-spreadsheets-data-api-to-build-a-recommended-reading-list-code-words.h) suggested a solution. It recommended the use of some basic scripting languages and shortcuts (e.g., jQuery, JavaScript, CSS, and HTML) in combination with atom feeds provided by Google Drive (drive.google.com) and an existing API from Open Library (openlibrary.org).

With some modification to the code, a WordPress plug-in for loading the CSS/JavaScript customized to each widget, and the addition of the ability to auto-link to the OPAC, I was able to provide subject guide authors with a simple and functional tool—one that would not require us to migrate to a different subject guide product. An added bonus for us was that choosing the Open Library API reflects our library's support for open technologies.

Basic Tools Needed

- Open Library API
- Atom Feed (courtesy of Google Drive)
- CSS/JavaScript for display
- OPAC that can search by ISBN

Finding a Source of Cover Images

In examining the options for building a LibGuides-like cover image feature, I needed to first find a data source that was open and available for this purpose. Luckily there are a number of options made available through public APIs. An API, or Application Program Interface, is a convenient way to share data—including images—with other organizations, and many organizations (both non- and for-profit) offer public APIs for this very reason. However, many APIs come with Terms of Service (TOS) agreements that control how the data may be used, and some policies have the potential to put privacy and/or convenience at risk. (On that note, it's important to read the TOS for any API you intend to use—especially the free ones.)

For instance, Amazon.com's TOS introduces a commercial aspect to the use of its cover images by requiring the image link back to Amazon's store (see affiliate-program.amazon.com/gp/advertising/api/detail/agreement.html). Because we wanted the cover images in our subject guides to direct users to our catalog, I did not consider Amazon as a source of the images we needed.

We considered the WorldCat API (oclc.org/developer/services/worldcat-search-api) as an image source; however, I felt that the WorldCat user interface might be difficult and confusing for student use, and this API offered a less than efficient way to discover authenticated ebook versions of the texts a student might be looking for.

A third source of cover images we considered was Google Books (books.google.com), but our concern was that Google makes frequent changes to its Book API (developers.google.com/books) and has been known to shut down projects without warning. Another thing to keep in mind with Google is the potential privacy concerns. The company considers your use of its services as commercially viable information, meaning that your organization's Google data, including data about your students' use of Google's services, is harvested by the company. To quote from the Google Books TOS (developers.google.com/books/terms):

> You must notify users of your websites and applications that any content they submit through the Books API, including their name or nicknames, may be made publicly available on Google services as described by the Books Privacy Policy and Help Center article.

The privacy concerns, combined with the increasingly commercial thrust of Google Books (which aggressively pushes its users to Google Play when viewing a book and possibly would require students to enter financial information into Google Wallet), made us view Google Books as a risky choice for our purposes.

That left us with Open Library, self-described as "an open, editable library catalog, building towards a webpage for every book ever published." It is an initiative of the Internet Archive (archive.org), which means that "the software is open, the data are open, the documentation is open" (openlibrary.org/about)—a phrase that rings like music to my ears. The data Open Library provides, including images, is available free of charge and without a restrictive commercial TOS. The succinct and straightforward user guidelines (openlibrary.org/dev/docs/api/covers) seem to boil down to one primary concern: the need to keep their servers from becoming overrun with requests. Because I keep a close eye on our website usage by watching our access logs, and given the modest size of our user base as a small community college, I did not believe this would be a problem.

Nuts and Bolts

Having chosen the source for our book cover images, I set about following the instructions set forth in Jason Clark's blog post to mash up the Open Library images with the syndicated feeds of a Google Spreadsheet to create a book cover widget we could install on our WordPress subject guides.

Preparing the Spreadsheet

Because Google provides an easy source of JSON, Atom, RSS, and CSV feeds, this project uses Google Spreadsheets (instead of a database) to keep a list of the books we want featured on our guides. In addition to offering several data feed options, it is also easy to use, set up, and manage. To use Google Drive you (or your institute) will first need to sign up for a free Google Account.[1]

Once your account is set up you can create your spreadsheet. You will want to visit Google Drive (drive.google.com) and then click on the red Create button on the left-hand side. You'll want three columns in your spreadsheet. One is for Title, which refers to the title you want to appear to the students on the website. The second column is for ISBN, and a third column, Callnumber, is for the call number your library uses as a locator. The project is also coded to be able to return a Description, using a fourth column, should we choose to annotate the item; so far we haven't found a good use for that feature.

In Jason Clark's original example, author and publisher information was also included, but this type of information was superfluous for our needs. Your columns, of course, will vary depending on the focus and scope of your project.

For our application, we wanted the book cover images to link to our library catalog so that students could quickly find location and availability data by clicking on *either* the image or the book title. For the most effective use of this feature, be sure to check your OPAC search options to be sure that searching by ISBN is possible. Once it's been fully configured, your spreadsheet is the only item you'll need to present to your content providers, which makes this a very

How to Find a Google Spreadsheet Worksheet ID

- Step 1: Go to File > Publish to the Web.
- Step 2: In the first part under "Sheets to publish" choose the worksheet whose ID number you wish to find.
- Step 3: Republish that sheet. You will temporary disable your book widget by doing this, but this would normally only be done once and most likely while you are building your widget.
- Step 4: In the second part called "Get a link to the published data," you will see two boxes of options to choose from. Click on webpage, choose Atom or RSS.
- Step 5: The resulting URL displayed in the box below that will contain the worksheet specific ID. The worksheet ID is located at the arrow tip in Figure 7.1. The will be different for each sheet in the spread, however od6 is always the default for the first sheet.

Figure 7.1   Where to find a Google Spreadsheet worksheet ID

user-friendly project even for technology-averse librarians. Subject guide authors will not need to edit code; all they will need to do is add the book they want linked to their guide from their spreadsheet and, like magic, the code in the back end will take care of posting the book to their guide and formatting it properly.

Sharing the Spreadsheet

The next step is to make the spreadsheet accessible to the outside world. To do this you want to share the spreadsheet as "Public - Anyone on the Internet can view. No login required." You can do this through the little blue Share box in the upper right corner of the sheet. You are going to want to retain editing rights so do not change the Access level. The Access level defaults to *can view* but can be changed to *can edit*, so be careful here.

You'll also want to publish the spreadsheet to the internet. You can do this by going to File > Publish to Web and then under Sheets to Publish. Click on the button labeled Start Publishing.

Finally, you'll want to take note of the worksheet KEY and ID. The KEY is the alphanumeric part that begins after "key=" located in the URL that you can find either in your address bar or when you click the blue Share button. The worksheet ID is a little more difficult to find. The default ID on the first worksheet is "od6" so if you have not created and used a new worksheet, than that will be the ID you can use. However, if you do need to find the worksheet ID (if you are using secondary sheets or deleted the first), see the sidebar "How to Find a Google Spreadsheet Worksheet ID."

Putting It All Together

Because we utilize WordPress rather than a proprietary product for our subject guides, we were able to take advantage of a plug-in that allows us to only load the JavaScript on the specific pages where the book widgets will appear, thus reducing the page-load on the rest of the site. A plug-in is an extra piece of functionality that you can install easily from the admin area and is a basic feature of any WordPress site; additional information including installation instructions and tutorials is available at wordpress. org. The plug-in we used is CSS & JavaScript Toolbox (wordpress. org/plugins/css-JavaScript-toolbox), which we chose because it lets us keep all our modifications in one convenient place (Figure 7.2), thus making it easy for us to manage our additions and other changes. CSS & JavaScript Toolbox also allows you to reuse pieces of code only on the pages where you need it, thus reducing page load time. You may find an alternative plug-in that meets your needs, or you can hardcode the JavaScript and CSS right into the individual page templates, but I personally found this particular plug-in to be the best use of our library's resources, and it was fairly self-explanatory.

CSS & JavaScript Block: Book Widget CSS

CSS & JavaScript Block: Book Widget: Philosophy

CSS & JavaScript Block: Book Widget: Sustainability

Figure 7.2 Script management plug-in

Preparing the JavaScript

The annotated scripting language follows and needs to be placed in the CSS & JavaScript Toolbox or anywhere in the <head></head> area of the specific webpage you would like to add the widget to; remember you will need a different div name for each widget:

```
//Calls in the jQuery library needed for this
function. For more information on jQuery,
navigate to (www.jquery.com)

<script type="text/JavaScript" src="https://
ajax.googleapis.com/ajax/libs/jquery/1.7.2/
jquery.min.js"></script>

//Begin widget specific script.

<script type="text/JavaScript">

//standard opening so that the script starts
after page is loaded.

$(document).ready(function() {

//Begin listBooks function. This is the
principle function that will be displaying the
book covers and hyperlinks.

$(function listBooks() {

//Begin getJSON function that gets the data
from the spreadsheet. Make sure the URL has
```

the correct spreadsheet key and ID. Name your div well and make note of it, you will need it for the HTML part. The name you choose for the class will be used in the CSS so make a note of that as well.

```
        $.getJSON
( "https://spreadsheets.google.com/feeds/
list/0AuwEG4hnNDDYdDJQR2xZTnJkUVd6RXZINEZ
KY1VtT3c/od6/public/values?alt=json-in-
script&callback=?", function (data) {

//This will return the results into an
unordered list

$('div#librarybooks').append('<ul
class="items"></ul>');

//Begin data.feed.entry function. This is where
you add the Open Library book covers API, link
to your OPAC and organize the display of your
unordered list. We use either the small or
medium book cover sizes.

$.each(data.feed.entry, function(i,entry) { var
item = '<span style="display:none">' + entry.
id.$t + '</span>';
item += '<a href="http://whatcom.library.ctc.
edu/vwebv/search?searchArg=' + entry.
gsx$isbn.$t + '&searchCode=GKEY^*&limit
To=none&recCount=50&searchType=1&page.search.
search.button=Search">' +
'<img src="http://covers.openlibrary.org/b/
isbn/' + entry.gsx$isbn.$t + '-S.jpg" />' +
entry.gsx$callnumber.$t + '</a>';

item += '<br/>' + entry.gsx$title.$t;

if (entry.gsx$notes.$t) {item += '<br/>
Description: ' + entry.gsx$notes.$t; }
```

```
$('.items').append('<li>' + item + '</span>
</li>');

  }); //ends data.feed.entry function
  }); //ends getJSON function
  }); //ends listBooks function
  }); //ends document.ready function
</script>
```

Preparing the CSS and HTML

Next we want to customize the look and feel of the widget. This is the CSS that I used; it has been modified from the original to a horizontal view. Remember that in the JavaScript I gave the function a class called *item*; we are going to use the same name here. This information also goes into the header, <head></head>, of the document and puts each "item" returned into a table cell for formatting. The original CSS had the covers displayed vertically; I wanted to display them horizontally, as vertical space on our webpages is at a premium:

```
<style type="text/css">
.items {display:table;list-style:none;
margin:0;padding:0;border-spacing:5px;}
.items li {display:table-cell; -webkit-
border-radius:10px; -moz-border-radius:10px;
border-radius:10px; border:1px solid #ccc;
padding:5px; margin:0 0 10px 0;}
.items li img {display:table-cell;
vertical-align:top;}
</style>
```

Next, place the HTML code that follows within the <body></body> in the place where you want your book cover widget to appear. The div ID is the name you gave your function; in our case it was *librarybooks*. Overflow is displayed natively as scrollbars and is recommended to accommodate the various widths of devices used to access your site:

```
<div id="librarybooks" style="width:100%;
overflow-x:auto;overflow-y: hidden;"></div>
```

You need to create a uniquely named function for each worksheet you use. The widget will pull in titles from the other worksheets after the initial sheet of book covers loads. To avoid this we used a different spreadsheet for each book widget we created except for our Sustainability Guide (library.whatcom.ctc.edu/guide/home/sustainability) because the sub-topics fit in well together.

Book Covers in Action

And that's it! This brings some visual pizzazz to our traditionally text-based subject guides and also showcases our physical collection. To see a basic widget in action, as shown in Figure 7.3, take a peek at our History Subject Guide (library.whatcom.ctc.edu/guide/home/history) or the second tab of our Philosophy Subject Guide (library.whatcom.ctc.edu/guide/home/philosophy).

In conclusion, even though we lacked experience working with APIs, JavaScript, or Atom feeds, by breaking down this project into small, manageable chunks we were able to accomplish what we set out to do. We avoided putting ourselves at the mercy of proprietary technologies from for-profit companies that might raise rates, cease supporting an application, or disappear entirely, and we were able to concentrate on features that our students would benefit from the most. In this case, we wanted to show what the book looked like physically and identify its location without making users click through to another page. The one optional link students are presented with is to our OPAC—not to Amazon or WorldCat—in order to provide an optimal experience during bibliographic discovery activities. By focusing on three columns on an online spreadsheet,

Figure 7.3 What a book cover widget looks like

we were able to keep it simple for all our librarians to contribute to their subject guides and, in addition, we were able to increase the visual appeal of our guides by including book covers in a sustainable way moving forward.

Endnote

1. If you are unfamiliar with these products, Google provides very good tutorials and help at their site (support.google.com/drive/?p=mktg_home&rd=3), and librarian Leah Kulikowski has created a cheat sheet on "Using Google Drive for Library Communication and Collaboration" (www.arsl.info/wp-content/uploads/2012/09/Cheat-Sheet-Getting-Started-with-Google-Drive.pdf).

## Part III

Mashing Up Library Catalog Data

## CHAPTER 8

Searching Library Databases Through Twitter

Bianca Kramer
Universiteitsbibliotheek Utrecht

Mashups offer a great opportunity for libraries to make new connections between users and digital content. In this respect, library mashups that do not require programming but instead make use of Web 2.0 tools are especially interesting. Their implementation is not limited by the librarian's ability to code or by access to the limited time of a developer. Such mashups could be conceived and made by any librarian irrespective of programming experience, unlocking creative potential and fostering a spirit of innovation. As an example, this chapter describes a demonstration version of the Twitterbot of Utrecht University Library, which allows users to search WorldCat from within Twitter.

In the Beginning Was *The Guardian*

In the fall of 2011, *The Guardian* introduced a new service called Guardian Tagbot[1] that enabled readers to send a tweet with a query to @GuardianTagbot (now defunct) and receive back a link to a selection of articles from *The Guardian* on the subject of their query.

This feature sparked the idea of creating something similar for our library. Having little experience in coding but an interest in web-based technologies, I explored the possibilities for creating similar functionality using Web 2.0 tools. Looking for useful leads, I searched Google for *Twitterbot no coding* and came across a blog post entitled "How to Make a Twitter Bot With No Coding" on the Digirati Marketing blog.[2]

Using the method described in this blog post as a blueprint, I set to work trying to create a Twitterbot for our library, adapting tools and techniques as needed. Due to changes both in the Twitter API and in our library's availability of search engines, the Twitterbot has gone through several iterations. The demonstration version described here was functional in October 2013 and might be further modified as circumstances change.

The Ever-Elusive RSS

The workflow of the Twitterbot is based on RSS-feeds. In its first incarnation, this was a straightforward feed based on the Twitter search functionality, albeit in Atom- rather than RSS-format due to Twitter's API v1 restrictions. With the launch of the Twitter API v1.1 in September 2012 and the final deprecation of the Twitter API v1 in June 2013, this was no longer a possibility, as Twitter dropped RSS and Atom in favor of JSON. In addition, OAuth authentication is now required for all API interactions, blocking easy access to Twitter feeds.

Fortunately, a clever solution was found by Amit Agarwal (@labnol) in July 2013 and described on his blog Digital Solutions.[3] This solution uses Twitter's own widgets that enable users to embed user timelines, favorites, lists, and search results. By transforming these widgets into regular RSS-feeds using a Google Apps Script,[4] it is once again possible to obtain a Twitter RSS feed that can be accessed without OAuth authentication.

Using this method, an RSS feed of relevant incoming tweets can be generated. As the original Twitterbot allowed users to interact with our library's regular Twitter account (@UniUtrechtLib), rather than having to address a separate Twitter account, a method was needed to distinguish tweets with a search query from other tweets containing our library's Twitter handle. This was accomplished by specifying that users should use the hashtag *#search* in their tweet in order to activate the Twitterbot.

For the current demonstration version of the Twitterbot, a separate Twitter account (@UBTestbot) is used. However, for demonstration purposes, the requirement of including a specific hashtag in querying the Twitterbot is maintained. An example query of the Twitterbot is shown in Figure 8.1.

Figure 8.1   Example of a tweet querying the demonstration version of the Twitterbot

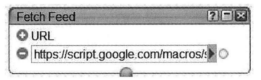

Figure 8.2   Yahoo! Pipes Fetch Feed module

For the Twitter account @UBTestbot a Twitter widget was created to collect tweets containing this Twitter handle and the hashtag *#search*. Since the search functionality within Twitter widgets appears to be case-sensitive, care was taken to include the most common variations in the capitalization of the Twitter handle. The widget is then converted into an RSS-feed using Amil Agarwal's Google script. This feed forms the input for our Twitterbot.

Yahoo! Pipes

We chose to use Yahoo! Pipes (pipes.yahoo.com) as a tool to convert the items in the incoming RSS feed into reply tweets. Yahoo! Pipes is a very versatile tool, with modular blocks that can be used to modify feed items in various ways. First, the Fetch Feed module is used to import the Twitter RSS feed into Yahoo! Pipes (Figure 8.2). After importing the feed, the first modification is to use the Filter module to eliminate any retweets in the feed, in order to prevent duplicate answers (Figure 8.3).

All remaining feed items follow the same format for the *item.title* element (see Figure 8.1 for the original tweet):

```
MsPhelps: @UBTestbot #search mobile technology
```

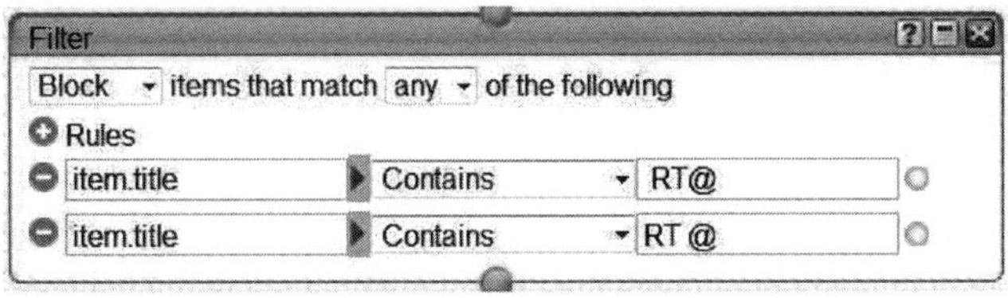

Figure 8.3 Yahoo! Pipes Filter module

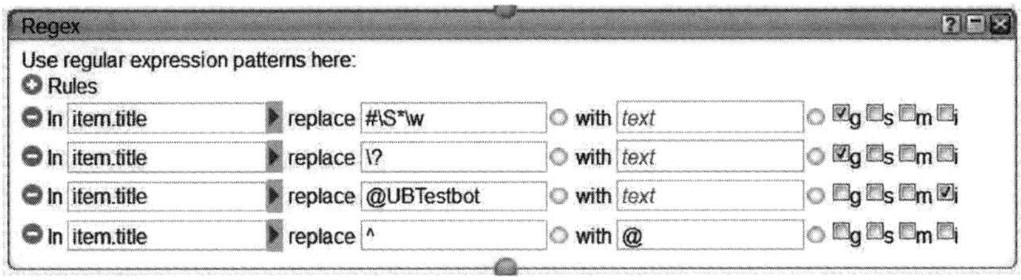

Figure 8.4 Yahoo! Pipes Regex module (1 of 4)

The *item.title* element is modified using the Regex module (Figure 8.4). This module allows replacing parts of the element using regular expressions. Though regular expressions are certainly not intuitive, copying existing examples (such as those in this Yahoo! Pipe) can go a long way to achieve the desired outcomes. Here, regular expressions are used to strip all hashtags (both the required *#search* hashtag and any other hashtag[s] the user might have added) from the *item.title* element. The first line in the Regex-module accomplishes this by replacing any string of non-whitespace characters starting with a #-character, until the end of the word is reached. In addition, any question marks are also removed, as was our Twitter handle. This leaves only the Twitter handle of the sender and the search query. Since the sender's Twitter handle is not preceded by @ in this RSS feed, a @-character is added at the beginning of the string. After these modifications, the *item.title* element reads as follows:

```
@MsPhelps: mobile technology
```

Subsequently, the search query (in this example, *mobile technology*) is modified to construct a link to the result of the query in a library database. Originally, our custom-made search engine Omega for digital publications was used. However, in September 2013, Utrecht University Library discontinued Omega in favor of facilitating discovery and delivery in existing search engines.

For demonstration purposes, the version of the Twitterbot discussed here uses WorldCat as its default search engine.

To build a WorldCat query, the *item.y.title* element in the RSS feeds is used, the contents of which are similar to the contents of the *item.title* element. A new Regex-module (Figure 8.5) modifies the contents of the *item.y.title* element. Using this module, not only all hashtags, question marks and our own Twitter handle are stripped, as previously described for the *item.title* element, but also the sender's Twitter handle. Line 4 in the Regex module accomplishes this by eliminating all characters from the beginning of the element until a whitespace is reached.

This leaves the search query as the only content of the element:

```
mobile technology
```

This search query is further modified by replacing any whitespaces by a +-character and replacing brackets and quotation marks by their URL-encoded counterparts (see Figure 8.5).

The modified search query in the *item.y.title* element now reads:

```
mobile+technology
```

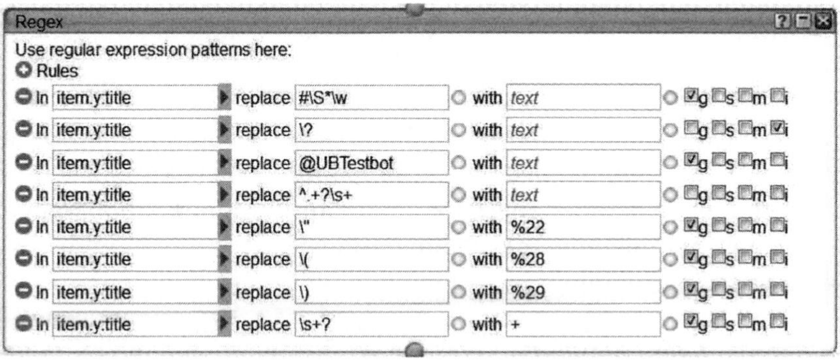

Regex					? □ ⊠
Use regular expression patterns here:					
⊙ Rules					
● In item.y:title	▶ replace #\S*\w	○ with *text*	○ ☑g □s □m □i
● In item.y:title	▶ replace \?	○ with *text*	○ □g □s □m ☑i
● In item.y:title	▶ replace @UBTestbot	○ with *text*	○ ☑g □s □m □i
● In item.y:title	▶ replace ^.+?\s+	○ with *text*	○ □g □s □m □i
● In item.y:title	▶ replace \"	○ with %22	○ ☑g □s □m □i
● In item.y:title	▶ replace \(	○ with %28	○ ☑g □s □m □i
● In item.y:title	▶ replace \)	○ with %29	○ ☑g □s □m □i
● In item.y:title	▶ replace \s+?	○ with +	○ ☑g □s □m □i

Figure 8.5   Yahoo! Pipes Regex module (2 of 4)

This modified search query can now be added to a base URL of the chosen database, so that the resulting URL represents a valid search. For WorldCat, this base URL is as follows:

```
http://www.worldcat.org/search?q=
```

Using another Regex module, this base URL is added to the beginning of the *item.y.title* element so that the whole element constitutes a valid search:

```
http://www.worldcat.org/search?q=mobile+
technology
```

In addition, a temporary placeholder for a whitespace ("add_space_character"; but any text will do) is added to the beginning of the element (Figure 8.6).

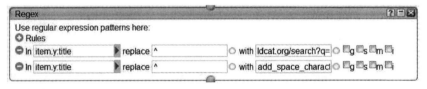

Figure 8.6 Yahoo! Pipes Regex module (3 of 4)

The *item.y.title* element now contains the following:

```
add_space_characterhttp://www.worldcat.org/
search?q=mobile+technology
```

Now it is time to put both elements (*item.title* and *item.y.title*) together to create the reply tweets. This is accomplished by the String Builder module, embedded in a Loop module to perform the action on each item in the feed (Figure 8.7). The resulting string is assigned to the item.title element, which now reads:

```
@MsPhelps: mobile technologyadd_space_character
http://www.worldcat.org/search?q=mobile+
technology
```

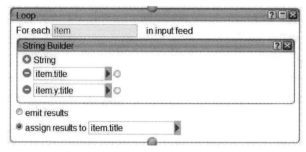

Figure 8.7   Yahoo! Pipes String Builder and Loop module

Figure 8.8   Yahoo! Pipes Regex module (4 of 4)

As a final modification, the placeholder "add_space_character" is replaced by an actual whitespace, employing the Regex module one last time (Figure 8.8). Though not a particularly elegant solution, more straightforward approaches to put a whitespace in front of the http-string did not seem to work.

In the final Pipe output, the *item.title* element now reads as follows:

```
@MsPhelps: mobile technology http://www.worldcat.
org/search?q=mobile+technology
```

The results from Yahoo! Pipes can be used as Twitter replies to the senders of the initial tweets. Posting to Twitter cannot be done from Yahoo! Pipes, though, so the Pipe output is exported as an RSS feed to take to a different web-based tool, IFTTT (ifttt.com).

The complete Pipe is public (pipes.yahoo.com/ubtestbot/ubtest bot_twitterbot_oct2013) and can be copied to adapt it to any library's needs and circumstances.

IFTTT

IFTTT (If This Then That) is a very intuitive tool that takes as input a multitude of online services, or channels, such as Facebook, Evernote, Dropbox, and Yammer. It can be used to connect these services to each other and to email, SMS, and other mobile functions. Using two of IFTTT's channels, RSS feeds and Twitter, a so-called recipe was created to tweet the results from Yahoo Pipes! via our library Twitter account.

Each recipe in IFTTT consists of a trigger and an action. In our case, the trigger is a new item appearing in the RSS feed from Yahoo! Pipes. The action is to post the item title as a tweet from the Twitter account of our Twitterbot. As the RSS feed export from Yahoo! Pipes unfortunately does not seem to include the @-character preceding the recipient's Twitter handle, this character is added to the recipe in IFTTT.

The IFTTT recipe is public (ifttt.com/recipes/122007) and can be copied to adapt it to any library's needs and circumstances.

The combined workflow of Yahoo! Pipes and IFTTT results in a tweet back to the user with a (shortened) link to the search results from WorldCat (Figure 8.9).

Possibilities

Using the tools and techniques described in this chapter, the Twitterbot can be adapted to fit the purposes of any library. By specifying the search terms in the Twitter widget that is used to generate the incoming RSS feed, a custom-made filter can be created. Either a library's own Twitter handle or a separate Twitter account, created for the sole purpose of the Twitterbot, can be included in the filter to pick up tweets directed at that account. Also, different hashtags can be employed, and it is even possible to search for keywords. Theoretically, by omitting a specific Twitter handle, tweets from the

Figure 8.9 Example of a reply tweet from the Twitter bot demonstration version

general public (i.e., not directed at the library) that contain certain hashtags or keywords can be filtered as well. Care should be taken, however, to make sure the responses from the Twitterbot are not perceived as spam, both because this is detrimental to the library's image and because it might lead Twitter to suspend the account deploying the Twitterbot.

Yahoo! Pipes offers many opportunities to modify the specifics of the Twitterbot. Most importantly, almost any database can be searched by inserting the respective base URL in Yahoo! Pipes. Figuring out the exact format of the base URL can usually be done by performing a search in the chosen database and looking at the URL of the search results. In our example, performing a search for *mobile technology* in WorldCat results in the following URL:

```
http://www.worldcat.org/search?q=mobile+
technology
```

Omitting the search terms from this URL gives the base URL used in the Twitterbot:

```
http://www.worldcat.org/search?q=
```

Similarly, by limiting a WorldCat search to, for example, ebooks (using advanced search) and examining the resulting URL, the following base URL could be constructed for a search for ebooks in WorldCat:

```
http://www.worldcat.org/search?fq=x0%3A
book+%2B+x4%3Adigital&q=
```

Other examples of databases that can be searched in this way include PubMed, Google Scholar, and several web-scale discovery systems such as Primo, Summon, and WorldCat Local.

The modularity of Yahoo! Pipes also enables further differentiation in the responses of the Twitterbot. Using the Split and Union modules (Figure 8.10), it is possible to split the incoming feed into two identical feeds that can be processed separately and then joined into one feed again to be exported. In this way, incoming tweets with different hashtags could be processed differently, for instance by searching different databases or providing search results in different

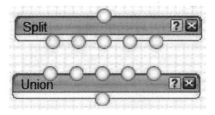

Figure 8.10 Yahoo! Pipes Split and Union modules

interfaces (i.e., different language interfaces depending on the language of the hashtag, or desktop and mobile interfaces).

The combination of Yahoo Pipes! with IFTTT offers the possibility of extending the ideas put forth in this chapter into channels other than Twitter. IFTTT supports a wide range of channels, including Facebook, LinkedIn, and Yammer, to which automated replies to queries could be posted. IFTTT can also be used to generate RSS feeds from different channels, which can then be further modified by Yahoo! Pipes and disseminated via various channels as described above. Thus, there is great potential for libraries to create new services. Some may be useful to facilitate behind-the-scenes activities, such as easily sharing promotional library photos or event announcements across different media, while others may facilitate direct interaction with library users, like our Twitterbot.

Limitations

Though web-based tools like Yahoo! Pipes and IFTTT have many advantages for the development of new services without the need for coding, there is an inherent limit to the extent of customization that is possible. In addition, there is always the possibility that functionalities may be discontinued, with or without warning. An example is the temporary removal of Twitter as a trigger channel in IFTTT following changes in the Twitter API. Currently, Twitter has been restored as trigger channel, but with limited functionality. Although our Twitterbot only uses the Twitter action channel in IFTTT, this example does illustrate the drawbacks of depending on external tools as opposed to doing in-house development.

One of the major limitations of the Twitterbot also results from this dependency on the functionality of external tools, namely the Twitterbot's slow response time. The time it takes for a reply to be sent in response to an incoming tweet depends on the update frequency of both Yahoo! Pipes and IFTTT, and proves to be between 0 and 15 minutes (for an example response time, see Figures 8.1 and 8.9), with an average of about 8 to10 minutes. While this might not be problem for an answering service using a different platform (such as email), it is a major issue for a service using Twitter, where near instantaneous responses are the norm.

Given this limitation in functionality, the Twitterbot was launched as an experimental service, and we kept marketing efforts to a minimum. The Twitterbot attracted attention from librarians from the Netherlands and abroad; however, use by library patrons was limited. Whether this limited response was due to unfamiliarity, dissatisfaction, or lack of interest in a service like this is currently unknown.

Future Developments

Despite the limitations mentioned, the Twitterbot offers interesting possibilities, mainly as proof-of-concept for employing web-based tools to develop new services, without having to rely on the support of software developers within the organization, who are often not able to accommodate *ad hoc* requests.

If an experimental service proves to be successful, or potentially interesting enough to merit further development, all or part of the workflow can then be scripted by the software development team and incorporated in the organization's website. This would overcome the drawbacks of web-based tools, such as the lag in response time described for our Twitterbot. It also allows for further customization of services.

An interesting initiative in this regard is pipe2py (github.com/ggaughan/pipe2py), a code generator available on GitHub (github.com) that automatically translates the functionality of a Yahoo! Pipe into Python code. It is also possible to create and run the resulting Python script online using pipes-engine (pipes-engine.appspot.com), a Google Apps Engine application that uses pipe2py.

These examples clearly go beyond the "no coding" level, but they illustrate the possibilities for further development of tools that were originally constructed by using web-based tools only.

Endnotes

1. Nina Lovelace, "Introducing @GuardianTagBot, your new Twitter-based search assistant," *The Guardian*, October 27, 2011, www.theguardian.com/help/inside guardian/2011/oct/27/guardian-tag-bot-twitter-questions.
2. Mark Cook, "How to make a Twitter bot with no coding," *Digerati Marketing*, September 23, 2009, www.digeratimarketing.co.uk/2009/09/23/how-to-make-a-twitter-bot-with-no-coding.
3. Amit Agarwal, "A simple way to create RSS feeds for Twitter," *Digital Inspiration*, July 13, 2013, www.labnol.org/internet/twitter-rss-feed/28149.
4. Amit Agarwal, "Twitter RSS feeds v2.0," *Google Apps Script*, July 30, 2013, tinyurl. com/mx7td2f.

## CHAPTER 9

Putting Library Catalog Data on the Map

Natalie Pollecutt
Wellcome Library

There is a wealth of detail in library catalog records, and libraries spend a great deal of money and staff time creating these rich resources. It makes sense to view this data in ways other than just through a catalog search. With online tools it's a fairly simple process to make record data available in new, interesting, and useful ways that offer an eye-opening and inspiring route into our collections. It is easy to export catalog data, prepare it with geo-information, and import into a Google Fusion Table (tables.googlelabs.com) to map and filter catalog data visually. Library users instantly understand what is available through the familiar interface of a Google Map (maps.google.com). The Wellcome Library (wellcomelibrary.org) has been able to use these techniques for our Medical Officer of Health collection (goo.gl/Ez3Tfl) and our AIDS posters (goo.gl/cHWBdR), and to show where we've sent our material on loan to other exhibitions (goo.gl/LyMKm5).

My first encounter with mapping tools wasn't related to mapping library records. But as soon as I saw the technology I could see the potential in it for our library. Maybe you shouldn't want to play with a shiny new toy and then look for what you might use it for. It would be better to have a need and then look for ways to satisfy that need. But maybe in the back of my mind, I was already aware of that need, and when I saw the tool I instantly saw how the two could fit together.

I had already seen other maps mashups on the web; they're very common and, of course, were covered in the first edition of this book. I follow *The Guardian Datablog* (theguardian.com/news/datablog), which always has interesting data visualizations, often using maps, for example, the poverty and deprivation map of London (guardian. co.uk/uk/datablog/interactive/2012/apr/12/poverty-deprivation-london-map). The OldSF (oldsf.org) map also interested me because it uses data from a library. What makes it even more interesting is that it was created by people not affiliated with the San Francisco Public Library. People who aren't members of the library staff are coming up with great ways to exploit library metadata and resources, in this case images from the library's image database.

Learning With Play

I originally began playing with very small sets of data. I would recommend this approach because that way you can familiarize yourself with the tools and see what you can do with them, without getting bogged down with masses of data. We had recently launched an online application for customers to order copies of images from our collections, so I decided to start there (Figure 9.1). I knew we collected data on where the customer was from and where they wanted the order sent to: two sets of geographical data per order. I could choose to look at just a month's worth of orders. I didn't need the customers' names or what they ordered, just their postcodes (or the equivalent).

Figure 9.1   Wellcome Library online photo requests (dark dots = invoice postcode, pale dots = delivery postcode)

I also looked at users who had registered with the library online and subsequently went on to complete their registration in person. It was interesting to see where people were—in other words, was it only or mainly people who were geographically distant from the library who registered online? I needed to use the subset of those who registered in person because it's only at that point that we capture any geographical (in this case, address) information for the person registering. Without the geo data, no map can be made. Again, all I needed was location data, so it's all depersonalized. I also keep the map private online.

Creating the Medical Officer of Health Reports Map

After I had shown this map to a few people, my manager suggested that our Medical Officer of Health (MOH) reports could be a good source for this kind of geographical data. Medical Officers of Health were locally appointed government agents whose job was to oversee the provision of health-related services to local communities. Their reports on health-related issues in their region were influential on health and social reform in Britain for over a century. The reports covered a wide range of subjects, including:

- Food and food safety

- Infectious diseases

- Maternity and child welfare

- Housing

- Pollution

- Industrial and commercial practices

- Sanitation

- Meteorology

The time period covered by the reports is from the mid-19th century to the late 20th century.

In addition to the wealth of public health information held in these reports, the fact that the Wellcome Library holds a very comprehensive collection of these reports made it a great collection for me to experiment with.

The other great aspect of these reports was that they covered a wide geographical area. I didn't realize how well Great Britain was covered by the MOH or by our collection of their reports until I produced the map.

The MOH reports were good to use because they:

- Are a good set of data (a few thousand records)

- Are a discrete set

- Are large enough to be interesting

- Are small enough to work with

- Have a good geographical spread

- Have good metadata (title, year, subjects, place)

Gathering Data

Once I'd identified this good set of records, I had to think about what data I wanted from them. I wanted to plot the reports on a map, so place names from the MARC 651 fields were necessary. Our MOH reports also have subject headings, which I thought might come in handy. I also wanted to have the record number, to refer back to the record in the catalog. I wanted to create a link from each plot on the map back to the catalog record that generated it. I was lucky that our library management system (LMS) uses record numbers to create succinct URLs for individual records, so having the catalog record number served a dual purpose.

With my record set created and my fields chosen, I could easily export the data I needed from our database. Now I had all my data. My next task was to think how to turn geographical place names from the 651 fields into plot points on a map.

I'd originally been introduced to the idea of mapping data when I'd heard of MapAList (mapalist.com). I looked at that and a few other options and discovered Google Fusion Tables (tables.google labs.com). They sounded useful, and I already had a Google account, so that was enough for me to start experimenting.

For the online photography requests map, I had used an online batch geocoding tool (doogal.co.uk/BatchGeocoding.php) to convert, or geocode, postcodes into latitude and longitude, the data that's needed to pinpoint a place on a map. I added the geocoded information to my spreadsheet and imported the whole lot into a Google Fusion Table.

Creating the Map

To geocode the MOH map, I chose to use the functionality built into the Google Fusion Tables that allows you to have just a place name in your spreadsheet; Google Fusion Tables then translates the place name into a plot on the map for you. This is a simpler method as it cuts out the step of having to geocode your data first.

I got my data from our catalog into a spreadsheet so that I could upload it to Google Fusion Tables. The steps are straightforward:

1. Go to Google Drive (drive.google.com) and sign into your Google account.

2. Click Create.

3. Choose Fusion Table.

From here you can choose to import a new table (Figure 9.2) either From This Computer or From Google Spreadsheets, or Create Empty Table (if you're not importing data but building your table from scratch in Google Fusion Tables).

I chose From This Computer and then did the following:

1. Click Choose File. At this point you could instead choose an existing Google Fusion Table that's flagged "public."

2. Click Next.

3. When asked some questions about the format of the data in your spreadsheet, answer as appropriate.

Once the questions about the data are answered, you'll have to make some decisions about your table.

Obviously a useful and descriptive name is important. You need to decide if you want your data to be available to others to export. If these are catalog records that anyone can view online, you might be happy to allow this. It's also good to make sure the data has the correct attribution information. Finally, some information that will be useful to you can be included in the description. Click Finish, and your data is imported.

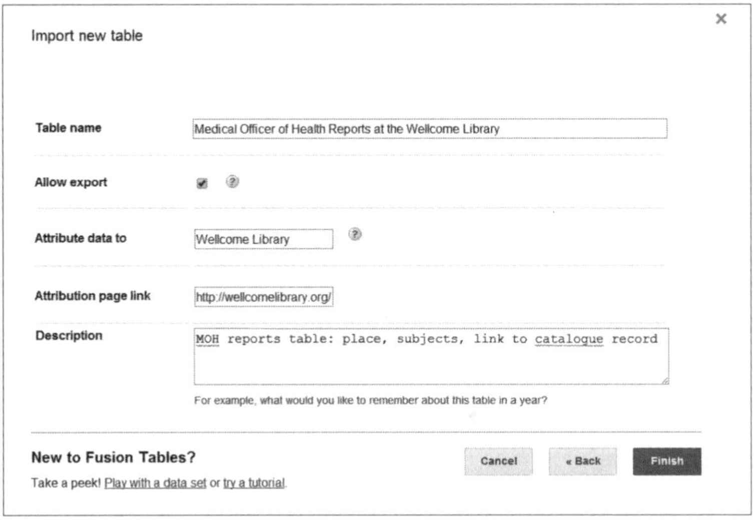

Figure 9.2　Importing a new table

So now your data is imported, but it's still just a table. We want a map. To get a map from your data choose File – Geocode. You will be asked which column in your table holds the location information. Choose that column and click Begin Geocoding. Your table is now geocoded. But it's still just a table! Where's the map? Just click the Map tab at the top of your table to see it.

You now have a map. You might need to adjust the map for the best presentation of it (e.g., zoom in or zoom out), but your map is now created.

Lessons Learned

It's probably worth starting out with a small but representative sample of your data. Assume that you'll have to try things a few times or in a few different ways before you get something good. After all, you won't really know what it's going to look like until you see it mapped. But this experimentation is good: It helps you get a feel for what the tool can do and how you can best expose your data with it.

After I had created my map and felt pretty happy with it, I told some people about it. One of my colleagues later asked me why there was only one point on the map for a place that had multiple reports and records. When I looked at the map and the underlying spreadsheet, it looked like only the latest row on the spreadsheet for that place was mapped. A bit more investigation revealed that all the records for that place were mapped, but because they were all for the same place each subsequent plot point overlaid those previously plotted, hence only the data for the latest row was visible. This called for some iteration with the data in the spreadsheet.

I chose to edit the spot on the map by editing the data on the spreadsheet. You can easily move a marker so that it is far enough away to be individually distinguishable on a map but still in the correct geographical area.

After I discovered this problem, I checked through the spreadsheet to find out how many rows shared the same place name, and there were a lot. I edited these by hand, but I wouldn't do it the same way again if I were recreating the map. Now I would check the spreadsheet for duplicate place names to prevent overlapping markers before creating a Google Fusion Table.

You don't have to use place names: Google Fusion Tables also accepts longitude and latitude to place a marker on the map. Where there are duplicate place names you can get the longitude and latitude and tweak the value, maybe with a spreadsheet formula to adjust a longitude and/or latitude value fractionally. This shifts the markers enough for each one to be seen on the map. In fact we used this technique on another map we subsequently made to show the geographical distribution of the source of the posters in our AIDS posters (goo.gl/cHWBdR)·

The interesting thing about the problem I've just described is that, with hindsight, it's fairly obvious that it would be a problem. On a map you want each of your plot points to be in a different place so that you can see them all. However, we're feeding our spreadsheet with catalog data. In a catalog we want all of our records that all have the same place name to have identical data. We deliberately use tools like authority files to ensure consistency of data throughout our database. But it's precisely the consistency that's valuable in one domain (our database) that caused the problems in a new domain (the map). This example shows why it's valuable to know your data well. If you don't know your data you can't exploit it fully, whichever tool you choose. And if you don't know your data, it's harder to solve problems when you come up against an issue like this.

When looking at a different set of records, I encountered another issue: not that the place name information was identical, but that it was too broad. For example, some records had "Great Britain" as the place name, when it could have been a lot more precise. If all of the records in your catalog exported data just have the place name "Great Britain," you're going to end up with only one plot point on the map in the middle of Great Britain. This is not much use if you're hoping to show the geographical spread across the country.

In this case I was able to give much more precise locations within my spreadsheet and enhance the map that way. However, my enhancements only sit within my spreadsheet. The source data—the catalog records—haven't benefited from the time I spent finding out and applying the extra information. Any time I want to export the same data set I'm going to have to do the same enhancement to my new spreadsheet. It would be much better to find a way to propagate this extra information back into the catalog records, so that it's then there for anyone who wants to use it. This data could be in the form of more precise place names in the 651 fields. This example also shows another benefit of exporting bibliographic record numbers: I'd know which catalog records to update.

Once you start taking data out of your catalog and then considering that you might want to put enhanced data back in, the question of resources is raised. Do you have the ability and the time or other resources necessary to add to your catalog records? Does this enhancement fit with local cataloging policy at your institution? If you don't have the resources, does your cataloging department? They might not have the time or inclination to add to existing catalog records, so it's worth taking some time to consider these issues when you come across them.

Additional Features

I found it useful to include the 650 subject headings in my catalog export. Most of the records I exported had the subject headings Sanitation, Water Supply, Disease Outbreaks, and Public Health. But I'd seen that some of the records also had the subject heading School Health Services, and others had the subject heading Harbors. Google Fusion Tables allows you to filter on your data. If you're just interested in MOH reports relating to Harbors you can filter on this data to find out where the library has reports, just by looking at the map.

To filter, click on the Filter button and choose the field column where your filter information is. Select the subject heading you want to see, and your map updates to show you the relevant places (Figure 9.3).

As I'd chosen to export the bibliographic record number in the data I took from the catalog, it was easy to append that to a URL catalog stem and create a link from the plot point on the map back to the catalog record that had generated it. Providing that link back to the catalog was useful for two reasons. Firstly, it made it obvious where this data was coming from, which helps the library to promote its resources. Secondly, for researchers, it made it very easy for them to get their hands on the item. Once a researcher finds a geographic area he is interested in, he can click the plot point to find out a bit more information. For example, researchers can see the subjects covered by the report from the subject headings in the catalog record. From there it's just one click to the catalog record they need to request the item they want to see. Making the process of discovery a step-by-step, click-by-click process—one that doesn't require having to think of or identify the precise subject headings—is a more intuitive and painless journey for the researcher. There's no need to stop and think. Researchers can flow along the pathways that are opened up

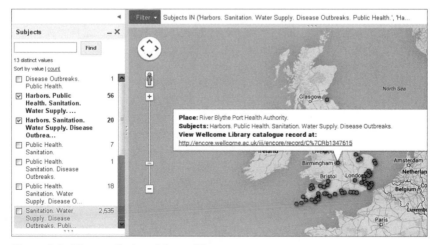

Figure 9.3 The result of applying a filter

to them. All of this information can be found directly via the catalog's search, but the map provides a different way in to the same material.

Sharing the Results

Once I'd created my map, I needed to think about where to put it. First I made my Google Fusion Table public. I clicked the Share button in Google Fusion Tables and set the Visibility options to Public on the Web (Figure 9.4).

However, I doubt that anyone would find the map with Google Fusion Tables: It's just not the place someone would think to go to look for maps of MOH reports. After showing the map to a few people in my library, I chose to blog about it. I used a blog post, "Putting Medical Officer of Health Reports on the Map" (blog.wellcome library.org/2011/03/putting-medical-officer-of-health-reports-on-the-map) to explain what I'd done, and how and why I'd done it. I also used a staff training session to show colleagues how it was possible to show data on a map without having to know much about the web. The main things you need to know are your source data and how to use a spreadsheet, skills, and knowledge that are prevalent in any library.

I was pleased that colleagues were able to suggest other collections or sets of data that this mapping could be applied to. It was out of this presentation that the AIDS posters map came to be (Figure 9.5). We created a map to show where our posters come from and also

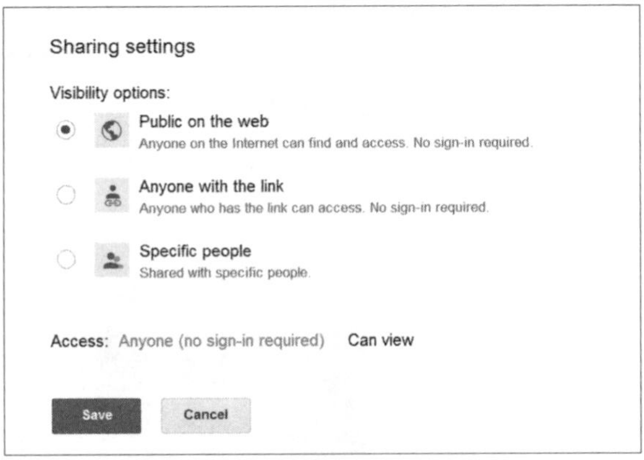

Figure 9.4 Sharing settings

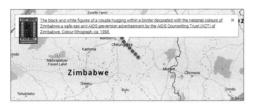

Figure 9.5   **AIDS posters map with thumbnail image and link to catalog record**

included thumbnails of the posters in the info bubbles, along with links to the full images and their catalog records.

I also got the chance to present the medical reports map at a Geospatial Engagement and Community Outreach event, Geospatial in the Cultural Heritage Domain (geco.blogs.edina.ac.uk/events/geospatial-in-the-cultural-heritage-domain-past-present-and-future). It's quite funny telling a group of geographers who use GIS technology how you used Google Fusion Tables to create a map. I did feel quite the fraud, as it was clear from their talks that I wasn't using "proper" GIS techniques. However, it was useful for me to talk to the organizers, as they'd previously helped others with getting geospatial information from library catalogs. They had some good suggestions for me, such as using longitude and latitude in catalog records, and I now know that the Geospatial Engagement and Community Outreach organization is a resource that I can draw on again if I need it.

Choosing the Right Tool

Like any technique, this is not flawless. One drawback is that once the data is exported from your catalog, if the catalog is amended your map won't reflect this. An API from your catalog might be more up-to-date, but it also requires more coding skill to exploit.

Another issue is that Google Fusion Tables are still labeled as "experimental." I first used the tool in 2011. Will it stay experimental? If not, will it be shut down by Google anyway? The new version of Google Maps introduced in 2013 has a new tool, the Google Maps Engine (mapsengine.google.com), which might eventually supersede Google Fusion Tables. However, new features have been added to Google Fusion Tables every year since it was first announced, up to 2013.[1]

Of course, there are other mapping tools available besides Google Fusion Tables. But the best thing to do to get started is to ask yourself: What data do I have that's interesting or could tell a story? and What would be a good set of data for a user to explore and for me to work with?

I was surprised that some of the best bits about making this map came after I'd finished it. One was when a colleague pointed out that we weren't seeing all of the data for a single place. I investigated why that was happening, and in the process, I found a way to improve the map by moving the markers in places where there were multiple records with identical 651 geographical subject headings. But feedback from our users was the best of all. It was clear that some people found it "fascinating" and "very useful." One noted that this visual way of presenting the information was extremely useful especially when there have been historical boundary changes: It's easier to pinpoint the record you want if you can just see the place on a map, rather than having to work out the correct municipal name for a place when that name could change depending upon the time period you are investigating.

Another user also commented that it was a simple way to get to the data that we already hold in our catalog, and that this simplicity makes it useful for scholars and the general public alike. I think that's the value of this kind of visualization: You've already got this data, so all you're really doing is just presenting it in a new form. And with tools like Google Fusion Tables that make this pretty straightforward for anyone who can use a spreadsheet, you can add value for your users with just a little bit of time and effort.

Endnote

1. "New features," support.google.com/fusiontables/answers/1656859.

## CHAPTER 10

Mashups and Next Generation Catalog at Work

Anne-Lena Westrum and Asgeir Rekkavik
Oslo Public Library

Oslo Public Library serves the county of Oslo and is Norway's largest public library. The services are available for free to everyone: individuals, institutions, students in the public school system and at the university level, the business community, and public administration. The library has approximately 250 employees spread over 16 branches in the city. In addition, there are several specialized departments, such as the Multilingual Library that serves the entire country with its collection in roughly 35 languages, and separate departments for music and children/youth.

Plans are underway for a new main library in the vicinity of the Oslo Fjord and the main railway station. The new library is scheduled to open in 2018. We place a major emphasis on the 24-hour library—web-based services that are available around the clock—in addition to our traditional on-site services. This focus will continue to be important as we look to the future and eventually move into our new home.

Digital Development Team

Over the last 5 years, the Digital Development Team has worked with the library catalog and different types of mashups. We have struggled our way through the library-specific protocols Z39.50 and SRU, but in the last 2 years we have experienced a breakthrough as we have managed to convert the catalog into linked RDF data.

We have developed the open source toolkit MARC2RDF (github. com/digibib/MARC2RDF) that converts MARC data into RDF and uses SPARQL methods to construct supplementary data to improve the quality of the catalog.

Our tasks range from software development, concept development, prototyping, and user testing to more advanced technological strategy planning. We are keeping a special focus on the future of the digital library through the planning process of the new library, and we consider the RDF catalog a possible basis for all of our content and end-user services in the years to come.

Current Status in Norway

Like most other Norwegian public libraries, we rely on a proprietary integrated library system (ILS) that takes care of everything from back-end functions such as acquisition, cataloguing, circulation, and logistics to end-user services and online presentation.

While the ILS works well enough as a tool for library employees, its end-user services are in no particular way customized or optimized for the needs of the individual library. One of the main challenges is how it lets library patrons browse and search big collections, and how it presents search results. This might be an insignificant problem for the majority of the ILS vendors' smaller customers, but for us this problem is very real. In our OPAC, a simple search for the Norwegian playwright Henrik Ibsen returns more than 1,000 hits, while Ibsen in fact published 26 plays and one book of poetry

Next Generation Catalog: The Active Shelf

The Active Shelf is a physical touch screen device (Figure 10.1) that makes use of open source software, RFID technology, RDF data, and external web service APIs to provide information about any library book a patron wants to know more about. The Active Shelf is our first end-user service based on the converted dataset.

The shelf has a built-in RFID reader, which identifies the book and triggers the application that collects the relevant information. Initially the application queries the RDF data for bibliographic data, book reviews, and a list of related books. The ISBN is used to retrieve

Figure 10.1   The Active Shelf, which is located alongside the fiction collection at the main library (Photo by Nikolaj Jonas Blegvad)

additional information from external source APIs, such as online bookstores and social websites for book lovers.

Why RDF and Not MARC?

The library-specific protocols Z39.50 and SRU proved early to be a difficult approach when creating mashups. The protocols are old and slow, and it is not possible to get multiple records and process them on the fly. The MARC data itself proved to be difficult to work, hampering the delivery of uniform, user-friendly services. Library-specific metadata and library-specific protocols have just not proven to be a good match for rapid and innovative development.

The traditional library catalog mainly focuses on the individual *manifestations* of the works it describes. This means that when a book is published in several editions, each edition is registered as an independent document, with no formal connections between them. This might be practical in those rare cases where it is essential for the user to find one particular edition of a book, but it is not a good basis for presenting and exploring the library collection in general.

First and foremost, there is no room in the MARC format to connect the records to the kind of information we want to display to our users. Secondly, the library-specific protocols do not allow us to query our data in the way we need to in order to get good results. And finally, the format hides relevant metadata, such as the number of pages in a book, in a text string. As a result of this there is a lot of recorded information that we cannot put to good use.

Our desired use of catalog data has revealed some obvious weaknesses in the MARC format. Since the format itself isn't meaningful or semantic, all programming requires an in-depth knowledge of the fields as well as an understanding of how they have been used within a particular catalog.

It is our view that the MARC format is caught somewhere between human and machine readability. The format itself becomes a massive hurdle both for us and, obviously, for the clever people outside the libraries who might like to do something interesting with our data.

While traditional library-specific tasks and transactions still rely on the ILS and the MARC catalog, the RDF representation—its semantic twin—has proven to be a much better basis for developing digital services.

The RDF linked data format and the SPARQL query language allow us to link our catalog data with other data and query them in new ways. Additionally it allows us to process our data to find connections and derive new information that adds value to the catalog. This is a significant improvement and a good way to make use of all the metadata that is hidden in the MARC format.

MARC2RDF: The Conversion Tool

The open source toolkit MARC2RDF is a Ruby toolkit for converting MARC records and producing an RDF representation of a library catalog. The tool also includes methods for refining and enriching the data.

We use several different vocabularies[1] in our dataset. Primarily we use vocabularies for bibliographic description, such as Dublin Core metadata terms (dublincore.org/documents/2012/06/14/dcmi-terms/ ?v=terms) and the BIBO Bibliographic Ontology (bibliontology.com). In addition we use other vocabularies where they are most suitable: music and movie ontologies for expressing data about these media types, FOAF (oaf-project.org) for information about people and organizations, SKOS (w3.org/2004/02/skos) for topics and classification, GeoNames (geonames.org/ontology/documentation.html) for geographical data, Lexvo (lexvo.org) for information about languages, and the Core FRBR (vocab.org/frbr/core.html) and FaBiO (purl.org/spar/fabio) vocabularies for expressing data about works and manifestations and the relationships between them. In addition we have established a significant number of classes and predicates within our own namespace, in cases where we have been unable to find the means to express what we want elsewhere.

After converting MARC data into RDF and storing it as triples in the Virtuoso Universal Server (virtuoso.openlinksw.com), the dataset is enriched by harvesting and linking to information from external sources, such as book reviews and cover images. In addition we run several methods to construct extra information by logical reasoning over the data already present. This is done by using the SPARQL query and update language.

The MARC2RDF toolkit includes methods for clustering the manifestations of works into unified records. The method creates separate unique identifiers for works and links their corresponding manifestations to them (Figure 10.2). This makes it possible to query the catalog for works, as well as for the traditional manifestations. It also makes it possible to unite metadata from records that describe the different manifestations to create richer descriptions of works. These enhanced descriptions serve as a valuable resource for the Active Shelf software to make assumptions about similar works.

Examples

The following example shows how to generate work for documents *Wuthering Heights* and *Sturmhöhe*.

RDF record "Wuthering Heights"

```
Creator: <http://data.deichman.no/person/
x12821000> (Emily Brontë's URI)
Title: Wuthering Heights
Title, urlized: wuthering_heights
Originaltitle: N/A
Original title, urlized: N/A
```

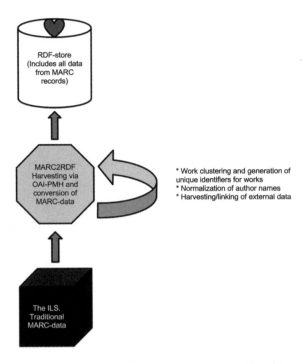

Figure 10.2 How we have built our stack of programs to facilitate the leap from "black box" to open data

RDF record "Sturmhöhe"

```
Creator: <http://data.deichman.no/person/
x12821000> (Emily Brontë's URI)
Title: Sturmhöhe
Title, urlized: sturmhoehe
Originaltitle: Wuthering heights
Original title, urlized: wuthering_heights
```

Rule 1: If document has creator AND original title, write statements:

```
<document URI> fabio:isManifestationOf <work URI>
..
<work URI> fabio:hasManifestation <document URI>
..
```

where work URI is constructed from:

- URI prefix http://data.deichman.no/work/x

- integer part of creator's URI: x12821000

- separating character: _

- original title, urlized: wuthering_heights

Rule 2: If document has creator, but does not have original title, write statements:

```
<document URI> fabio:isManifestationOf <work URI>
. .
<work URI> fabio:hasManifestation <document URI>
. .
```

where work URI is constructed from:

- URI prefix http://data.deichman.no/work/x

- integer part of creator's URI: 12821000

- separating character: _

- title, urlized: wuthering_heights

Rule 1 applies to *Sturmhöhe* while Rule 2 applies to the English *Wuthering Heights*. Both result in the URI

```
<http://data.deichman.no/work/x12821000_
wuthering_heights>
```

The clustering of documents by work aims to identify which parts of a bibliographic record describe the individual manifestation specifically and which parts it shares with other manifestations of the same work. Basically, you could say that the work clustering is based on the assumption that if two documents have the same title and were created by the same person, they are most likely manifestations of the same work.

The process makes use of authority IDs for creators and other contributors as well as strings describing titles and original titles. The simplest case is where two records differ only by manifestation dependent data, such as publisher, place and time of publication, ISBN, and number of pages.

Document 1

```
Title: Wuthering Heights
Author: Emily Brontë
Publ.: Edinburgh : Grant, 1924
Pages: XVII, 499 p.
```

Document 2

```
Title: Wuthering Heights
Author: Emily Brontë
Publ.: Leicester : Galley press, 1987
Pages: 320 p.
ISBN: 0-86136-661-1
```

The only data in these records that describe the work in general are the title and author statements. Neither of them identifies the work precisely on its own, so the identification depends on a combination of the two. The title is necessary for distinguishing between the novel *Wuthering Heights* and any other work created by Emily Brontë, such as her poetry. The author statement is necessary for distinguishing between the novel and any other work with the same title, such as the Kate Bush song or any of the many movie adaptations of the novel.

But not all manifestations of this novel are entitled *Wuthering Heights*. In those cases where one of the manifestations is a translation into another language, or where both are translations into different languages, we will have to look at uniform or original titles.

Document 3

```
Title: Les Hauts de Hurle-vent
Author: Emily Brontë
Publ.: Paris : Payot, 1939
Pages: 494 p.
Orig.: Wuthering Heights
```

Document 4

```
Title: Sturmhöhe
Author: Emily Brontë
Publ.: München : Goldmann, 1996
Pages: 413 p.
ISBN: 3-442-72043-5
Orig.: Wuthering Heights
```

In these cases, the ordinary title statements do not contain information about the work. Instead it is the combination of author and original title that identifies these books as manifestations of the same work. This way the ordinary title statement is only used to identify a work if no uniform or original title is given in the record.

These are all pretty straightforward cases, where one manifestation corresponds to one work precisely, and where there is exactly one creator behind the works. Other rules are needed in those cases where there is more than one creator, where no creator is given, where a manifestation contains more than one work, or where a work is split between several manifestations.

Constructing Identifiers and Linking Data Together

Both manifestations and works are identified by HTTP URIs in the RDF dataset, and they are linked together with semantic links or predicates. A work URI is constructed from the information that is shared by the different manifestations of that work. So for the *Wuthering Heights* example, we combine a standard URI prefix, Emily Brontë's authority file identifier, and an urlized version of the preferred type of title statement. This results in the identifier:

```
<http://data.deichman.no/work/x12821000_
wuthering_heights>
```

This should be absolutely unique for this work, and it should be identical for all manifestations of the work, provided the quality of the bibliographic records is good enough, with correct use of title statements and without duplicate authority records.

For expressing the distinction between manifestations and works, and for linking them together, we use the Fabio vocabulary (the FRBR aligned bibliographic ontology). This provides us with a simplified FRBR model in which works are linked directly to manifestations, without the expression level in between.

So an individual document in the library catalog is expressed in RDF as an instance of the type *fabio:Manifestation*, which is linked to one or more instances of the type *fabio:Work* with the semantic link *fabio:isManifestationOf*. A work is in its turn linked to one or more manifestations with the link *fabio:hasManifestation*.

RDF Record: A Manifestation of *Wuthering Heights*

```
@prefix fabio:   <http://purl.org/spar/fabio/> .
@prefix bibo:    <http://purl.org/ontology/bibo/> .
@prefix dct:     <http://purl.org/dc/terms/> .
@prefix deich:   <http://data.deichman.no/> .
@prefix dbpedia: <http://dbpedia.org/resource/> .
@prefix lexvo:   <http://lexvo.org/id/iso639-3/> .
@prefix iface:   <http://www.multimedian.nl/projects/
n9c/interface#> .


<http://data.deichman.no/resource/tnr_226404>
a fabio:Manifestation ;
    a bibo:Document ;
    dct:identifier    "226404" ;
    deich:cataloguingDate    "901107" ;
    dct:audience <http://data.deichman.no/audience/
adult> ;
    deich:literaryFormat    dbpedia:Novel ,
        dbpedia:Fiction ;
    dct:language lexvo:eng ;
    deich:bibliofilID "146920" ;
    dct:format    <http://data.deichman.no/format/
Book> ;
    deich:location_dewey    "82" ;
    deich:location_signature "Bro" ;
    deich:publicationPlace    <http://data.deichman.
no/publicationPlace/leicester> ;
    dct:issued    "1987" ;
    dct:isPartOf <http://data.deichman.no/series/
x14896800> ;
    bibo:isbn    "0861366611" ;
```

```
    dct:title      "Wuthering heights" ;
    deich:titleURLized "wuthering_heights" ;
    dct:publisher       <http://data.deichman.no/
organization/galley_press> ;
    bibo:numPages        "320" ;
    deich:signatureNote        "xbsj901107" ;
    deich:bindingInfo  <http://data.deichman.no/
bindingInfo/ib> ;
    dct:creator  <http://data.deichman.no/person/
x12821000> ;
    fabio:isManifestationOf   <http://data.deichman.
no/work/x12821000_wuthering_heights> ;
    iface:altDepictedBy       <http://covers.open
library.org/b/id/120437-M.jpg> ,
        <http://www.bokkilden.no/SamboWeb/servlet/
VisBildeServlet?produktId=6449905> ,
        <http://covers.openlibrary.org/b/
id/105715-M.jpg> ,
        <http://covers.openlibrary.org/b/
id/109038-M.jpg> ,
        <http://www.bokkilden.no/SamboWeb/servlet/
VisBildeServlet?produktId=951434> ,
        <http://covers.openlibrary.org/b/
id/109039-M.jpg> .
```

RDF Record: The Author Emily Brontë

```
@prefix foaf:      <http://xmlns.com/foaf/0.1/> .
@prefix dct:       <http://purl.org/dc/terms/> .
@prefix radatana:       <http://def.bibsys.no/xmlns/
radatana/1.0#> .
@prefix deich:  <http://data.deichman.no/> .
@prefix xfoaf:  <http://www.foafrealm.org/
xfoaf/0.1/> .

<http://data.deichman.no/person/x12821000>a
foaf:Person ;
    dct:identifier     "12821000" ;
    foaf:name     "Emily Brontë" ;
    radatana:catalogueName    "Brontë, Emily" ;
    deich:lifespan     "1818-1848" ;
```

```
    xfoaf:nationality   <http://data.deichman.no/
nationality/eng> ;
    foaf:lastName       "Brontë" ;
    foaf:firstName      "Emily" .
```

Technical Implementation of the Active Shelf

The Active Shelf application uses the SPARQL query language to query the RDF representation of the library catalog. As described in the MARC2RDF section, we can identify editions of the same work, meaning that we don't have to list all editions of each book when the user looks for related titles. We also make new connections between books, based on similarities between the metadata describing them, so the application can suggest other titles that might be interesting.

When a book is placed on the Active Shelf, the RFID reader automatically detects and identifies the item (github.com/digibib/rfidgeek), and the process of collecting additional information is initialized. The software collects data from the RDF store and uses the semantic data as a basis for retrieving supplementary information, such as book reviews, cover images, and reader ratings.

The user can flip through reviews and get an impression of the book, or he can use the book as a starting point for exploring other books. Furthermore he can choose to look at other books by the same author and books that are assumed to be similar to the one he started with (see Figure 10.3, in which at the bottom left are more books by the same author and on the right are similar books by other authors). If he selects a book from one of the lists, the application initiates a new series of queries and provides new reviews, reader ratings, and a list of related books. It also provides information about whether the book is available.

Content

A vital part of the Active Shelf mashup is the ability to make use of the actual metadata hidden in the MARC format.

The first version of the Active Shelf supports fiction books and audiobooks. Movies and music are entirely different content and require other types of supplementary information. This information is easy to find but may be more difficult to link. With books we have the ISBN as a starting point to collect information from other

Figure 10.3 Review view of the title *The Curious Incident of the Dog in the Night-Time* by Mark Haddon

sources, but for music and films there are other identifiers we'll have to research further.

The Active Shelf collects data from open and free sources. The only exception is the database NoveList (ebscohost.com/novelist), which we already had a subscription for.

Mashing Internal Data Sources

The Active Shelf displays title, author, and summary from the RDF catalog. Behind the scenes the ISBN is important for gathering information from external data sources, while topics, literary format, audience, and Dewey classification codes are used as variables to present similar books.

By using the RDF data we are able to display a single representation of a work, instead of the multiple editions in the library's collection. This is a huge improvement from the traditional OPAC search results.

The shelf also displays book reviews from a book reviews database (anbefalinger.deichman.no). These reviews are written by library staff from all over Norway and are collected via a REST API (github.com/digibib/data.deichman.api) developed by our team.

Book Review Database

While developing the Active Shelf we have built a database and an API to collect reviews from Norwegian libraries. The reviews are stored in RDF format in a shared open database and are connected to the same RDF version of the library catalog as the Active Shelf application.

The reviews are made accessible via an open API, so that other developers can easily produce services that utilize and expose the reviews. External services can submit ISBN, book titles, author names, and other metadata to the API, and get book reviews and metadata in return for use in other services. It is also possible for other libraries to use the API to submit their own reviews to the database, and there is even a WordPress plug-in for publishing blog posts as reviews directly to the API.

In the web application (anbefalinger.deichman.no) library staff can write reviews or look up reviews written by others. Since the reviews are linked to our RDF data, library staff can use the metadata that describe books to put together lists of reviews. The flexibility of RDF data becomes evident when it is used to compile lists of, for example, reviews of children's fantasy books, reviews of books by American authors, reviews of novels for adults with less than 250 pages, or reviews of Jo Nesbø's crime novellas. Lists can be exported as RSS feeds and used as dynamic elements on blogs and webpages.

Mashing External Data Sources

During the development of the Active Shelf application, we evaluated several external data sources and their content. Starting out with a list of 21 interesting sources, we ended up with using only five of them (Table 10.1). These were the five that suited us the best based on ease of use, the richness of the data, stability, quality, and cost.

It was important for us to get as much content as we could from as few sources as possible. This requirement was due mainly to stability and performance issues. As we collect data on the fly when the book is placed on the shelf, we rely on a quick response. It is also a goal for us that the application itself be easy to manage.

The external APIs return data in XML and ratings from Bokelskere, and item holdings from our ILS vendor are returned in JSON. The "tone" of the book from NoveList is included in the RDF dataset and used as an extra variable to derive similar books (Figure 10.4).

Table 10.1   The External Data Sources We Used

Source	Content used
Bokkilden (bokkilden.no)	• book covers • publisher presentations
Bokelskere (bokelskere.no)	• ratings
Goodreads (goodreads.com)	• ratings • a simple description of the book
Novelist (ebscohost.com/novelist)	• reviews • ISBN-numbers • "tone"
ILS vendor cover database and item holdings	• book covers • publisher presentations • availability

Figure 10.4   Books similar to *The Curious Incident of the Dog in the Night-Time* by Mark Haddon

data.deichman.no

data.deichman.no (github.com/digibib/data.deichman.api/blob/master/README.md) is the gateway to raw RDF data from our library and a potential platform for developers to access the library data to build applications and mashups.

The main part of data.deichman.no is the enriched RDF version of the library catalog and its authority files. This includes data about books, music, movies, persons, organizations, topics, and genres. The dataset consists of an RDF version of the entire MARC catalog, enriched with book cover URLs harvested from external datasets. Most importantly it consists of a FRBR-like work-manifestation structure that identifies the unique works described in the catalog, and clusters the different editions and translations of each work.

The dataset is updated daily to account for additions, deletions, and changes made in the catalog. The updates are harvested via OAI-PMH from our MARC catalog and converted via MARC2RDF.

As of July 2014, data.deichman.no contains descriptions of approximately:

- 415,000 documents (books, CDs, DVDs, periodicals, etc.)
- 200,000 persons
- 75,000 organizations
- 65,000 topics
- 2,000 genres
- 7,500 book reviews

Future Challenges

The Active Shelf and the book reviews database are the first two services we have created based on the RDF version of the library catalog. It will be very exciting to see what other services and mashups we can build based on this data.

Our future goal for the Active Shelf is to integrate it into the bookshelves in the new library building and connect it with shelf ID to display where you can find the book.

It is also a priority to use the RDF data as a basis for a new OPAC search. Mashing the content from the Active Shelf and creating a rich

OPAC will be a natural extension of this work. This will bring the idea behind the Active Shelf application one step further, reaching the users where they are, whenever they want, from smartphones, tablets, and other gadgets that will emerge in the years to come.

The catalog data requires continuous work, and it is crucial to find content that supports the library's nonfiction collection and the large collections of film and music. The challenge will be to figure out how we can identify a work of film or music in external data sources and mash information from those sources with our data, as these are items without an ISBN. With that in mind, we also have similar challenges aggregating content about books published before 1970, when the ISBN was introduced, if the book was not subsequently republished with an ISBN.

We believe it is important to present a rich catalog to our users. Linking to, and using, external content by creating different variations of mashups will most likely continue to play an important part in this work.

Those who are interested in trying to convert their MARC records and build an Active Shelf application or a book reviews database are invited to have a look at our GitHub account (github.com/digibib). We are sharing every line of code, for everything we do!

Authors' Note: You can watch a video presentation of the Active Shelf in use on Vimeo (vimeo.com/68687814).

Endnote

1. A controlled way to organize and describe knowledge for subsequent retrieval lov.okfn.org/dataset/lov.

## CHAPTER 11

Delivering Catalog Records Using Wikipedia Current Awareness

Natalie Pollecutt
Wellcome Library

As librarians we know we have a lot of interesting and useful information in our collections. We can better connect people with our material when they are more receptive to it, for example, when our information is linked to news and current affairs. One method that I explored for my library, the Wellcome Library in London, was to build a current awareness service using Google Drive (drive.google.com) and Google Apps Script (developers.google.com/apps-script).

Google Apps Script is very similar to JavaScript. The result of the current awareness service is a timely and relevant email sent straight to your inbox, with links to the first few relevant records from your catalog and further search results. Staff can set Wikipedia search criteria themselves, making the search as narrow or broad as they like. Links to top catalog records give them a one-click route to your library's holdings to quickly gather information for a tweet or blog post.

The idea for this project came from a suggestion on the Mashed Library wiki (mashedlibrary.com/groups/wiki) to "Link book titles from search to news items from various news sites" (mashedlibrary.com/wiki-content/cookbook/menu_suggestions). I, however, ended up doing this the other way round, going from a news website back to our catalog.

I considered a few sources, such as the BBC's or *The Guardian*'s websites, but alighted on using Wikipedia (wikipedia.org). Wikipedia is a very well-known site and lots of library users are aware of it. For my purposes, the daily featured article is a very clear top story of the day. The featured article can also be quite topical, so using it does retain some of the original idea of topicality from the Mashed Library wiki suggestion, even if it is not actually news from a news site. For these reasons Wikipedia seemed like a good place from which to begin experimenting.

Around this time I also came across an online video explaining how to use Google Drive for gathering data from the web (appsumo. com/google-docs-unleashed/). It struck me that I could use these same techniques and apply them to gathering data from Wikipedia, specifically the featured article. Then it would just be a matter of using the data from Wikipedia and seeing if there was anything relevant in our library catalogue.

Getting Started

My first task was to get the data from Wikipedia and put it somewhere that I could use it. From the online video and from reading the Google Apps documentation, I knew this was a relatively simple thing to do. First, I needed to create a new spreadsheet in Google Drive. Secondly, I needed to get the URL of the site I wanted to use and identify which specific bit of the page I needed.

The URL I want is en.wikipedia.org/wiki/Main_Page, because that's where the featured article is on the English language version of Wikipedia. I put this in cell A1 of my spreadsheet.

I then use the Google Drive built-in ImportXML formula and target the URL I've just put in cell A1. This imports the XML of the page I need. Essentially I'm importing the code used to present the page on Wikipedia, so I can mine it for information. I use XPath (developer. mozilla.org/en/docs/Xpath) to retrieve only the specific part of the page that I'm interested in: the title of the featured article. My XPath:

```
//div[@id='mp-tfa']//b[1]
```

is saying

```
'get the content of the first <b> tag (//b[1]),
which is in the div which has an id of 'mp-tfa'
(//div[@id='mp-tfa']
```

How do I know where the title of the featured article is on the page? By using the Chrome browser's developer tools (developers. google.com/chrome-developer-tools). [*Author's Note:* If you've never used Chrome's developer tools before, you can find them easily by clicking the Chrome menu on the browser toolbar, selecting Tools and then Developer Tools.] Using the developer tools, I can see that the featured content is in a div with an id of mp-tfa, and that the title of the article is wrapped in the first <b> (bold) tag (Figure 11.1).

Combining these in my ImportXML formula automatically places the data I'm targeting, in this case the article title, "Joseph B. Foraker," into my spreadsheet.

So far I've only got the title of the article, but I also want all the text of the featured article on Wikipedia's home page. I can place this on a new sheet in the same way that I retrieved the article title. This time I want the whole article so the ImportXML function needs to retrieve the entire article, not just the title. So this time I'm retrieving all the data from the div with an id of 'mp-tfa':

```
=ImportXML(A1,"//div[@id='mp-tfa']")
```

You can see the data in column C of this new spreadsheet (Figure 11.2). I now have the article data and the article title. But that just tells me what Wikipedia is doing. It doesn't link this Wikipedia information with anything that I'm interested in or with my library catalogue.

My Interests List

I can list the topics in which I'm interested in a column on a new sheet. Let's call this sheet "searchTerms." I create a heading in cell A1 so I know what this sheet is for and then list all the topics below that

Figure 11.1 The data retrieved from XPath

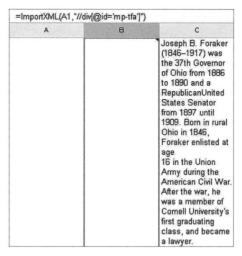

Figure 11.2 **Data from the webpage in the spreadsheet**

in column A. As with any Google Drive spreadsheet, this list can be edited at any time, so it is very flexible.

Now I have the topics I'm interested in, and I have the data from Wikipedia. But how do I compare these two parts to find out if my topics are in today's Wikipedia featured article? I need to:

- Get the text of the featured article

- Get my list of terms

- Check the text of the featured article to see if it contains any of my terms

To do this I have to use the Google Apps Script that's available to me in my Google Drive spreadsheet. Google Apps Script is "a JavaScript cloud scripting language that lets you extend Google Apps. ... Scripts are developed in Google Apps Script's browser-based script editor, and they are stored in and run from Google's servers" (developers.google.com/apps-script/overview). If you have some familiarity with JavaScript, you'll be able to pick this up very quickly. To get to the browser-based script editor, go to Tools > Script editor in your spreadsheet. This will open up a new script editor for you (Figure 11.3), where you can now start writing your custom functions.

Figure 11.3   Where to write your custom functions

At the beginning of my script I created an object to store values I knew I'd need more than once later:

```
var SS = {};
SS.activeSpreadsheet = SpreadsheetApp.get
ActiveSpreadsheet();
SS.name = SS.activeSpreadsheet.getName();
SS.url = SS.activeSpreadsheet.getUrl();
```

Going back to my list, the first thing I have to do is get the text of the featured article. I'm going to store the text of the featured article in a variable called "text":

```
var text = featuredArticle();
```

I use this script:

```
function featuredArticle() {
var featuredArticleSheet = SS.activeSpreadsheet.
getSheetByName("featuredArticle"),
// gets value from C1
featuredArticle = featuredArticleSheet.get
Range(1,3).getValue().toLowerCase();
   // puts value in F1
   featuredArticleSheet.getRange(1,6).setValue
(featuredArticle);
// returns Wikipedia featured article
return featuredArticle;
}
```

I identify the sheet that has the featured article and store that in a variable:

```
var featuredArticleSheet = SS.activeSpreadsheet.
getSheetByName("featuredArticle")
```

If you remember I can see the text of the featured article in cell C1 on the "'featuredArticle" sheet. On the spreadsheet this isn't the text itself, but the visible result of the ImportXML formula. I get the text of cell C1 via the getRange(1,3) method. I also change it to lower case with the toLowerCase() method (I'll explain why I do this a bit further on):

```
// gets value from C1
featuredArticle = featuredArticleSheet.get
Range(1,3).getValue().toLowerCase();
```

To put this data into cell F1 (1,6), I identify the cell with get-Range(1,6) and set its value with the setValue() method, using what's stored in my featuredArticle variable:

```
// puts value in F1
featuredArticleSheet.getRange(1,6).setValue
(featuredArticle);
```

Finally, I return this value when the featuredArticle() function is called:

```
// returns Wikipedia featured article
return featuredArticle;
```

Doing all this means that my variable text will store the text of the featured article:

```
var text = featuredArticle();
```

My second task is to get my list of terms. I identify the sheet that has the terms:

```
searchTermsSheet = SS.activeSpreadsheet.getSheet
ByName("searchTerms")
```

Then in the variable range I use the getLastRow() method to find the last row on the spreadsheet with data in it:

```
termsRange = searchTermsSheet.getLastRow()
```

Google Apps Script (like JavaScript and many other languages) starts counting from 0: It is zero-indexed. So where we count the range of rows:

```
1. Terms to look for in Wikipedia's main article
2. Wellcome
3. history of medicine
```

Google Apps Script counts the range of rows:

```
0. Terms to look for in Wikipedia's main article
1. Wellcome
2. history of medicine
```

Where we count the last row as 3, Google Apps Script counts it as 2. To make the 2 into the 3 we're expecting, we just need to add a 1 to get the correct number for our last row:

```
termsLastRow = termsRange + 1;
```

I need to check each term against my featured article text, not just the first term. For this I need to loop through my list to count how many terms there are.

My for loop uses my range of row 2 to termsLastRow to make sure I get the term from each row with a term in my sheet, and then stop at the last row. I also put the term in lower case:

```
for (var i = 2; i < termsLastRow; i++) {
      // gets term from searchTermSheet cell A2
row2 colA
      //  puts to lower case
    term = searchTermsSheet.getRange(i,1).get
Value().toLowerCase();
```

So my term is in lower case. My featured article is also in lower case; remember we did that earlier. This makes it easier to look through the text of the featured article and compare it with each term. As both sets of data are now in lower case I don't have to worry whether my Google Apps Script sees *Wellcome* and *wellcome* as the same or different. I've eliminated that uncertainty by making everything lower case before I compare them. It's good to do this in the script for two reasons: 1) I have no control over how Wikipedia uses cases, and 2) if I give this to a colleague I have no control over how they enter their terms on the spreadsheet. My code can take any data that it's given, make everything lower case, and be in a good position to compare the list of terms with the featured article.

Now I have my featured article in lower case stored in my variable text, and I have each term in lower case stored in the variable term at every run through the loop. The next thing to do is check the text of the featured article to see if it contains any of my terms

This is easy to achieve with the built-in match() method:

```
text.match(term)
```

That's all there is to it. What it's doing is taking the value of text (the text of the Wikipedia main article) and trying to match term (each search term I'm interested in) against it.

If There's a Match, Check Against the Catalog

That's good as far as it goes, but what if there is a match? I can write this is as:

```
if (text.match(term))
```

If a match is found, I want to do something. I want the code to tell someone that it's found a match and send them some matching catalogue information. That way they will know that Wikipedia has a featured article that might be relevant to the library's collections. They will have a good starting point of some catalogue records to look at so that they can see what the library holds on that topic:

```
// if the search term is in the text of the
featured article
```

```
if (text.match(term)) {
opacSearchUrl = getOpacSearchUrl(term);
        opacRecords = getOpacRecords();
```

First I need to generate a search URL for my catalogue. I do this by passing my term to the getOpacSearchUrl() function:

```
function getOpacSearchUrl(term) {
   var opacUrlSheet = SS.activeSpreadsheet.get
SheetByName("opacUrl"),
     // get value from A2
        opacSearchUrl = opacUrlSheet.get
Range(2,1).getValue();
   // add search path and encoded article title
   opacSearchUrl = opacSearchUrl + "/search/Y" +
encodeURI(term);
   // set value at B2
   opacUrlSheet.getRange(2,2).setValue
(opacSearchUrl);
   return opacSearchUrl;
}
```

I get the sheet in which I've already stored my catalogue's URL in cell A2:

```
var opacUrlSheet = SS.activeSpreadsheet.getSheet
ByName("opacUrl")
```

I get the value from cell A2:

```
opacSearchUrl = opacUrlSheet.getRange(2,1).get
Value;
```

I construct the full search URL by linking together the catalogue URL with "/search/Y" to make it search the right index and finally add the matching term to search for. I use the encodeURI() method on it to format it correctly:

```
opacSearchUrl = opacSearchUrl + "/search/Y" +
encodeURI(term);
```

I put the result in cell B2 (2,2):

```
opacUrlSheet.getRange(2,2).setValue(opac
SearchUrl);
```

Finally, I return this value when this function is called:

```
return opacSearchUrl;
```

To recap:

- I have my article title from Wikipedia.
- I have my article text from Wikipedia.
- I have all my search terms from my spreadsheet.
- I have checked my terms against the full text from Wikipedia.
- If my term is found in the article text I create the full search URL using my term.

However, I don't want those records to stay in the spreadsheet. I need to email them out. To do that, I need to get the titles and links from the catalogue records in a usable format. For that I use my getOpacRecords function and store the results in a variable, opacRecords:

```
opacRecords = getOpacRecords();
```

This is the function:

```
function getOpacRecords() {
var records = "",
     opacRecordsSheet = SpreadsheetApp.get
ActiveSpreadsheet().getSheetByName("opac
Records"),
     opacUrl = opacRecordsSheet.getRange(2,1).
getValue();   opacRecordsSheet.getRange(2,2).
setValue(opacUrl);
  for (var i = 2; i < 7; i++) {
```

```
      var recordTitle = opacRecordsSheet.get
Range(i,3).getValue();          recordTitle =
opacRecordsSheet.getRange(i,4).setValue(record
Title);
      var link = opacRecordsSheet.getRange(i,6).
getValue();
      link = opacRecordsSheet.getRange(i,7).set
Value(link);
      records = records + recordTitle.getValue();
      records = records + ' ' + link.getValue() +
'\n\n';
      }
   records = records + ' ' + '\n\n';
   return records;
}
```

This is how getOpacRecords() works. First I set up an empty variable to store my output:

```
var records = "";
```

I set a reference to the sheet I'm using where the record titles and links will be:

```
var opacRecordsSheet = SpreadsheetApp.get
ActiveSpreadsheet().getSheetByName("opac
Records");
```

With these variables set up I can start doing something. In cell A2 I have already set up a reference to the search URL generated by our getOpacSearchUrl(), with =opacUrl!B2.

I get the value of A2 (2,1) and put it in B2 (2,2):

```
opacUrl = opacRecordsSheet.getRange(2,1).get
Value();
opacRecordsSheet.getRange(2,2).setValue(opacUrl)
```

The search URL is in place. Other cells in this same sheet, "opac-Url," are already set up to use the ImportXML formula with the search URL. More XPath gets the titles and links from the catalogue records retrieved by the search.

The XPath you use will vary depending on how the titles and links are marked up in your own catalogues. For my catalogue I use =ImportXML(B2, "//span[@class='briefcitTitle']") in cell C2 to identify record titles, and =ImportXML(B2, "//span[@class='briefcit Title']//a/@href") in cell E2 to identify record links. I now have a list of record titles in column C, and record links in column E.

I want to get the first five records, as this is only meant to be a taste of what the catalogue has, not a comprehensive list. I set up a for loop to loop through the first five records, from rows 2, 3, 4, 5, and 6:

```
for (var i = 2; i < 7; i++) {
```

Each time I loop through the rows I get the record title and copy it to another cell on the same row. We did something similar in the featuredArticle() function to copy the value referenced from one cell to be an actual value in another cell. The title from the retrieved catalogue record is copied from column 3 into column 4 for each row (i) in the for loop:

```
var recordTitle = opacRecordsSheet.getRange(i,3).
getValue;
recordTitle = opacRecordsSheet.getRange(i,4).
setValue(recordTitle);
```

Then I do the same thing with the links for each record as I loop through the rows, copying to get the actual value into a new cell:

```
var link = opacRecordsSheet.getRange(i,6).get
Value();
link = opacRecordsSheet.getRange(i,7).set
Value(link
```

Now I have a title and a link for each of the first five catalogue records. I want to present them in the email in the format "title link," which is what this next bit of code does. The "\n\n" part puts two new lines between each "title link." This is how the records variable is built up with a recordTitle and a record link for each row, building up to 5 records (recordTitles and links):

```
records = records + recordTitle.getValue;
records = records + ' ' + link.getValue() +
'\n\n';
```

After the end of the loop I put two line spaces after the 5 sets of titles and links:

```
records = records + ' ' + '\n\n';
```

Finally I make sure to return all of this when the getOpacRecords() function is called:

```
return records;
```

Now we have all the information from Wikipedia and we've compared it with our terms. Where there is a match we've collected the first five records from our catalogue that match the Wikipedia article title. The final step is to put all of this information into an email.

Emailing From the Spreadsheet

Google Apps Script enables us to send emails from a spreadsheet via a Gmail address. This script is what allows us to send our email alerts.

Just as we have a list of search terms, we also need a list of email addresses to which we want to send our email alerts. This list can be just your own email address, or any number of email addresses.

On a sheet called "emailAddresses," I list the email addresses in column A. The user of this spreadsheet can easily update this list of email addresses.

This is the script that gets the email addresses:

```
function getEmailAddresses() {
   var emailsAddsSheet = SS.activeSpreadsheet.get
SheetByName("emailAddresses"),
       rangeEmailAdds = emailsAddsSheet.get
LastRow(),
       emailAdds = '';
   for (var i = 2; i <= rangeEmailAdds; i++) {
     emailAdds = emailAdds + emailsAddsSheet.get
Range(i,1).getValue();
```

```
    if ( i < rangeEmailAdds ) {
      emailAdds = emailAdds + ',';
}
  }
  return emailAdds;
}
```

You can see that this script uses techniques explained in previous functions. I start by setting up the variables I will need.

I identify the sheet with list of email addresses:

```
var emailsAddsSheet = SS.activeSpreadsheet.get
SheetByName("emailAddresses")
```

I get the last row that contains data, so I know how many goes through the loop I will need:

```
rangeEmailAdds = emailsAddsSheet.getLastRow()
```

I set up an empty variable emailAdds as a placeholder for where I want to store the email addresses in this function:

```
emailAdds = '';
```

A for loop goes through each row on the sheet that contains an email address (rows 2–4), building up email from an empty string to a string containing all the email addresses:

```
for (var i = 2; i <= rangeEmailAdds; i++) {
```

I get the value of the cell containing the email addresses and add it to the emailAdds variable:

```
emailAdds = emailAdds + emailsAddsSheet.get
Range(i,1).getValue();
```

If I'm not at the end of the loop, I add a comma to separate the email addresses. This makes multiple email addresses usable by Gmail:

```
if ( i < rangeEmailAdds ) {
  emailAdds = emailAdds + ',';
}
```

Finally, I return this list of email addresses:

```
return emailAdds;
```

My last task is to build the email that I want my script to send. For this I use Google Apps Script's MailApp.sendEmail() method. This method needs three parts to construct an email (address, subject, body):

```
// address, subject, body
MailApp.sendEmail(
    // next line gets email addresses
    getEmailAddresses(),
    // next line is email subject
    "Your search term '" + term + "' is
mentioned in today's main article of English
Wikipedia, '" + articleTitle() + "'",
    // next line is email body
    "See http://en.wikipedia.org/." + "\n\n" +
"The first five catalogue records are: \n\n" +
opacRecords + "Search for more Library holdings
on the OPAC (" + opacSearchUrl + ")." + "\n\n"
+  "This spreadsheet is " + SS.name + " at " +
SS.url
        )
```

To get the email address, I call the getEmailAddresses() function we've just seen to get my list of email addresses.

For the subject of the email I concatenate strings with variables and function returns to create a full subject line. The strings are the exact text I want. Variables use the data I've previously stored in them, and functions do the same with the values they return after they have been run by the script. For the body of the email I do the same thing, concatenating strings, variables, and function returns.

Email Trigger

I now have all of the code I need to create an email with information from Wikipedia and my catalogue when there is a match between data from both sources. But what's the trigger to send my email? How do I make the code run?

I don't want to have to open this spreadsheet every day to run the code. If I'm doing that I might as well just look at Wikipedia and see if the featured article is of interest to me. I want this to run in an automated way, so that if, and only if, there is a match, an email will be sent to me. Then all I'll have to do is open the email and follow the links in it if I decide to investigate the Wikipedia article or our catalogue records further.

Luckily the Google Apps Script has a number of ways to trigger the code to run. I can use a trigger based on use of the spreadsheet (an action-based trigger), or I can use a trigger based on time (a time-based trigger).

I know from looking at Wikipedia that the featured article is updated once per day. That means I only need to run my code once a day. To set a daily trigger I need to click the Current Project's Triggers button (the one that looks like a clock). So far I have no triggers set up. I click the link to add a trigger.

I use the options to choose (Figure 11.4):

- Which function to run

- What type of trigger to use, time-driven or from the spreadsheet

- The type of timer

- The time period each day that I want it to run

From experimentation I know that an early morning trigger will cause my code to be run after the Wikipedia featured article is updated and before I get into work. If Wikipedia's featured article relates to my search terms there will be an email in my inbox waiting for me with all the information I need. Job done!

Of course, I want to check that my script works right now, rather than wait until tomorrow to see if I get an email. I can do that by selecting the function I want to test from the drop-down list of functions

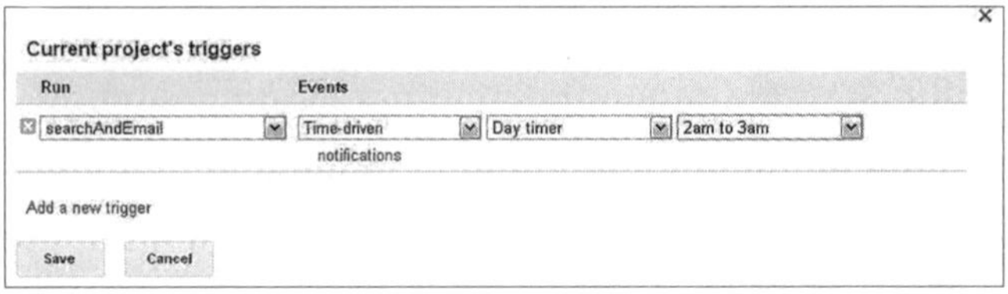

Figure 11.4 Setting the current project's triggers

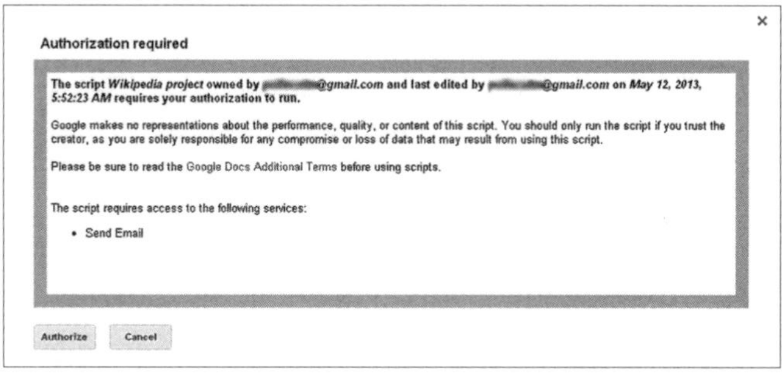

Figure 11.5   Authorizing the use of email from your Google account

and clicking the right-facing arrow button. This runs the function immediately.

And it turns out it's a good job I checked. Before I can send any emails from my spreadsheet, Google asks me to authorize this use of the email account associated with my Google login (Figure 11.5). Just click the Authorize button to do this. You will only be asked for authorization the first time you try to send an email.

And there you have it: a Wikipedia current awareness service tailored to your own collections. The whole script is around 100 lines. Those lines, plus the set-up in the spreadsheet itself (e.g., your search terms), plus the trigger, are everything that's needed.

If you'd like to use my spreadsheet as a starting point, with the script I wrote, it is available online at goo.gl/ZsmjRY.

## Part IV

Visualizing Data With Mashups

## CHAPTER 12

Telling Stories With Google Maps Mashups

Olga Buchel
Counting Opinions (SQUIRE) Ltd.

We live in the time of geospatial revolution. We have a variety of open source tools and application programming interfaces (APIs) for developing mashups and visualizing information. Moreover, some of these tools, such as Google Maps (maps.google.com), can be used not only for transforming data from tabular or structured text format to static spatial representations, but also for designing interactive front-end interfaces for document collections. Notwithstanding the wide availability of tools and the abundance of geospatial references in library knowledge organization systems (e.g., classifications, meta-data, and gazetteers), which suggest that geospatial mashups are suitable for representing collections, libraries are not eager to jump onto the bandwagon of adopting geospatial mashups as interfaces to their collections.

There are many obstacles that preclude them from doing so. Some of these obstacles are associated with the lack of technical skills to link map interfaces to library databases; others can be explained by the lack of theory for making useful mashups. On the one hand, the gap in theory can be explained by the difficulty of understanding how to merge different knowledge organization systems, and on the other hand, by the difficulty of estimating potential benefits from such mashups. A mashup linking documents to a map will not necessarily help users with searching, browsing, and other tasks. Asking users how to improve such interfaces might be fruitless, since few users would know how to improve something that they have not even had a chance to use before.

To understand what can be done with map mashups besides linking, mashup designers need to account for conceptualizations and techniques developed in information visualization, cartography, geovisualization, and human computer interaction. These conceptualizations already have theories of storytelling about data, metadata, ontologies, and other knowledge structures; frameworks for conceptualizing tasks and interactions; and a variety of encoding techniques. Together all these theories, frameworks, and techniques might improve the usability of mashups, as many of these techniques have already been tested and verified in user studies in information visualization, geovisualization, and cartography.

A Brief Survey of Storytelling Techniques

Generally speaking, all map-based stories in cartography can be divided into narratives and cartographic stories about statistical data. According to Mei-Po Kwan and Guoxiang Ding,[1] the former are characterized by temporal dimensions; they take place in specific places and focus on the personal and the social. An example of a narrative map that relates a story in space and time is Robert Roth's Exploring the Trail of Tears map (geography.wisc.edu/faculty/roth/interactive/TrailofTears_DemoVersion.swf), which is an interactive animation of the forced relocation of the Cherokee Nation in 1838. An example of a cartographic story about statistical data (more on this later in the chapter) is Hans Rosling's Gapminder[2] (goo.gl/wpMr69), which shows inequalities among nations over time.

To design narrations, cartographers use a wide variety of techniques to render a sense of each location. They can supplement maps with artifacts such as antiques, sketches, paintings, photographs, collages, and ambient sounds to depict how a place looked in the past, or they might combine representations of real places with imaginary places to show map users how other people perceive a place.[3] They may provide different spellings of place names (local and official) and local dialectal words to give a better sense of place. They can use color hues to encode emotions about places and different scales to separate stories about states or provinces from stories about streets in a city.[4]

To combine episodes into and to facilitate the flow of a narrative, cartographers include multiple map frames and map insets in animations and cartographic movies. Frames in animations often have arrows that indicate direction of the narrative. Frames are either stacked (overlaid on top of each other as in Gapminder) or arranged as tours. Tours (described in Alan MacEachren[5]) rely on the use of graphic scripts, basic sequences called graphic phrases, and tightly coupled representations that show how changes in one representation are affected by changes in another representation.

To personalize stories, some designers propose the use of metaphors. For example, Cartwright[6] suggests the theatre metaphor, as storytelling has many similarities with theatrical concepts. Much like theatrical plays, storytelling is orchestrated through scripting, staging, and directing. If these concepts were applied to cartographic storytelling, the stage would be the part of the landscape and the actors would be the elements that act upon or move through the landscape. The theatre metaphor would allow users to be engaged and pleased with the experience.

Narrative maps can have many practical applications. Jeremy Crampton[7] and Kwan[8] give many examples of narrative maps that convey oral histories, performances, human discourses, and narratives. Narrative maps have been found effective at outlining journeys and for telling stories about people,[9,10] diseases,[11] natural disasters, emotions and sentiments in communities,[12] and revealing geographies of novels.[13]

Cartographic stories are also about statistical data, as mentioned earlier. "Data stories" differ in a number of ways from traditional forms of storytelling. First of all, they are about statistics and analytical reasoning,[14] not about voyages or history. Second, unlike narrative maps, data stories do not include direct quotes or artifacts that recreate a sense of place; rather they are composed of tightly coupled charts, graphs, and maps. Third, users of such storytelling maps are expected to be active thinkers and sense makers who will likely ascribe meaning to charts and graphs and tell their own stories about the data.[15] To understand a data story, users will need to have special skills to carry out spatial exploratory analyses, which are based on visual comparisons, associations, differentiations, and many other visual tasks.[16] Most importantly, users should be able to generate hypothesis, find correlations, and notice some other patterns in statistics.

Data stories can be designed either from statistical data or metadata. Gapminder, for example, is built from statistical data. Data stories designed from metadata usually show main facets: subjects, genres, years of publication, places of publication, time periods, and some other facets. VisGets visualization[17] and the tool for selecting geospatial metadata described by Paula Ahonen-Rainio and Menno-Jan Kraak[18] are examples of mashups that tell data stories about metadata facets. For representing different facets, such visualizations supplement maps with additional representations, including time-lines, tag clouds, and parallel coordinates.

In visualizations that tell data stories, interactions play an important role. In this context, *interactions* refers both to the actions performed on representations and to the subsequent responses of those representations to those actions.[19,20] In other words, interactions help users complete visual tasks (i.e., compare, associate, make connections and analogies). Interactions link representations and aid users to discover the maximum number of insights. For example, showing markers on a map mashup is a linking interaction. But it is only one type of interaction. Theories in information visualization and geovisualization recommend that designers use an array of other interactions, such as navigating, filtering, selecting, annotating, drilling, comparing, and gathering. All these interactions enhance users' reasoning and cognition.

Examples of Library Mashups

Let's look at a few examples of mashups designed according to geo-visualization and information visualization principles. Because of their thorough conceptual models that adhere to visualization principles, they are referred to as visualizations in this chapter. These mashups were created with Google Maps JavaScript API (developers. google.com/maps/documentation/javascript). Besides maps, the mashups also employ additional representations that are embedded in information windows. Some of these additional representations are Flash-based graphs and charts from FusionCharts (fusioncharts. com); others were developed in D3.js (a JavaScript framework for visualizing documents). The designer used these additional charts to illustrate that other web-based charts can be embedded in information windows in Google Maps (e.g., charts made with Raphael, HTML Canvas, and other JavaScript visualization frameworks). Additional charts and graphs help users tell better stories about data. Besides charts and graphs, the designer has also used an array of interactions. Some of these interactions were developed from examples described in Google Maps JavaScript API documentation, while others were custom-developed.

Each of the mashups described in this section visualizes a collection. Here, a collection refers to a group of documents characterized by thematic cohesiveness (e.g., by topic area, holding institution, type of materials), searchability, and a unique point of entry.[21] I am deliberately making a distinction between collections and non-collections to emphasize that the mashups discussed here do not simply visualize books or documents; rather they visualize thematically related documents. One of the mashups visualizes a local history of Ukraine; the other visualizes collections of medical citations retrieved from PubMed.

VICOLEX

Visual Collection Explorer (VICOLEX; abuchel.apmaths.uwo.ca/ ~obuchel/maps/VICOLEX.php) is a prototype that I developed for my dissertation.[22] VICOLEX visualizes a test bed collection of 343 records from the Library of Congress Catalog. This collection has call numbers that begin with DK508. DK508 in the Library of Congress Classification corresponds to the Local History of Ukraine. There are several reasons that I chose this collection for the visualization: It is mature, and its coverage is most likely complete, in that it includes all books that were published about the local history of Ukrainian locations. The temporal coverage of the collection in the visualization ranges from 1837 to 2007, which was the cut-off year and also the year the data was collected. VICOLEX uses almost all the bibliographic properties of the documents for visualization (subjects, physical properties, languages, years of publication and acquisition, and authors). It groups these properties by locations and facets, which are shown on multiple additional representations.

VICOLEX takes advantage of classes in DK508 that group documents by locations. Each class is linked to the main map that shows books about local history of locations in Ukraine. The test bed collection contains 32 classes, which correspond to 32 locations in Ukraine. Since the classes do not include coordinates, necessary for locating documents on a map, VICOLEX uses a custom-built gazetteer (a dictionary of place names including locations, their coordinates, and types). Gazetteers, as we show later, are necessary for making mashups more interactive.

Figure 12.1 shows that the map has two timelines: One timeline shows years of publication, and the other shows years of acquisition. Markers on the map are linked to scatter plots, pie charts, histograms, additional geographic maps, tag clouds, and Kohonen maps. Each of these representations reveals the structure of a particular facet of the documents linked to a location. Scatter plots diagram book sizes in the collection of documents about the location. Pie charts show the proportion of languages in the collection. Histograms present color-coded years of publication and numbers of books published. Colors in the histograms show historical time periods (e.g., "before the October Revolution of 1917," "the Soviet times," and "after 1991").

In VICOLEX each location has its own timeline, which is different from the main timeline linked to the map. Whereas the main timeline shows quantities of books purchased during the time the collection existed, the local timelines show local historical periods. In addition to timelines, locations also have their own maps. These maps show where the documents were published. On the main map, all the locations are part of Ukraine; on the maps of publication places, markers can be found in different parts of the world. Tag clouds show authors and the numbers of works they published. Kohonen maps show frequencies of subjects. The selection of these representations is justified by the following rationales: 1) These representations are fairly simple to understand for ordinary users, and 2) these representations are suitable for representing major properties of the documents (i.e., languages, subjects, places and years of publication, book sizes, and authors).

All representations in VICOLEX are subject to the following interactions: linking, filtering, selecting, grouping, and annotating. Filtering allows users to sift out document properties (subjects, genres, physical properties, and time) and location properties (i.e., type of location); see Figure 12.1. Types of locations (small, large, and other) are not part of the bibliographic records. These were added as descriptors of place names in the gazetteer in VICOLEX. In VICOLEX, types are represented by the population sizes of locations. Types of locations enhance filtering; they allow users to discover hidden relationships among documents and locations. Filtering on the map affects the representations inside the markers. Because of filtering on the map, the representations inside the markers become more legible and easier to understand. Such filtering allows users to complete tasks not only at the level of documents, but also at the level of their properties.

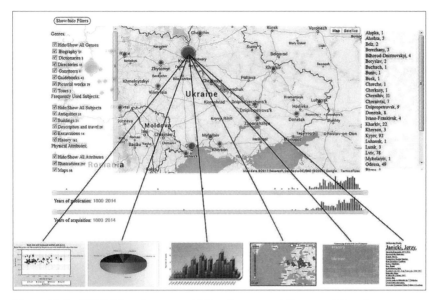

Figure 12.1   VICOLEX main map, additional representations, and timelines

In addition to filtering, VICOLEX allows users to select regions on the main map by drawing a bounding box around markers (Figure 12.2). This interaction is necessary for regions that do not have exact place names (e.g., northern Ukraine, western Ukraine). Once a region is selected, VICOLEX represents the documents from that region using additional facets. For example, Figure 12.2 shows how documents from a selected region are re-represented on a scatter plot.

VICOLEX supports several types of annotation: automated, structured, and free-text. Automated annotation is supported by different colored markers that appear in places visited by a user. This type of interaction shows the user's path through the information space. Users can modify this path by changing the colors of the markers to custom colors. Changing the color of markers is an example of structured annotating. The resulting annotations provide users with information about relevant, irrelevant, and visited locations. VICOLEX also supports free-text annotations. Free-text annotations generate user-created metadata, which capture users' judgments, observations, opinions, problems, and solutions.

At first glance, all these interactions are ordinary. They can be found in many other mashups. However, they are rarely used

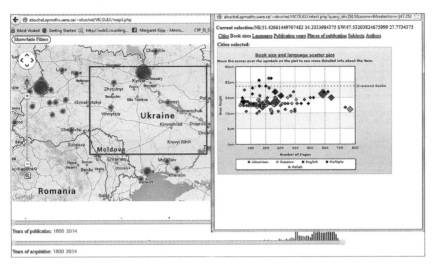

Figure 12.2 Selection in VICOLEX

together in a single mashup. This is partly because users and designers do not fully understand the interactions' roles in tasks and activities with information. Literature in information visualization and geovisualization shows that if these interactions are used together, they can increase the number of insights that people gain from the visualization.[23,24]

Representations and interactions in VICOLEX provide numerous stimuli for its users. For example, scatter plots can indicate which books have more illustrations or which books have more pages. Pie charts shed light on languages of publications. Color-coded histograms emphasize trends in publishing (e.g., during the Soviet times, the publication rates about local history were low, and they became higher after 1991 when Ukraine became independent). They show differences among collections and growth rates over time. Embedded publication maps tell users where books about a particular city were published. Knowing the places of publication for this particular collection is useful, as some of these items were published by authors in Ukraine and some were published by émigrés. Kohonen maps show the landscape of subjects for each location at a certain period of time. Tag clouds aid users in finding the most prolific authors in a short period of time.

VICOLEX was evaluated in a formal user study. The study employed a variety of methods: a think-aloud protocol with visual tasks, a semi-structured interview, and a questionnaire. The purpose of the study was to determine the effectiveness of the representations and interactions in supporting users' understanding of the collection. The study was conducted mostly with English-speaking participants. The results of the study demonstrate that additional representations stimulate users to generate hypotheses and conjectures, and to make other generalizations even when they do not know the language of the collection.

GeoPubMed

Another prototype is GeoPubMed, a geographic search interface for PubMed (ncbi.nlm.nih.gov/pubmed), the premier medical database with more than 22 million citations. This prototype is described in my presentation "Redefining Geobrowsing."[25] GeoPubMed retrieves records from PubMed via the Entrez Programming Utilities (E-utilities), the API that facilitates various types of searches (metadata, full-text, or combination of these) as well as mapping queries to standardized Medical Subject Headings (MeSH). Documents in the E-utilities have authors' names, authors' affiliations, article title, journal title, MeSH terms, and retrieval filters. Citations include references to geographic place names that can be found in authors' affiliations and MeSH geographic subject headings. Authors' affiliations tell where the researchers work. MeSH geographic subject headings describe the geographic aboutness of citations. However, MeSH geographic subject headings are present in only about 8.66 percent of records.

Technically, what GeoPubMed does is build a geographic index for each search. Each search is subdivided into a number of queries, and each query is expanded with geographic place names from a gazetteer. For example, if a search is about cancer, the query *cancer* is combined with the names of countries, provinces/states, and smaller locations. The index contains information about geographic locations and numbers of matching results. This index is later shown on a map. The map has multiple layers: a country-level map, a state/province level map, and a city-level map. An example of how search results look in GeoPubMed is shown in Figures 12.3, 12.4, and 12.5. These are the results for the query *depression*. Currently, the coverage in

GeoPubMed is incomplete. Users can retrieve countries, states, and provinces in the U.S. and Canada, and some cities in the U.S. (namely, 19,000 U.S. locations have been disambiguated so far).

Essentially, what GeoPubMed users can see is a multi-scale map. The small-scale map summarizes the results at the level of countries (Figure 12.3), the mid-scale map summarizes the results at the level of states/provinces (Figure 12.4), and the large-scale map summarizes the results at the level of cities (Figure 12.5). Maps of different scales support different kinds of user tasks and activities. Namely, they allow users to compare different objects (countries, states/provinces, and cities) at each scale. This is important as users often ask questions at different levels of specificity. The transitions from one level of specificity to another in GeoPubMed are easy for users to understand.

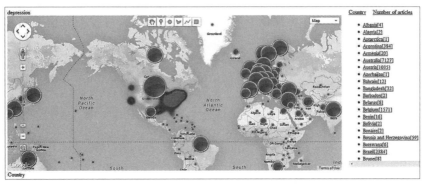

Figure 12.3 Small-scale map summarizing the results at the level of countries

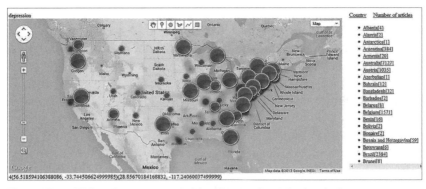

Figure 12.4 Mid-scale map summarizing the results at the level of states/provinces

Figure 12.5   Large-scale map summarizing the results at the level of cities

Markers on the maps contain additional representations about collections. (Here I refer to collections retrieved about specific locations. For example, a U.S. bubble represents publications from the U.S.; graphs inside the bubble represent therapies, treatments, and ages of patients described in papers published in the U.S.) These representations were designed from PubMed filters and other document properties. GeoPubMed does not visualize all PubMed filters yet. Currently it has clinical queries and ages of patients queries. The clinical queries filter describes 14 facets of health-related research (Figure 12.6), and the age filters have 13 categories that retrieve documents about certain age groups (Figure 12.7). Years of publication can go as far back as 1880 (Figure 12.8). Filters allow users to see a bigger picture since they group multiple subject headings and keywords. For example, the filter on the cancer subset includes nearly 1,200 terms from different branches of MeSH hierarchies as well as

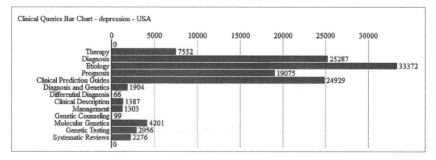

Figure 12.6   Additional representations of clinical queries in GeoPubMed

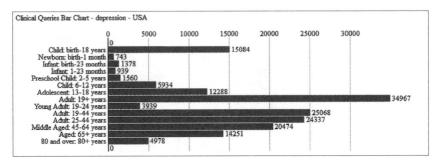

Figure 12.7 Additional representations of ages in GeoPubMed

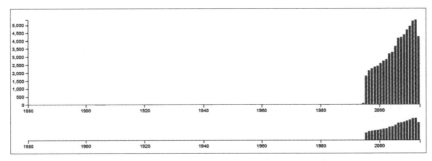

Figure 12.8 Additional representations of years of publication in GeoPubMed

keywords from abstracts and MEDLINE journal titles. In the future versions of GeoPubMed, MeSH can be linked to filters to help users understand filters in detail.

Interactions in GeoPubMed are similar to interactions in VICOLEX. Here users can also select regions and take advantage of a variety of annotation techniques. Spatial selection is especially powerful in GeoPubMed as this visualization has more place names than VICOLEX. Consider, for example, a query expansion for the query *tuberculosis AND Central AND South America*:

```
tuberculosis AND (Guadeloupe OR ("Argentine
Republic"[Affiliation] OR Argentina[Affiliation])
OR Guatemala OR Panama OR Peru OR Guyana OR
Honduras OR Haiti OR Puerto Rico OR Paraguay
OR Bolivia OR Brazil OR Jamaica OR Ivory Coast
OR Chile OR Colombia OR Costa Rica OR Cuba OR
Dominican Republic OR Ecuador OR Trinidad and
```

Tobago OR Uruguay OR Venezuela OR Grenada OR
French Guiana) AND ((systematic review [ti] OR
meta-analysis [pt] OR meta-analysis [ti] OR
systematic literature review [ti] OR
(systematic review [tiab] AND review [pt]) OR
consensus development conference [pt] OR practice
guideline [pt] OR cochrane database syst rev [ta]
OR acp journal club [ta] OR health technol assess
[ta] OR evid rep technol assess summ [ta] OR drug
class reviews [ti]) OR (clinical guideline [tw]
AND management [tw]) OR ((evidence based[ti] OR
evidence-based medicine [mh] OR best practice*
[ti] OR evidence synthesis [tiab]) AND (review
[pt] OR diseases category[mh] OR behavior and
behavior mechanisms [mh] OR therapeutics [mh] OR
evaluation studies[pt] OR validation studies[pt]
OR guideline [pt] OR pmcbook))OR ((systematic
[tw] OR systematically [tw] OR critical [tiab] OR
(study selection [tw]) OR (predetermined [tw] OR
inclusion [tw] AND criteri* [tw]) OR
exclusion criteri* [tw] OR main outcome measures
[tw] OR standard of care [tw] OR standards of
care [tw]) AND (survey [tiab] OR surveys [tiab]
OR overvie*[tw] OR review [tiab] OR reviews
[tiab] OR search* [tw] OR handsearch [tw] OR
analysis [tiab] OR critique [tiab] OR appraisal
[tw] OR (reduction [tw]AND (risk [mh] OR risk
[tw]) AND (death OR recurrence))) AND (literature
[tiab] OR articles [tiab] OR publications [tiab]
OR publication [tiab] OR bibliography [tiab] OR
bibliographies [tiab] OR published [tiab] OR
unpublished [tw] OR citation [tw] OR citations
[tw] OR database [tiab] OR internet [tiab] OR
textbooks [tiab] OR references [tw] OR scales
[tw] OR papers [tw] OR datasets [tw] OR trials
[tiab] OR meta-analy* [tw] OR (clinical [tiab]
AND studies [tiab]) OR treatment outcome [mh] OR
treatment outcome [tw] OR pmcbook)) NOT (letter
[pt] OR newspaper article [pt] OR comment [pt]))

The size of this query demonstrates how labor intensive it is to for-mulate such queries in PubMed. GeoPubMed saves users' time and efforts in constructing similar queries. The selection in GeoPubMed is scale-dependent. If a user makes a selection at the level of countries, only countries are selected; if states or provinces are selected, only states/provinces are selected.

GeoPubMed generates representations that stimulate stories at three levels of spatial detail: countries, states/provinces, and popu-lated places such as cities and towns. Inside the map markers, users find representations that stimulate stories about patients and clin-ical aspects: etiology, prognosis, diagnosis, treatment, molecular genetics, and ages of patients. Interactions with the visualization may reveal differences and similarities in the treatments of different diseases in different parts of the world.

Conclusion

I hope that I have demonstrated here that mashups designed accord-ing to the principles of geovisualization and information visualization can stimulate users to tell narratives and data stories. While narratives are usually encoded explicitly, data stories are presented implicitly in visualizations. For users, the nature of data stories means learning to interact with the visualizations in order to discover patterns. For mashup designers, it means paying greater attention to the theoretical frameworks, additional representations, and interactions discussed in information visualization and geovisualization. Map mashups should have more than one representation, since multiple representations provide more stimuli for users to tell stories. Representations should show the properties of the visualized objects (e.g., documents) from different perspectives. Interactions should facilitate linking, selecting, filtering, annotating, and easy transitions between the various forms of representation. Representations and interactions together should stimulate users to gain insights not only about the visualized objects (e.g., documents) but also about the locations on the map.

I have illustrated how these visualization principles work using the VICOLEX and GeoPubMed prototypes as examples. Both of these prototypes facilitate storytelling about data (metadata) in library col-lections. Rich sets of additional representations and interactions in these prototypes allow users to explore spatial, temporal, and other patterns in collections, and guide them to hypothesis generation, storytelling, and knowledge discovery at various levels of spatial detail.

Endnotes

1. Mei-Po Kwan and Guoxiang Ding, "Geo-Narrative: Extending Geographic Information Systems for Narrative Analysis in Qualitative and Mixed-Method Research," *The Professional Geographer* 60, no. 4 (2008): 443–465.
2. Hans A. Rosling, "Visual Technology Unveils the Beauty of Statistics and Swaps Policy from Dissemination to Access," *Statistical Journal of the IAOS: Journal of the International Association for Official Statistics* 24, no. 1 (January 1, 2007): 103–104.
3. Margaret Wickens Pearce, "Place Codes: Narrative and Dialogical Strategies for Cartography," *Proceedings of the 24th International Cartographic Conference*, 2009, http://icaci.org/files/documents/ICC_proceedings/ICC2009/html/non ref/22_7.pdf.
4. Mei-Po Kwan and Guoxiang Ding, "Geo-Narrative: Extending Geographic Information Systems for Narrative Analysis in Qualitative and Mixed-Method Research," *The Professional Geographer* 60, no. 4 (2008): 443–465.
5. Alan M. MacEachren, *How Maps Work: Representation, Visualization, and Design* (New York: Guilford Press, 1995).
6. William Cartwright, "Applying the Theatre Metaphor to Integrated Media for Depicting Geography," *Cartographic Journal*, 46, no. 1 (February 2009): 24–35. doi:10.1179/000870409X415561.
7. Jeremy W. Crampton, *Mapping: A Critical Introduction to Cartography and GIS* (Chichester, U.K., John Wiley & Sons, 2011).
8. Mei-Po Kwan and Guoxiang Ding, "Geo-Narrative: Extending Geographic Information Systems for Narrative Analysis in Qualitative and Mixed-Method Research," *The Professional Geographer* 60, no. 4 (2008): 443–465.
9. Pedro Lasch, "Guias de Ruta / Route Guides," in Alexis Bhaga and Lize Mogel (eds.), *An Atlas of Radical Cartography*, 77–80 (Los Angeles: Journal of Aesthetics and Protest Press, 2008).
10. Alice Maugeri, "Itinéraires Clandestins," Les Blogs Du Diplo, September 24, 2007, blog.mondediplo.net/2007-09-24-Itineraires-clandestins.
11. Michael Stryker, Ian Turton, and Alan MacEachren, "Health GeoJunction: Geovisualization of News and Scientific Publications to Support Situation Awareness," paper read at Geospatial Visual Analytics Workshop, GIScience 2008, September 23, at Park City, UT.
12. Michael Coulis, "Hermeneut on a Bike: Eleven Geo-logical Lessons in Love and Landscapes," in Matthew Rangel, David L Jones, and Michael Coulis (eds), *Journeys Beyond the Neatline: Expanding the Boundaries of Cartography* (Edmonton: William C. Wonders Map Collection, University of Alberta Libraries, 2010).
13. Barbara Piatti, Hans Rudolf Bär, Anne-Kathrin Reuschel, Lorenz Hurni, and William Cartwright, "Mapping Literature: Towards a Geography of Fiction," in *Cartography and Art*, 177–192. (Berlin: Springer, 2009).

14. Mikael Jern, "Explore, Collaborate and Publish Official Statistics for Measuring Regional Progress," in Yuhua Luo, ed., *Cooperative Design, Visualization, and Engineering*, 189–198. Lecture Notes in Computer Science 6240 (Berlin: Springer, 2010).

15. B. Mirel, "Usability and Usefulness in Bioinformatics: Evaluating a Tool for Querying and Analyzing Protein Interactions Based on Scientists' Actual Research Questions," in *Professional Communication Conference, 2007. IPCC 2007. IEEE International*, 1–8, 2007, doi:10.1109/IPCC.2007.4464064.

16. Natalia Andrienko and Gennady Andrienko. *Exploratory Analysis of Spatial and Temporal Data: A Systematic Approach* (Berlin: Springer, 2006).

17. Marian Dörk, Sheelagh Carpendale, Christopher Collins, and Carey Williamson. "VisGets: Coordinated Visualizations for Web-based Information Exploration and Discovery," *IEEE Transactions on Visualization and Computer Graphics* 14, no. 6 (November 2008): 1205–1212, doi:10.1109/TVCG.2008.175.

18. Paula Ahonen-Rainio and Menno-Jan Kraak. "Deciding on Fitness for Use: Evaluating the Utility of Sample Maps as an Element of Geospatial Metadata," *Cartography and Geographic Information Science* 32, no. 2 (2005): 101–112, doi:10.1559/1523040053722114.

19. Kamran Sedig and Mark Sumner, "Characterizing Interaction with Visual Mathematical Representations," *International Journal of Computers for Mathematical Learning* 11, no. 1 (April 2006): 1–55, doi:10.1007/s10758-006-0001-z.

20. Kamran Sedig and Hai-Ning Liang, "Interactivity of Visual Mathematical Representations: Factors Affecting Learning and Cognitive Processes," *Journal of Interactive Learning Research* 17, no. 2 (April 2006): 179–212.

21. Timothy W. Cole and Sarah L. Shreeves, "Search and Discovery Across Collections: The IMLS Digital Collections and Content Project," *Library Hi Tech* 22, no. 3 (2004): 307–322.

22. Olga Buchel, "Designing Map-based Visualizations for Collection Understanding," In *Proceedings of the 11th Annual International ACM/IEEE Joint Conference on Digital Libraries*, 429–430 (Ottawa, Canada: ACM, 2011), doi:10.1145/1998076.1998169; Olga Buchel and Kamran Sedig, "Extending Map-based Visualizations to Support Visual Tasks: The Role of Ontological Properties," *Knowledge Organization Journal* 38, no. 3 (2011): 204–230; ———. "Using Map-based Visual Interfaces to Facilitate Knowledge Discovery in Digital Libraries," in *ASIST Proceedings*, New Orleans, LA, 2011, www.asis.org/asist2011/posters/99_FINAL_SUBMISSION.docx .

23. Kamran Sedig and Paul Parsons, "Interaction Design for Complex Cognitive Activities with Visual Representations: A Pattern-Based Approach," *AIS Transactions on Human-Computer Interaction* 5, no. 2 (June 2013): 84–133.

24. Robert E. Roth, "Interactive Maps: What We Know and What We Need to Know," *Journal of Spatial Information Science* 2013, no. 6 (2013): 59–115, doi:http://dx.doi.org/10.5311/JOSIS.2013.6.105.

25. Olga Buchel, "Redefining Geobrowsing," in *Proceedings of the 76th ASIS&T Annual Meeting*, vol. 50, 2013.

## CHAPTER 13

Visualizing a Collection Using Interactive Maps

Francine Berish
George Brown College

Sarah Simpkin
Markham Public Library

Index maps are a long-established finding aid in map collections. These maps, typically marked with boxes outlining what areas are covered by maps or air photos within the collection, are common sights in many libraries. Whether digital or online, index maps offer a number of advantages to users: They provide information on the library's holdings, give users a quick visual reference to the coverage and scale provided by a given map, and provide a call number or other reference information for locating a copy of the item within the collection.

Online index maps, however, hold a number of advantages over their paper counterparts.[1] First, they are accessible at any time and from any location with web access. Next, these maps can incorporate useful linkages with catalogue records as well as opportunities for people to download digital materials and view additional metadata from the maps themselves. Finally, users can potentially interact with the maps themselves: By zooming, panning, and adding various reference layers, researchers can be confident that their target map covers their intended area.

With the rise of Google Maps (maps.google.com) and other web mapping services, many libraries are using map mashups to visualize collections in different ways. Sometimes these mashups are used to overlay scanned historical maps or airphotos on top of modern-day base maps.[2] Staff at the University of Connecticut have chosen this technique to showcase a broad collection of data; everything from racial change maps[3] to airphotos[4] and home value indexes[5] have been superimposed on top of standard Google Maps.

These interactive web maps are also an ideal way for users to browse and download geospatial data files. Scholars GeoPortal (geo2. scholarsportal.info) is a geospatial data discovery layer supported by the Ontario Council of University Libraries. Based on the ArcGIS JavaScript API, the Scholars GeoPortal web application features an embedded map view that can display geospatial datasets hosted by the service (Figure 13.1).

Beyond simply viewing the data on top of a basemap, Scholars GeoPortal users can toggle layers on and off, adjust transparency levels, view location-specific attribute data, share permalinks to particular data views, and even download a zipped file containing data for their area of interest.[6] The need to offer users a download feature was the primary driver behind our own library mashup at Western University, which we describe in detail here.

Choosing a Data Visualization Tool

The Map and Data Centre at Western University in London, Ontario is home to Canada's second largest collection of sheet maps (220,000),

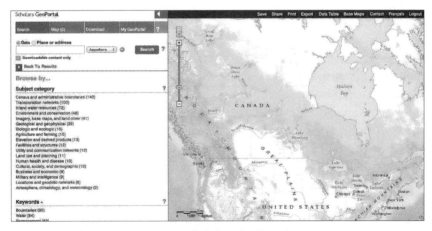

Figure 13.1 Geospatial datasets on Scholars GeoPortal

atlases (2,040), air photos (58,000), and related cartographic mate-rials.[7] Among these are a collection of uncatalogued early Ontario maps that are housed in wall-mounted frames and in display cabi-nets under acrylic glass. Dating from the early 1700s to the early 20th century, these maps are a rare glimpse into the history of European settlement in North America. When we began our mashup project in 2011, these maps were largely uncatalogued and unknown to users relying on the web to locate materials. Without the budget for paid web mapping services, we chose to build our online map index using Fusion Tables, a free interactive data visualization tool from Google (google.com/fusiontables).

Fusion Tables initially looks like a standard spreadsheet table: Datasets are organized into rows and columns, and the values in individual cells can be manipulated using functions. The power of Fusion Tables, however, lies in the visualizations it is able to gen-erate on the web. Instead of producing a chart or map that must be updated every time a data point changes, Fusion Tables will update embedded charts and maps with the latest data available from the table. Unlike regular spreadsheets, these tables can also contain information to control how parts of the map will display. Finally, Fusion Tables will also automatically detect table columns with loca-tion information (coordinates, place names, addresses, etc.), making the mapping part easy.

Fusion Tables was a good fit for our project for a few reasons. First, the tool is available at no cost. Next, multiple users can be granted permission to view and edit the data behind each visualization. This feature allowed multiple contributors to edit the data table simulta-neously and also allowed editing privileges to the people who would continue expanding the project. Since Fusion Tables is well inte-grated with the popular Google Maps service, we also felt it would provide an intuitive interface for users to browse. Finally, embedded Fusion Tables maps always contain the most up-to-date information from their tables, ensuring that users will always see the latest infor-mation that has been added.

Privacy Settings and Sharing

Google Fusion Tables operate in a web-based environment where information is stored using the cloud, and data entered or edited within the table are reflected on the map index automatically. This said, choosing the appropriate privacy settings is integral to the success of your mashup. How you manage sharing and editing in your Fusion Table completely depends on the content and context of your project. In our case, the information in the map index had to be published and publically accessible, with editing restricted to those with access to the library's Google account. If anyone could edit the map mashup, it would update in real-time and the library could be liable for any misinformation or if copyright laws are broken.

A mashup could also contain sensitive information (e.g., one identifying your child's favorite play areas). You may want to make these sorts of mashups private or limit sharing to a particular audience of friends and family. Access can be restricted by specifying which email addresses can view and edit the Fusion Table or by sending authorized users a link to a unique URL.

Copyright and Citation/Bibliographic Information

When making a mashup that combines information from different sources, the rights of the original creator of the works that you are using must be considered; it may be illegal to reproduce data and images without the author's permission. Copyright law varies by country and by context. For example, there may be exceptions for educational use. This can get complicated in a mashup with numerous layers and sources of information. In Canada, maps fall under the category of artistic works, receiving the same treatment as paintings, drawings, photographs, sculptures, plans, and so on. The process through which the items were digitized also matters. In our case, we were scanning the maps ourselves. If you are using maps or photos scanned by another organization, that organization could be the current copyright holder, which would mean that the scans cannot be reproduced without their permission.

Without an education in law, it can be difficult to comprehend the legalese used to describe copyright regulations and apply them to your particular project. It is therefore important to use existing resources to your benefit when decrypting how the law applies to your mashup. If you are working within a larger organization, you may have access to a copyright consultant or specialist. Professional associations affiliated with your line of work may also provide assistance. It also can't hurt to walk into your local library and ask for copyright help resources.

In short, have no fear if you're working independently or making a mashup just for fun. Never underestimate the power of the blogosphere for finding experts in your region who are working in a similar discipline or tackling a related project. Following blogs can also help you keep abreast of current copyright trends. Canadian readers may already be familiar with Michael Geist (michaelgeist.ca), a law professor and copyright expert who regularly writes and blogs about Canada's current copyright legislation. Copyright laws are subject to change, making it essential to stay informed.

When it's within your rights to reproduce a work (e.g., when the copyright expires), it is still necessary to give credit to the original creator or author of the work. When dealing with photographs one must ask who, if anyone, holds the copyright. It may not acceptable to use photos combed from Google Images (images.google.com) or Facebook (facebook.com). As a general rule, it is much easier to create a mashup if you are the copyright holder, if the datasets included have been made openly available by their creators, or if the material in question is out of copyright. In our case, the maps we scanned were out of copyright.

When it comes to citations, think about established conventions. What is the best way to describe the information you're delivering? Some citation styles are best-suited to certain disciplines, so choose the one that best suits your subject matter. For our project dealing with historical maps, we chose to follow the citation format used in Joan Winearls' influential book, *Mapping Upper Canada, 1780–1867: An Annotated Bibliography of Manuscript and Printed Maps.*[8]

Since our mashup was intended to fill a gap in the library's collection, it was also essential that these previously uncatalogued historic maps be made searchable within the library catalogue as well as downloadable via a link directly from the map mashup (Figure 13.2).

Because Western's Map and Data Centre was in the process of transitioning to the widely adopted MARC/AACR2 standard, we were advised to catalogue the maps accordingly for the sake of consistency. These standards are fairly common practice for map libraries: Over 55 percent of research libraries in North America reported that at least 70 percent of their map catalogue records used MARC.[9]

Of course, every mashup is different. While our first example included data layers that we created and cataloged ourselves, many

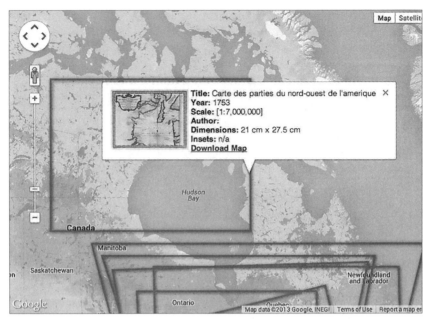

Figure 13.2   Browsing and downloading maps embedded on the Western Libraries website directly from the index

mashups simply combine existing information in unique visualizations, an example of which is described later in the chapter.

Image Quality

When adding images to mashups, or in our case, providing JPEGs of scanned maps, there are important considerations for image quality. Balancing usability and access can be challenging, since the size of each file can increase significantly with the image's resolution. When incorporating scanned documents, mashup creators will need to determine the number of pixels per inch at which the maps will be scanned and made accessible online. In our case, the maps had to be of a high enough quality to be useful for researchers, while balancing the needs of users with slower internet connection speeds. We decided on a 400 dots per inch (dpi) JPEG format as a compromise between image quality and accessibility. While there is an audience looking for higher quality lossless TIFFs, the user could always visit or contact Western Libraries to attain these. Ultimately, image quality settings will vary depending on your target audience and your institution's digital storage limitations.

Scale

Scale is a fundamental theoretical consideration for displaying any information on a map. In our case, the majority of the maps selected covered large regions (e.g., Ontario and Hudson's Bay). This means that the majority of bounding boxes showing the geographical coverage of each map are located in the same general area, making the content of the index viewable at a glance. One exception was an interesting map of a small town in Southwestern Ontario called Goderich. Unfortunately, in the Google Maps interface, the bounding box for this map is not visible until the user has zoomed in to the (less than 10 km^2) town, making the majority of the Upper Canada maps covering larger spatial areas disappear from view.

This interface is, therefore, less ideal for displaying maps of different scales in the same view. For example, a mashup including photos from both the Arctic and small island nations in the South Pacific may be challenging to visualize in its entirety, without zooming in to certain areas on the map. This said, the platform also has advantages including the up-to-date base maps provided by Google Maps, which are a big help for users affording the ability to locate known reference points on the map (place names, roads, physical features, and other points of interest).

Displaying large- and small-scale maps together is a challenge that can be somewhat overcome by the interactivity of Google Maps. While Goderich is one example of a difficulty posed by scale, our collection is still reasonably easy to visualize by zooming in and out of the map index. As the project is expanded to include more maps, Google Maps may impose different limitations, such as visualizing maps covering Mars or other extraterrestrial bodies.

According to theory in visual acuity, it is hard for humans to visualize too much information at a glance; therefore, adding excessive layers and data sets may make for a visually confusing mashup.[10] Since the brain can only process so many colors and features at one time, it may be necessary to add more interactivity. This can be achieved by reducing the number of layers shown at a time and by offering checkboxes to limit the display to specific layers or a timeline slider that would restrict data to a certain time period. It is important to keep scale in mind even when creating a mashup for posting travel pictures. If your trip included a thousand pictures capturing views spanning the entire globe, it may be overwhelming to visualize all the photos at once.

Creating a Mashup in Fusion Tables

One disadvantage to using a web-based service like Fusion Tables to create your mashup is that you are at the whim of an external provider. While our historical map index is available on the Western Libraries website and continues to function as a valuable tool, since its creation Google has changed the features we used to create our map index so they do not function in exactly the same way. That said the index still acts as a valuable demonstration of the theoretical areas that need to be considered when making a map mashup. The following example is meant to demonstrate the functionality of the current version of Fusion Tables for making mashups.

We decided to create a camping mashup—a hobby we both enjoy—that would combine our travel pictures on a map with travel information. Although we decided to create our own data set in our historical map index example by scanning the maps ourselves, that doesn't mean that you have to do the same. Your mashup could be as simple as combining existing data like photos from Flickr (flickr. com), Instagram (instagram.com) or Pinterest (pinterest.com) on a map in an interesting way.

When creating any type of table, be sure to name and format your columns appropriately. Ensuring that column titles are descriptive will facilitate editing by additional contributors and will help you remember what information about the locations you've included in the mashup. As an aside, many mapping software packages place restrictions on the names of datasets and the attribute (column) titles within. Some general rules to keep in mind: Begin titles with letters and not numbers, keep names brief, and do not use any spaces or special characters such as exclamation marks (underscores are acceptable). Following these guidelines will reduce the likelihood of encountering errors if you choose to open your data in mapping software later on.

In Fusion Tables the format of your column is communicated to the map side of the visualization, so having places/coordinates columns formatted as location type attributes is integral for populating the map view. This can be done in the Edit > Change Columns > Format menu.

When exporting a data set from another source, it may have to be converted to a file type readable by Fusion Tables. ESRI Shapefiles (.shp) are used in ArcGIS software and are a common proprietary format for geospatial data. Fusion Tables and Google Maps cannot display these files unless they are converted to Keyhole Markup Language (KML) first. Online services like Shape Escape (shpescape.com) can convert these files without the need for specialized software. Alternatively, open source GIS software such as GRASS (grass.osgeo.org) is available at no cost and also includes file conversion tools. It is possible to avoid file conversion altogether by starting your search for datasets using the .kml file extension.

When importing a data layer from an external source, you may find that there are more fields of data than necessary for your map. In this case, it is possible to filter the fields shown on the map by deleting unnecessary columns. You may also wish to delete rows of data that fall outside of your target region in order to speed up the map's loading time.

When you are creating a Fusion Tables mashup for the first time, there are helpful resources, tutorials, and forums provided by Google and other mapmakers that may be useful if you get stuck. Since web-based software is frequently subject to change, you may find that some features have been moved to different locations within menus or have even disappeared completely. If this happens, chances are that other projects have also been affected. Blogs, forums, and websites can be a good source of solutions and workarounds.

In our camping example, we decided to include data from different sources. Because the attribute data fields for one dataset can be completely different from those in another set, we have found that the easiest way to assemble all of the pieces into one map is to use a third-party tool called the Fusion Tables Maps Layer Wizard (fusiontables-api-samples.googlecode.com). This free and open source tool works by automatically generating the Google Maps JavaScript API code necessary to display several Fusion Tables maps as layers in a single, embeddable map. In order to get started with this process, we first created three separate Fusion Tables.

Our first data layer is one we created ourselves. We documented our past camping trips with photos and decided to show locations where we've taken these pictures as points on the map. To do this,

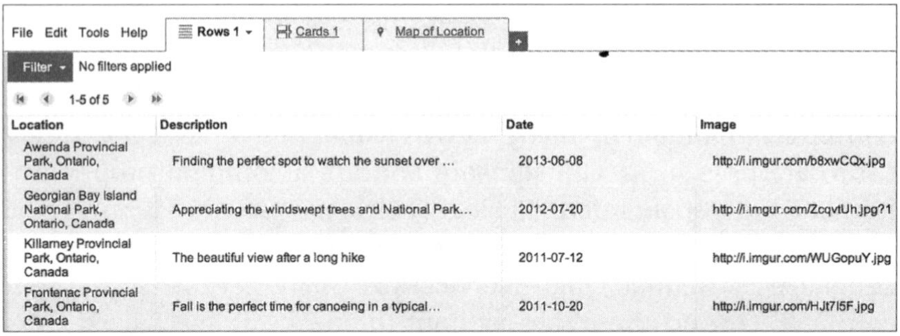

File Edit Tools Help | Rows 1 | Cards 1 | Map of Location

Filter No filters applied

1-5 of 5

Location	Description	Date	Image
Awenda Provincial Park, Ontario, Canada	Finding the perfect spot to watch the sunset over ...	2013-06-08	http://i.imgur.com/b8xwCQx.jpg
Georgian Bay Island National Park, Ontario, Canada	Appreciating the windswept trees and National Park...	2012-07-20	http://i.imgur.com/ZcqvtUh.jpg?1
Killarney Provincial Park, Ontario, Canada	The beautiful view after a long hike	2011-07-12	http://i.imgur.com/WUGopuY.jpg
Frontenac Provincial Park, Ontario, Canada	Fall is the perfect time for canoeing in a typical...	2011-10-20	http://i.imgur.com/HJt7I5F.jpg

Figure 13.3 A Fusion Tables layer used to create the camping mashup

we created a new Fusion Table with fields for location, photo descriptions, the date each photo was taken, the URL for uploaded photos, and, finally, the Google-provided icon name we chose to represent these sites (Figure 13.3).

Geographic data that references a location must be contained within a location-formatted field and must also be geocoded within Fusion Tables in order for it to appear in the right location on the map. Fortunately, Fusion Tables is good at "guessing" potential locations, and it can interpret street addresses, some placemarks, pairs of coordinates, and uploaded KML files. If data in these fields are highlighted yellow, click on the yellow text, open the geocode corrector tool, and confirm the location of each item.

Once our table was complete, we added our image files to the pop-up information window for each point by choosing the Tools > Change Info Window Layout setting and adding some custom HTML that references the field where images are located. This technique was also used in Western's historical map mashup in order to provide download links for the scanned maps. Here is some sample code to produce this kind of downloadable image, where text within {}s references the exact name of the columns in question:

```
<div class='googft-info-window'>
<a href="{ImageURL}"> <img src="{ImageURL}"
width="200px"> </a> <br>
<b>Date:</b> {Date}<br>
<b>Description:</b> {Description}<br>
</div>
```

Our second data layer was found online. The Government of Ontario provides information about carpool lots within the province as a free downloadable KML file on their website (ontario.ca/driving-and-roads/carpool-lots). We felt this information would be useful for reference and downloaded the file. It was then uploaded to Google Drive, opened as a new Fusion Table, and customized with different icons using the Tools > Change Map Styles setting.

Finally, we chose to include driving directions between a campsite and its nearest carpool lot. Because Google Maps allows users to create custom maps (titled "My Places") that can be downloaded as KML files, we just needed to generate a set of directions within Google Maps to connect both locations. Once "My Places" maps have been saved within Google Maps, a KML download option appears. From there, the files can be uploaded to Fusion Tables using the same Google Drive step previously described. Fusion Tables has no trouble interpreting this KML line data since coordinates are already ascribed to each segment of the line. The mashup combining the three distinct layers can be seen in Figure 13.4.

Figure 13.4 Mashup featuring a personalized photo layer, carpool lot locations, and directions to camping spots

Conclusion

Google Fusion Tables are an ideal way to develop mashups because the included data layers can be updated from anywhere and in real-time. Built in the Google environment, mashups made in Fusion Tables can be easily embedded and shared. The two mashup examples described in the chapter demonstrate how a map index can also be a mashup and highlight the important considerations needed to build one. Map mashups are a compelling way for users to browse, identify, and access spatial information.

Endnotes

1. Kristi L. Jensen, Linda R. Musser, and Paige G. Andrew, "Index Maps for the Digital Age," *Information Technology and Libraries* 23, no. 2 (06, 2004): 81–87.
2. Eva Dodsworth and Andrew Nicholson, "Academic Uses of Google Earth and Google Maps in a Library Setting," *Information Technology and Libraries* (2012): 102–117.
3. University of Connecticut Libraries Map and Geographic Information Center - MAGIC. 2012, "Racial Change in the Hartford Region, 1900–2010," magic.lib. uconn.edu/otl/timeslider_racethematic.html.
4. University of Connecticut Libraries Map and Geographic Information Center— MAGIC. 2012, "Neighborhood Change in Connecticut, 1934 to Present," magic. lib.uconn.edu/otl/dualcontrol_aerialchange.html.
5. University of Connecticut Libraries Map and Geographic Information Center— MAGIC. 2012, "Home Value Index in Hartford Region, 1910–2010*," magic.lib. uconn.edu/otl/timeslider_homevalue.html.
6. Elizabeth Hill and Leanne Trimble, "Scholars GeoPortal: A New Platform for Geospatial Data Discovery, Exploration and Access in Ontario Universities," *IASSIST Quarterly* 36, no. 1 (2012): 6–15, www.iassistdata.org/iq/issue/36/1.
7. Bruce Fyfe, Elizabeth Hill, Vince Gray, Eeva Munoz, Courtney Waugh, and Cheryl Woods, "Report and Recommendations of the Map, Data, and Government Information Working Group," *Western Libraries*, Last modified July 15, 2010, www.lib.uwo.ca/files/aboutwl/wlmad-report-20100715.pdf.
8. Joan Winearls, *Mapping Upper Canada, 1780–1867: An annotated bibliography of manuscript and printed maps* (Toronto: University of Toronto Press, 1998).
9. Harry O. Davis and James S. Chervinko. "Map Cataloging and Classification: The Basic Who, What, and Where," In *Maps and Related Cartographic Materials: Cataloging, Classification and Bibliographic Control* 27, no. 1/2 (1999): 9–37.
10. Amit P. Sawant and Christopher G. Healey, "A Survey of Display Device Properties and Visual Acuity for Visualization," *TR-2005-32, North Carolina State University*, (2005): 1–22, www.csc.ncsu.edu/faculty/healey/download/cstr.05a.pdf.

## CHAPTER 14

Creating Computer Availability Maps

Scott Bacon
Kimbel Library, Coastal Carolina University

During the fall semester of 2012, the Kimbel Library and Bryan Information Commons conducted a LibQUAL+ (libqual.org) survey to gauge how patron needs were being met. Many survey respondents commented that there were not enough computers for use in the library buildings. This issue was remedied by the addition of over 70 percent more computer workstations in the new commons building, a move that was well received by patrons. However, these desktops still filled up quickly, especially during midterms and finals, so the library decided to create a dynamic system to show patrons which computers were available for use at any given time. This is how the Kimbel Library Computer Availability Map project (coastal.edu/library/maps/availability) was born.

To create this service the library needed to involve several departments and needed to tie several different data points together. After reading Kim Griggs's *Code4Lib Journal* article "How to Build a Computer Availability Map,"[1] we decided that a computer availability map mashup would be the perfect solution. Our project used Griggs's code as a foundation of the mapping system.

What Are Computer Availability Maps?

Simply stated, computer availability maps provide an interface that shows patrons the location of computer workstations and whether those computers are available or are in use. This is usually accomplished by adding a programming script to the machines, which records the status of the computer ("available" or "in-use") and then sends this data to the database. The database is then queried to show different icons depending on the computer status, usually something like a green circle for available or red circle for in-use (Figure 14.1).

Computer availability maps can be purchased by using a proprietary mapping service such as LabMaps (labstats.com/products/labmaps). In this chapter, however, I will detail how to create an in-house solution using open source code and a little programming. I will outline the steps Kimbel Library took to create our mapping system and provide links to our code (coastal.edu/library/maps/availability/zipfiles/availabilityfiles.zip) so that anyone with a little coding and programming knowledge can create maps for their institution.

Why Should You Make Computer Availability Maps?

Librarians serve their patrons in many ways by providing access to resources and services. Maps help patrons orient themselves with your access points and provide a visual path to these points. Our patrons like Kimbel Library because it is a place to study, meet friends, and utilize technology. They also see our librarians as forward thinking, using technology to provide them with faster, more modern, and more integrated services such as these maps. Building

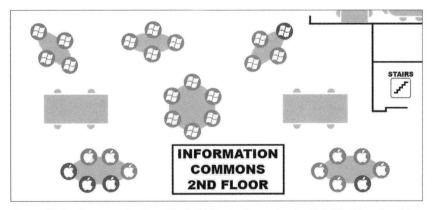

Figure 14.1   An example of an Kimbel Library Computer Availability Map, in which colors (red and green) and symbols are used to provide further distinction for each machine

services for your patrons helps to establish relationship and forms a good impression of the library in their minds.

What Makes These Maps Mashups?

A broad definition of a mashup might read: creating a single online service by joining data together using other services. This is how our computer availability maps were built. We used our MySQL database to load computer IDs, pixel positions, and map locations. We used a Perl script on the computers to tell the database whether the computer was logged in or logged out. We designed a PHP- and HTML-based user interface that included the maps and computer icons. We designed a graphical user interface console that allowed library administrators to change icon locations through drag-and-drop functionality. Finally we developed several ways for patrons to access the maps: through the help desk monitors, the full website, and our mobile website. Our maps illustrate how several different data points and applications can be mashed up to create new functionality for patrons.

Working Together

The Kimbel Library Computer Availability Maps project involved not only several different library services working in concert, but also several different library staff members. The Web Services and Emerging Technologies Librarian was in charge of the project. He designed the library maps, expanded the original script to include both buildings, mobilized the maps, and created the dashboard script for the help desk monitors. A web design student assistant carried out the map and computer icon designs using graphic design software. A computer science student took some of the code provided by other sources and revised it to suit Kimbel Library's needs. He also created and coded the administrative console and graphical user interface. Kimbel Library's information resource consultant (IRC) embedded the Perl script on the machines and performed computer maintenance and troubleshooting operations.

This project may appear daunting to those unfamiliar with coding and programming, especially noting the variety of expertise of the library staff members involved. But a basic application of this project can be created as long as there is an amenable IT staff member with access to the institution's database and directory structure. The script will need to be loaded on all of the machines as well. Not much else is needed to create maps tailored to each institution. Some HTML and PHP experience will be helpful in understanding how all of the files fit together and knowing what code to plug in to what area. A bit of knowledge about Adobe Photoshop or Adobe Illustrator is helpful in creating maps and icons.

Architecture and Implementation

The following sections describe in greater detail the system design and architecture of the availability maps and the steps involved in its implementation. The mapping system runs in a standard LAMP stack development environment (Linux, Apache, MySQL, PHP). We programmed the application to link to the university's MySQL database, which displayed information about each computer involved in the mapping system. The most important bit of information in the database was the login/logout Perl script, which switched from 0 to 1 to denote whether machines were available or in-use. PHP was used to display this computer status through the application programming interface (API) and to allow administrative functions through the administrative console. The front-end interfaces were coded using PHP, HTML, and Java-Script. This mashup of web programming, API, database, and scripting resulted in a user interface where patrons could see whether computers were available by finding green icons throughout the library buildings.

To track the operations of each computer, we created a MySQL database that contained each computer's name, status, type, positioning (relative to the top left of each map), the time of the last update, and location. You will need to create a database with at least these values in order to recreate our availability maps.

Figure 14.2 shows a sample of the structure of the MySQL database. We can see that Mac workstation 10883 has a status of 1 (in-use). Its icon will be located on the image map 609 pixels from the left and 394 pixels from the top. The Bldg column shows that the computer is located on the second floor of the Bryan Information Commons (BIC2).

Loading Perl Script on Computers

In order to track the status of each computer, a Perl script was loaded onto each machine's login and logout scripts. The Perl script sends

computer_name	status	computer_type	left_pos	top_pos	updated_at	bldg
BIC10883.COASTAL.EDU	1	mac	609	394	2013-07-02 11:14:22	BIC2
BIC10879.COASTAL.EDU	0	mac	655	341	2013-07-01 09:43:00	BIC2
BIC10863.COASTAL.EDU	0	mac	575	314	2013-06-24 09:30:22	BIC2
BIC10885.COASTAL.EDU	0	mac	609	284	2013-06-26 17:59:44	BIC2
BIC10868.COASTAL.EDU	1	mac	656	230	2013-06-18 16:48:38	BIC2

Figure 14.2 Database table sample

HTTP requests to a PHP script, changing when the computer is logged on or off by recording a value of 1 or 0, respectively. These values are stored in the database's status column, which is queried by the API to determine which icon to show on the map. A red icon shows if the status is 1 (in-use); a green icon shows if the status is 0 (available). These scripts were used verbatim from the Griggs article.

PHP and HTML Coding

Once the scripts were loaded on the computers, we set out to code the functionality of the application. The following section details each of the files created to make the maps work.

First, we needed to establish a database connection so the login/ logout scripts could talk to the database and record each computer's availability status. The _sql_header.php file helped establish a connection to the database. The statuschanger.php file queried the database to set the computer status. The database values were in a constant state of flux, so we also made sure to include a JavaScript refresh on the maps to give the most up-to-date information to patrons. We chose a 2-minute refresh in our map system in order to provide a balance between having real-time data and easing the load of updates to our servers.

User interface functions were created to make for a better user experience. For the interface, we determined that we needed differing floor locations, system metrics, a timestamp, and a symbol key. We identified four different locations for which we needed to create maps for our system: first floor library, first floor commons, second floor library, and second floor commons. A drop-down menu was created to enable switching between these locations; the _maps.php file contains this drop-down code. The Bldg column of our database was queried to assign computers to the correct map, as is seen in the

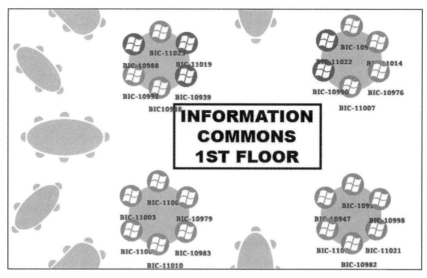

Figure 14.3 Example of the Admin Console sample, in which the computer_name values appear near icons when administrators are logged in

change map .php file. The metrics section shows users the real-time availability of Macs and PCs for each location. The timestamp shows users when the page was last updated. The symbol key shows what each icon represents.

Administrative console functionality was the next component to be coded. The administrative console is an API that was created using AJAX and the jQuery UI library to enable employees to login and drag-and-drop each computer icon to its proper location throughout each map (Figure 14.3). This functionality was designed to avoid much back-end work within the database and allow those without programming skills to change the computer locations in the event that computers needed to be moved to different tables or different rooms.[2] Functionality such as this is also helpful due to the fact that different browsers "read" pixels in different ways. Shifting icons slightly becomes necessary if a browser used in your institution reads the icon positioning slightly different than other browsers. The positioning of the icons on the maps is coded in the file update_map_. php and is reflected in the database columns left_pos and top_pos in real-time.

Other important administrative console functions are contained in the following files:

- index.php contains, among other things, the code that links the correct icon to the correct map.

- _links.php allows users to log in to the console.

- _clear_msgs.php clears messages upon session start or shows an error message if there is a login error.

- _protected.php contains authentication code, which lets authenticated users into the console or re-directs unauthenticated users to _links.php options.

- admin.php file is the code for the user login screen, which allows users to authenticate to gain access to the console.

- login_.php checks the username and password entered in the admin.php page in order to allow entry into the console.

- logout_.php allows logout functionality.

- create_user.php and user_create_.php allow the site administrator to create new users while also storing username and password information in the database.

Making the Maps

The next step in the project was to create the maps. Test maps were originally created by taking screenshots of building blueprints. The maps were then conceptualized and re-designed by hand for the website pages. At this point, Kimbel Library's web design student assistant designed the maps in Illustrator. She also designed the icons, incorporating Apple and Microsoft symbols in the icon design to allow users to differentiate between these machines.[3] Icons were placed atop the map using CSS.

Several design decisions were made in the making of these maps. Since the maps were going to be published to a variety of different devices in a variety of sizes, we needed to provide visual markers that would help map viewers orient themselves relative to each location. We ended up using the library help desk, circulation desk, and equipment checkout room as orientation points on the maps. Other important practical objects that we included on the maps were elevators, stairs, vending machines, and restrooms. Maps were positioned to match as near to true north as was appropriate design-wise. In general, the maps were broader and less detailed design-wise in order to mitigate potential design updates. Room numbers were left blank and non-essential building features were not included.

Publishing and Display

Before proceeding with the coding and design of the maps project, it is important to decide in what form the maps will eventually be presented to the public. The Kimbel Library maps were styled for the web and linked to the library website for use on desktop, laptop, and tablet devices. Maps were displayed on monitors above the main library help desk so that patrons could quickly find an open computer when they arrived at the library. We also mobilized the maps for display on mobile devices, so patrons could check the maps before coming to the library to determine if it was too busy to visit. We chose to use the same map for all three types of publication and display: web use, help desk monitors, and mobile devices.

Webpages

Patrons can access the API from our library website pages. A map 800 pixels wide by 872 pixels high was created for each floor. Positioning was measured in pixels from the top left of the map. This created a matrix of that same size where the computer icons could be placed. This consistency aided us in using one master map and one master database table to display the same map matrix on several different devices.

Help Desk Monitors

Patrons in the library can see computer availability on monitors at the main help desk. We have two LCD monitors above and behind this central information desk, located at the intersection of the library and information commons buildings. The Web Services Librarian created a new dashboard index page for each building, which consists of a JavaScript dashboard script that calls the two main HTML map pages. The script cycles through the floors at 7-second intervals, allowing patrons to get a full view of all computers on both floors in a relatively short time.[4]

Maps were displayed on the monitors by linking each monitor to a PC through a VGA cable. We had to use the "display full screen" function and had to decrease the browser window zoom level to 85 percent to enable optimal display on these monitors. Institutions could have the opportunity to choose monitors with the appropriate screen size and resolution based on the size and shape of their specific availability map system.

Mobile Pages

The maps were mobilized by utilizing several mobile optimization steps. The header was not called in the mobile pages. We added style sheet elements to use mobile tabs for navigation as opposed to drop-down functionality. Users could therefore quickly see which computers were available without having to interact with any unnecessary bells and whistles (Figure 14.4). We optimized the site for mobile

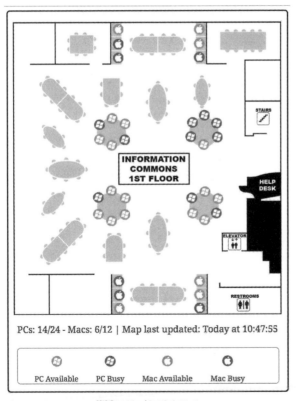

Figure 14.4   Map optimized for mobile devices

devices by linking to a mobile CSS style sheet. CSS media queries seemed like a good idea until we encountered the difficulty of representing pixels differently for the same computer on three different screens. In order to show three different map sizes, we would have needed to build three different database tables to pull data from top and left positions, which was not optimal for our environment. We did use the viewport metatag[5] to control the layout on mobile browsers, specifying a viewport width of 850 in order to maintain consistency across devices. During testing we found that the icons and maps were large enough even in mobile devices with screen widths of 480 pixels, which we felt was acceptable for our needs.

If we had a chance to do this project again, we might have created a series of three maps as others have done: one for large display (900 pixels wide), one for desktop display (600 pixels wide), and one for mobile device display (300 pixels wide). Many institutions mobilize their computer availability maps by porting text-only descriptions to the device screen, but we made a decision that we wanted to replicate the web experience as much as possible across all devices. Our icons were large enough when tested in many iOS and Android devices that we were satisfied with our basic web map design.

Testing

Several tests should be performed during a project of this nature. The login/logout script should be tested once the scripts are loaded onto the machines, to ensure that the database is recording and displaying 1s and 0s accordingly. Script values should be reflected in two places: in the database's status column, which switches to 1 if available (logged-out) or 0 if in-use (logged-in); and in the front-end map interface, which should show the green PC or Mac icon if the status value reads 1 and the red PC or Mac icon if it reads 0.

API functionality should be tested by logging into the administrative console, moving icons with a cursor, checking that the database is recording, and displaying the updated positioning. This should be reflected in the database by the left_pos and top_pos values and in the maps by changing icon positions.

Cross-browser testing should be performed, taking into consideration the technology utilized by each institution's population. Analytics should be used early in the project to determine which operating systems and browsers will be tested.[6] Mobile device testing should be performed to ensure users can access the mobile optimized service without too much scrolling, pinching, and squinting.[7]

Conclusion

Various issues that we encountered during the implementation of this project can be avoided to some extent with diligence and maintenance. Maintenance should be performed on the mashup components at regular intervals. Consult your IRC or systems librarian to set up a predetermined maintenance schedule in order to ensure that the scripts are running properly. The IRC should also check the script functionality whenever computers are re-imaged, for example.

Databases should be optimized, backed up, and free of any inconsistencies such as duplicate records. Refresh scripts should be checked to ensure that pages are not catching, pausing, or freezing during the cycle. Updates to operating systems, browsers, and software should be performed on a regular basis.

Many institutions have a wide variety of computers, which contain different operating systems, browsers, browser versions, software versions, antivirus, spyware blockers, and so on. A myriad of technology issues can cause machines not to send the login/logout status correctly. Scheduled updates and a diligent IT staff can help to mitigate many of these issues.

One issue that Kimbel Library has experienced deals with patron login/logout functions. The library does not require authentication for patrons to use computers. Since patrons do not need to log in to use computers, they do not need to log out either. The default logout event on our computers (when the screensaver takes over) is triggered by a script after 10 minutes of inactivity. Changing this metric may cause problems with students who are sitting at a computer taking notes; they are still at the computer but have not moved the mouse or used the keyboard. Forcing a logout may cause them to lose their unsaved work. The library is still actively working to find solutions to this issue and is contemplating several workarounds due to the fact that we are not authorized to add authentication on any library computers at this time. Each project team must work with their IRC or IT department to figure out the best workflow for their organization's technology environment and plan their availability map project accordingly.

Maps are helpful because they provide a visual representation to patrons. They help patrons locate library services by visualizing those services. Helping patrons save time by offering services that are accessible online from multiple devices further serves to endear them to the library. Tying several different data points and services together to create a computer availability map mashup is not only fun, but can also contribute to patron happiness and appreciation. Create a mashup at your institution and you should observe a noticeable rise in patron satisfaction.

***

I would like to thank the major coding and design contributors in this project: Joshua Carlson-Purcell, Jordan Ratti, and Jason Leary. Their contributions make up the bulk of this chapter, and anything of worth is most likely theirs. Any mistakes are my own.

Endnotes

1. Kim Griggs, "How to Build a Computer Availability Map," *The Code4Lib Journal,* December 21, 2010, accessed September 18, 2014, journal.code4lib.org/articles/4067. See github.com/griggsk/availability-map for the complete availability map code package. Use this package along with Kimbel Library's API files to create maps similar to the Kimbel Library maps.
2. This moving and shifting of computers actually happened several times during project development. Be sure to save computer locations frequently while in the administrative console. Otherwise the page resets upon refresh, losing any unsaved computer movement.
3. Many institutions include an "offline" designation for computers, which allows the icon to stay in position on the map while signaling to the user that the computer is unavailable, yet is also not in use. We chose to forego using the offline signifier (we have not experienced many offline problems, as we have an extremely responsive IRC dedicated to quickly fixing library computers).
4. See index_dashboard_bic.html and index_dashboard_klib.html in the Kimbel Library code files. Both files contain the full dashboard script.
5. We placed the viewport meta tag code within the head tag, <meta name="viewport" content="width=850" />
6. We used Google Analytics to determine which operating systems and browsers to test on. We also used analytics to track map usage by using a PHP include statement to call an analytics file into several of our map pages.
7. Cross-browser testing was performed on the majority of operating systems and browsers used by our patrons. We tested for mobile functionality using COWEMO's mobile phone emulator, www.mobilephoneemulator.com

## CHAPTER 15

Getting Digi With It:
Using TimelineJS to Transform
Digital Archival Collections

Jeanette Claire Sewell
Houston Public Library

Thanks to the increased availability of digitization equipment and the popularity of digital initiatives, many archival collections and libraries are making their unique holdings accessible online. Software programs such as CONTENTdm (contentdm.org), DSpace (dspace.org), Omeka (omeka.org), and Shared Shelf (artstor.org/shared-shelf/s-html/shared-shelf-home.shtml) make the cataloging and discovery of digital objects possible; however, the resulting content often remains relatively static and non-interactive. In an effort to make our digital archival collections more dynamic and discoverable, the Houston Public Library began creating timelines for the Houston Area Digital Archives (digital.houstonlibrary.org) using TimelineJS (timeline.knightlab.com). This free and easy-to-use internet application enables us to mash up our existing content with a variety of other exciting features included in the TimelineJS interface.

This chapter will give an overview of the features of TimelineJS and explain how to make it work with existing digital objects. Further, this chapter will also discuss how these timelines work successfully for the Houston Public Library's Houston Area Digital Archives website by attracting and engaging more visitors, displaying connections between different types of digital objects, and increasing positive feedback.

Transforming Existing Digital Content

Transforming existing digital content is often a challenge, but it is the necessary next step that should be taken to engage users. In 2011, the Houston Public Library began providing open, online access to digitized books, audio and video materials, documents, photographs, manuscripts, maps, memorabilia, and more with CONTENTdm, making them freely available for research and study through the Houston Area Digital Archives. Currently, the archival website includes more than 10,000 digital objects, with more added each day.

TimelineJS has been a very successful tool for the Houston Public Library in transforming these digital objects so that they come alive. The first timeline was based on a small born-digital archival collection and told the story of C.F. Richardson, Sr., a local African-American newspaper publisher. From there, the next subject chosen for a timeline was the Houston Astrodome, due to increased local interest surrounding the historic structure and because there were various images, oral histories, and finding aids already online that could each be seamlessly connected within the timeline.

It is precisely these kinds of connections that enable digital content to become more interactive and discoverable. As users navigate through a timeline, they can clearly see how an image is related to a finding aid, an oral history, and more. TimelineJS also provides the ability to display the most interesting items in a digital collection as well as the opportunity to highlight and increase usage of hidden collections. The collaborative aspects inherent in Google Drive (drive.google.com) encourage cooperation among staff members, and the final timeline output adds to the promotional possibilities of digital collections.

Creating a Timeline: Step-By-Step

For continuity and ease of use, each timeline that is created for the Houston Area Digital Archives follows a pattern: The timeline begins with an introductory title slide, followed by six to 10 images alongside a selection of text in chronological order, and ends with a Links and Sources slide. Spend some time exploring the timelines on the Houston Area Digital Archives website (digital.houstonlibrary.org/timeline/index.html) to become familiar with the functionality of a complete timeline. This will also help you to see how the Google Drive spreadsheet coordinates with the TimelineJS output.

The instructions that follow will take you through creating a time-line, step-by-step, in the format used for the Houston Area Digital Archives. Please note that the term *slide* is used to refer to each chronological event shown on the timeline, and *row* and *column* correspond to the Google Drive spreadsheet.

Step 1: Get Started

First you will need to create a Google Drive account or log into your existing account. Next, go to the TimelineJS website (timeline. knightlab.com), and click Make a Timeline Now.

Step 2: Copy the Template

Next, click Google Spreadsheet Template. At the top of spreadsheet, click Use this Template and a copy of the TimelineJS Template will appear in your Google Drive. Re-name the template to match the subject of the timeline. There is a lot of "junk" on the template that you will want to delete and replace. In the future, once you've created a few timelines, I recommend creating your own blank template. Then you can just make copies of your own template. This is especially useful if the majority of the images you will be using are from the same website or source. For now, leave the existing text there as a placeholder and replace it as you go along.

Hint: The original template includes some helpful reminders at the bottom about the function of each column in the template spreadsheet. This text will not appear in the copy of the template, but you can hover over the column titles at the top of your copied template to view the same information.

Step 3: Format the Dates Columns

To make entering the dates for each slide easier, highlight the Start Date and End Date columns (Figure 15.1), and then click Format, then Number, and choose Plain Text at the bottom of the menu. This enables you to enter specific dates, such as 7/1/2013, or just a year.

Step 4: Create a Title Slide

Row 2 of the spreadsheet corresponds to what will be the title slide of the timeline (Figure 15.2). The image you choose for the title slide

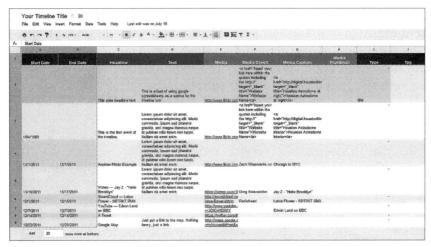

Figure 15.1   Highlight the Start and End Date columns on your spreadsheet

does not necessarily have to be the first image chronologically in the timeline, but it will be the image that is seen first. Think of it as an introduction to the timeline. The instructions for adding an image will be covered in Step 5.

The Start and End Date is optional for this row since the order of this slide is indicated by the word "title" in the Type column to the right. Next, replace the template's placeholder text in the Headline and Text cells of Row 2 with your text. In the final timeline output, the Headline text will display larger and in bold, whereas the Text below will be smaller and gray. For instance, think of the Headline as a title and the Text here as a subtitle. Steps 5 through 7 continue with creating a title slide in Row 2 of the spreadsheet (Figure 15.3).

Step 5: Add an Image

To add images to TimelineJS, you will need a unique, direct link for each image. You can use Flickr (flickr.com), Dropbox (dropbox.com), or Photobucket (photobucket.com) to upload your images and create a link. Then copy and paste the direct link to your image in the Media cell of Row 2.

Hint: The Windows Snipping Tool (or Command + Shift + 4 for Mac computers) is the best way to "grab" images from a CONTENTdm based website. Shrink the image until it fits within the viewing window, then crop and save it using the snipping tool. Even though

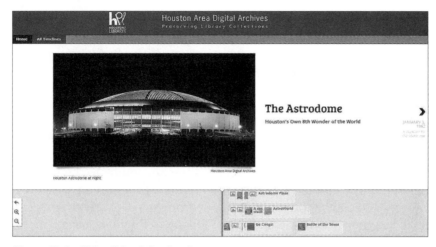

Figure 15.2   Title slide of the timeline

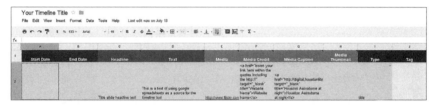

Figure 15.3   Row 2 of the sample spreadsheet

TimelineJS will automatically resize images to fit within the timeline structure, by shrinking and cropping the image you will have a perfectly sized .jpg to link to within the spreadsheet. This method also enables you to use your existing content quickly and easily without having to rescan or retrieve image files from a digital dark archive.

Step 6: Link to Your Website

Use the following html code in the Media Credit cell of Row 2 to create a direct link to your website:

```
<a href="Insert your link here within the
quotes including the http://" target="_blank"
title="Website Name">Website Name</a>
```

This will create a hyperlink in blue text at the bottom right corner of the image that will open in a new browser tab when it is clicked. It is a great feature because it enables you to give credit to your organization while also providing easy access to its homepage.

Step 7: Input a Caption

Add text to the Media Caption cell to create a caption that will appear slightly below the Media Credit text at the bottom left of the image.

Hint: Go a step further and create a direct hyperlink to the landing page of the image. For example, use the same title of the image on your website and copy it into the same code from Step 6 to create a hyperlinked caption. This time, instead of linking to the homepage, link to the specific landing page of the image as in the following example:

```
<a href="http://digital.houstonlibrary.org/
cdm/singleitem/collection/images/id/197/rec/12"
target="_blank" title="Houston Astrodome at
night">Houston Astrodome at night</a>
```

Step 8: Continue to Row 3

Row 3 will be the beginning of the chronological timeline sequence (Figure 15.4). Enter the Start Date that corresponds with the image that you will be using. An End Date is optional.

Hint: If some of the images you want to use in your timeline have the same date, simply enter them in the rows in the spreadsheet in the order in which you would like them to appear in the timeline. The bottom gray portion of the final timeline will not display as nicely, but the visual and text content will not be compromised.

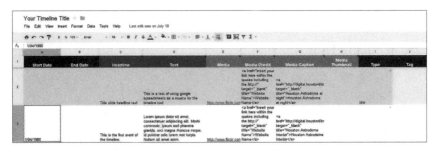

Figure 15.4 Row 3 of the spreadsheet, which will be the beginning of the chronological timeline sequence

Create a Headline as in Step 4. You may want to come up with something in your own words that introduces the image in a creative, snappy way, or you can use the name of the person, place, or thing that is featured in the image.

Next, in the Text cell of Row 3, begin to tell the story of your timeline. Think of the text here as your opportunity to expand on the image in a way that you are unable to within your metadata. Here you can really illuminate the historical significance and impact of whatever is taking place or featured in the image. TimelineJS will automatically generate a scroll bar in the text area of the timeline if your description runs a bit long; however, it is a good idea to keep the text succinct and related to the image that you are featuring in the slide.

Repeat Steps 5 through 8 for each additional row of the spreadsheet corresponding to the number of images and events that will be represented in the timeline. Remember to replace the Media Caption link and text for each image as you go along.

Step 9: Create a Links and Sources Slide

This slide is optional for ending a timeline, but it is important to give credit to any quoted or cited resources in the Text cells. It also reminds users one last time of the website for your library or organization (Figure 15.5).

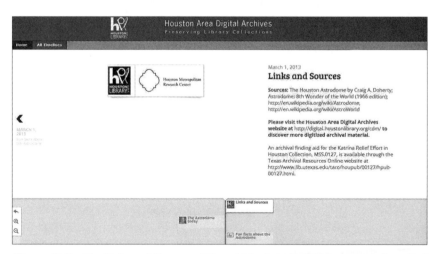

Figure 15.5   The Links and Sources slide, which gives credit to any quoted or cited resources and reminds users one last time of the website for your library or organization

In the Media cell, add a link to your library or organization's logo. Another nice option is to add a link to a photo of your library or organization's building. Then, enter the date that the timeline was created in the Start Date field of the spreadsheet (this ensures that this slide will always show up at the end of the timeline), and add Links and Sources in the Headline cell. Finally, in the Text cell, add citations for sources that were quoted or referenced in the timeline.

As a last reminder, you can also add a statement with a link to your website. For example, the following statement appears on the Links and Sources slide of each Houston Area Digital Archives timeline: "Please visit the Houston Area Digital Archives website digital.houston library.org/cdm to discover more digitized archival material."

Step 10: Publish to the Web and Preview

Once you have added all of the information to your spreadsheet, the next step is to publish it to the web. Click File and then Publish to the Web (Figure 15.6). In the window, check the box next to "Automatically republish when changes are made" and then click Start Publishing. Highlight and copy the link that is generated in the box at the bottom of the window. Click Close.

Hint: Choosing the Automatically Republish option means that any changes or updates you make to the Google Drive spreadsheet in the future will update automatically in the timeline once it is embedded on your blog or website. This makes it very easy to change an

Figure 15.6 Publish your spreadsheet to the web

image or edit the text as you go along, without having to re-publish the spreadsheet or re-embed the code.

Next, return to the TimelineJS website scroll down to the third step on the page, "Copy/paste spreadsheet URL into the generator box below." Paste the link that you copied in Step 10 into the Google Spreadsheet URL box to the right. If you click on the More Options button below the size options, you can explore a few more features, the most fun of which is Fonts. Choose a font from the menu, and then click the blue Preview button.

Voila! You now have a preview of your beautiful timeline. To view it as it will appear on your blog or website, click on the Link to Preview button. You can also copy that link and send it to colleagues as a proof. To choose another font, select another option from the menu and click the blue Preview button until you find the one that best complements the images and text of the timeline.

Step 11: Embed on Your Website

The last step is to copy the code that is automatically generated in the Embed Code box in the fourth step on the TimelineJS page and paste it wherever you would like the timeline to appear on your website.

Step 12: Enjoy Your Creation

Sit back, relax, and wait for the compliments—and increased statistics for your digital content— to roll in! Of course, colleagues and users will most likely have feedback as well. Listening and responding to any suggestions they may have is an important part of the process that can help you to improve the timelines you create, so that each one becomes more appealing to users.

Using Advanced Additions

Using advanced additions will help to further display the relationships between digital objects and add even more interactivity to any timeline. Once you have successfully created a timeline or two, you may want to try some of the following options:

1. Create short paragraphs within the Text cells by adding the HTML tags <p> </p> around text you would like to separate.

2. Add links to related content from other websites, such as an archival finding aid, within the Text cells. Create a statement that will encourage users to click on the link and explore further. For example:

```
<a href="http://digital.houstonlibrary.org/cdm/
singleitem/collection/film/id/193/rec/9"
target="_blank" title="Please click here to watch
a 1965 Astrodome promotional film clip.">Please
click here to watch a 1965 Astrodome promotional
film clip.</a>
```

3. The target="_blank" tag will open the link in a new browser tab so that users can continue to view the timeline without interruption in the current tab. You can also add the <p> </p> tags around this code sequence to separate it from the descriptive text.

4. Utilize the Block Quote feature in the Media cell. This is a very simple addition but one that can make a big impact. Instead of utilizing the Headline and Text cells, add text surrounded by the <blockquote> </blockquote> tags to the Media cell, and it will appear centered in that slide of the timeline. You can still use the Date, Media Credit, and Media Caption cells as well. An example of this feature can be seen in the timeline, When Camelot Came to Houston, available at (digital.houstonlibrary.org/timeline/kennedy.html).

5. Use the Media Thumbnail to indicate linked content. Copy and paste a thumbnail URL from your website, if available, into the Media Thumbnail cell of the spreadsheet. Your image will then show up next to the Headline text in the gray bottom section of the timeline within the corresponding tab. Alternatively, create thumbnails by resizing the same larger images that you used in the timeline and upload them as described previously to generate URLs.

6. Experiment with the other TimelineJS features, such as adding links in the Media field to other websites, Google

Maps (maps.google.com), Vimeo (vimeo.com), or Twitter (twitter.com). Integrating these features will not only make your timelines even more interactive, but they can also broaden your online presence and increase page views of individual digital objects.

Other Ideas for Using TimelineJS

Other ideas for using TimelineJS could include creating a timeline about the implementation of a library program or even highlighting your own career progress for a resume or presentation. TimelineJS can also be a great showcase for something like a summer reading program, in which both patrons and library staff could collaborate during the creative process. For example, staff members could enlist patrons of the program to take photos at events and upload them to Flickr for inclusion in a timeline. The timeline could also include other elements such as tweets from the library and block quotes to highlight positive feedback from customers. A Vimeo video clip of the program in action would also make a great addition—the possibilities are limitless.

Conclusion

TimelineJS is an incredibly effective tool for the Houston Public Library's Houston Area Digital Archives. Ten timelines on various historical subjects relating to the city of Houston have been created so far (available at digital.houstonlibrary.org/timeline/index.html) The Houston Astrodome timeline has received a substantial number of views since being featured on the Houston Area Digital Archives homepage, and the other timelines continue to generate interest and increased usage statistics across the website as a whole.

## Part V

Mashups for Value-Added Services

BookMeUp: Using HTML5, Web Services, and Location-Based Browsing to Build a Book Suggestion App

Jason Clark
Montana State University

Do you have a book, like, on clouds? In the spotlight?
The one with a dog.
        —Anonymous elementary school library patron[1]

The library service Reader's Advisory has been a component of public library reference services going back to the beginning of the 20th century.[2] This practice of conducting a reference interview to find out people's interests and tastes and then offering books to read has wavered as traditional reference services have become less about guiding readership and more focused on research needs. Beyond the physical mediation of the librarian, principles of serendipity—the act of making fortunate discoveries by accident—are literally encoded into our library classifications schemes. Our own Library of Congress classification system works by grouping similar items in browsing settings, but more importantly, it places like materials on the physical shelf to allow for a person to discover similar materials as they physically navigate the collection (e.g., books about biology are located on shelves with other books about biology.) Many people talk of the library's physical arrangement value in terms of this serendipity, but little research has been done on how to recreate this value in our newer library systems and services.[3]

In thinking about library traditions of reader's advisory and serendipity, I became interested in the ways we might move these customs into our digital library environment. The problem is that in our earlier approaches, we were inevitably tied to the physical and the analog. The rise of apps and mobile devices opened the door to small, dedicated software programs that are focused on singular tasks. From my perspective, these apps offered an opportunity to build a focused digital service aimed at allowing someone to enter a search for a title or subject, match an item, and then receive suggested related items. In essence, it was user-mediated reader's advisory and serendipitous browsing. The result was BookMeUp (lib.montana. edu/beta/bookme), a web app incorporating many of the emerging features of HTML5 to work across smartphone and tablet platforms as well as the traditional desktop.

Going the Way of HTML5

As I worked through the idea of a book suggestion app, I started to sketch out a few requirements. Among the top-level functional requirements were:

- Ability to run in any web browser on any platform
- Compatibility with existing skill sets in the organization
- Ability to rapidly iterate and prototype
- Access to the internet for using web services and APIs
- Access to geolocation hardware or settings on desktop computers and mobile devices
- Ability to scale app into multiple design environments (e.g., desktop, smartphone, tablet, etc.)
- Ability for other libraries to understand and apply the techniques and development tools used in building the app

With these basic requirements in place, and because they are required core skills of our digital team, it became clear that we should build the tool using HTML, PHP, JavaScript, and CSS. I also assumed

HTML Resources

- HTML5 Geolocation (w3schools.com/html/html5_geolocation.asp)
- HTML5 Rocks (html5rocks.com)
- HTML5 Please (html5please.com)

that most libraries would have these similar skills in place as they have been hiring for website support and development for a number of years.

Additionally, the instant publishing model of an HTML-based web app allowed me to work live and rapidly develop using only a web browser and an internet connection. During development, I could test and work through bugs immediately and wasn't subject to App Store restrictions, laggy patching, and software deployments. If I had gone with a native application development kit, changes in design would have to be been done via software patching and updates, which was not responsive enough for our needs. The web app option also gave me access to the network where my app could make continual HTTP requests for remote web service data and other dynamic data for page views. JavaScript and the Geolocation API (related to the HTML5 spec) enabled a location-based facet for the app. Finally, the use of CSS with an eye toward responsive design would allow the app to scale into multiple environments like smartphones, tablets, and desktop computers. With all of these advantages, I looked at what was possible to make web apps behave like the native apps you might find in the App Store. Voice input with Google Chrome and some simple HTML markup was one of these experiments (Figure 16.1).

Once I started to grasp some of the possibilities with the Device APIs (hacks.mozilla.org/category/device-apis) coming from the HTML5 specification, the argument to build the app using common web development techniques became even more compelling. The Device APIs include functions like voice input, tracking of device movement and orientation via embedded accelerometers and gyroscopes, accessing device calendaring info and contact information, and even camera input for pictures and video (w3.org/TR/dap-api-reqs). Access to these newer functions meant that I could use the web

Figure 16.1 BookMeUp voice input

browser to emulate a native "app-like" experience using standard HTML, JavaScript, CSS, and a server-side language.

The Algorithms That Make BookMeUp Suggestions Possible

Data mining and machine learning algorithms have been around for quite a while.[4] Finding ways to personalize user experience by filtering a view of data as it relates to a particular person is just one application of data mining and algorithms. More recently, similarity algorithms and the "More like this" relations paradigm have become commonplace in search and browse interfaces.

Until recently, libraries have been using very simple methods to describe and define similarity relationships between items. Library of Congress subject headings, tags, and even simple related keywords have been used to build a network of related items. These methods often rely on matching related patterns of strings and work by associating exact alphanumeric strings from one record to another. This model can hold up on a very generic level, but eventually the nuances of the relationship break down. And here's where similarity algorithms can be applied to pick up the slack. Consider the uncannily accurate Amazon recommendation system (Figure 16.2), which suggests similar products that other customers have purchased as related to the current product.

Suggestions for related items on Netflix are powered using "association learning" models in a similar way. Association learning models work to recreate the intentions of the user by recording and learning similar behaviors between common items and the people who

Figure 16.2   Amazon recommendations

browsed these items. The move away from simple pattern matching to intention recording and learning the relationships between similar people using the systems is what makes these newer forms of recommendations compelling.

Applying Web Services for Recommendations and Book Cover Thumbnails

Fortunately, these association algorithms are not completely hidden. Many internet companies and organizations are making pieces of their service data available via web services. The Amazon Product Advertising API (affiliate-program.amazon.com/gp/advertising/api/detail/main. html) is one of these web services that can be used under certain terms of service (affiliate-program.amazon.com/gp/advertising/api/ detail/agreement.html) to collocate related items using Amazon's data. Another feature of this API is a rich amount of book data related to each item returned: standard metadata like ISBN, thumbnails, author(s), prices, etc. Using this API requires registering as an Amazon Associate and acquiring a developer key that gives Amazon the ability to identify you and your application. BookMeUp also uses the Open Library Covers API (openlibrary.org/dev/docs/api/covers) when there are gaps in thumbnail coverage on Amazon.

Once registered as an Amazon developer, I was able to build a PHP script that made a call to Amazon's web service using the search form input on the main page view of the BookMeUp app (Figure 16.3). When the results are returned to the BookMeUp app public interface, you are given the option to check within WorldCat to find the location of the item. When you touch or click the Check WorldCat link, a subsequent

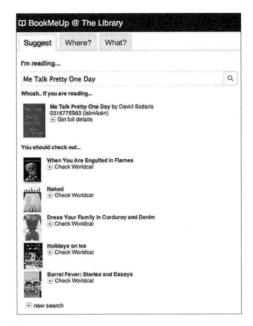

Figure 16.3 BookMeUp results

query against the WorldCat Search API searches for the book and allows you to push through to a WorldCat listing that shows you the holdings of the closest library (oclc.org/developer/documentation/worldcat-search-api/using-api). The request from the PHP script to the Amazon API has the following parameters:

```php
<?php
...
$parameters=array(
"region"=>"com",
"AssociateTag"=>"jasonclarkinf-20",
"Operation"=>"ItemSearch",
"SearchIndex"=>"Books",
'ResponseGroup'=>'Images,ItemAttributes,
EditorialReview,Reviews,Similarities',
"Keywords"=>"$q");
...
?>
```

One thing to note is that the programming in the BookMeUp app is specifying that only books within Amazon's catalog are to be searched. SearchIndex is the parameter controlling this option, and it can be set to look at other indexes or everything in the Amazon catalog. A successful call to the Amazon API returns formatted XML that is used to create the display for a specific book item and the related books that the app uses as suggestions. Here's an excerpt from the XML file that has the suggestions:

```
<TotalResults>27</TotalResults>
<TotalPages>1</TotalPages>
    <Item>
    <ASIN>B0007MZV3C</ASIN>
    <ItemAttributes>
            <Manufacturer>Back Bay Books</
Manufacturer>
            <ProductGroup>Book</ProductGroup>
            <Title>Me Talk Pretty One Day</Title>
            <SimilarProducts>
                    <SimilarProduct>
                            <ASIN>0316777730</ASIN>
                            <Title>Naked</Title>
                    </SimilarProduct>
                    <SimilarProduct>
                            <ASIN>0316078913</ASIN>
                            <Title>Holidays on Ice</
Title>
                    </SimilarProduct>
                <SimilarProducts>
        </ItemAttributes>
    </Item>
```

Within the XML file returned by the Amazon API, the SimilarProducts tag is where the BookMeUp app gets the suggestion info. That info is the key behind the whole BookMeUp app. I don't mean to trivialize the workings of the PHP script because there is a whole lot going on. To see all the details, please have a closer look at the code by downloading the BookMeUp source code available at github. com/jasonclark.

Building Location-Based Recommendations

One other feature that I had sketched out in my requirements was a location browse point. Part of my logic here was that an important part of reader's advisory was context. That is, where a person was standing in time and space could be of interest in determining what they might want to read. To this end, one can write JavaScript that can be used to call the Geolocation API (w3.org/TR/geolocation-API) and get some info about where a person is located. The following is the BookMeUp JavaScript geolocation:

```
if (navigator.geolocation) {
    navigator.geolocation.getCurrentPosition
(getSubjects);
    console.log('geolocation done');
} else {
    alert('Error: Your browser doesn\'t support
geolocation.');
}
```

The results returned from this request are geographical coordinates (latitude and longitude) based on where a person's device is located on the network. Once you have these location values, you can start to use them to create some interesting relationships between someone's current location and items related to that location (Figure 16.4).

In the case of BookMeUp, the coordinates are used to make a call to OCLC's mapFAST Service (oclc.org/research/activities/mapfast. html?urlm=159681), an experimental web service that matches geographic subject headings to latitude and longitude values. An example

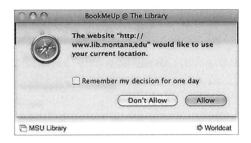

Figure 16.4 BookMeUp geolocation prompt

request from the BookMeUp JavaScript to the mapFAST service might look like:

```
http://experimental.worldcat.org/mapfast/
services?geo=" + lat + "," + lon + ";crs=wgs84&
radius=100000&mq=&sortby=distance&max-results=25
```

In this example, lat and lon would be the retrieved values from the previous Geolocation request. The real power of mapFAST is that this request returns the subject heading in the form of structured data that can be used to create an HTML display of subject headings. Using this information, the BookMeUp "where" page (lib.montana.edu/beta/bookme/index?view=where) prints out links of subject headings that can then be passed to the search of the Amazon Product Advertising API, and recommendations based on subject headings of your current location are returned (Figure 16.5).

Figure 16.5   Location-based recommendations based on a mapFAST subject heading search

Next Steps and Future Plans for BookMeUp

With the prototype for BookMeUp in place, I brought the demo to the public services team. I was hoping to bring a small project group together to refine the service and see if the project had any legs. In my experience, pitching the project always works better if you have a working product to help shape the discussion. Design and commentary on the interface and suggestions for integrating the service into established library software came first. The discussion brought forward a number of interesting possibilities:

- Integrating the service to point at item-level records in the local library catalog

- Opening the suggestions scope to include a wider range of items like movies

- Introducing and promoting the project through library channels like the blog and Facebook

As the discussion ended, I started to think about places where the technical pieces of the app could be improved:

- Caching (goo.gl/of5Crs) the most commonly used files in the app to help with performance (cache manifest file)

- Using CSS3 media queries (goo.gl/AEhbke) to create unique displays for multiple environments

- Using CSS3 to create "touchable" buttons that work better in handheld environments

- Creating search suggestions to help guide the user to successful queries

- Being able to share and bookmark book recommendations

- Encoding book recommendations in common formats like BibTeX, EndNote, or RefMan

- Setting up SMS and or texting capabilities to allow the app to push recommendations to phones

And even beyond these technical improvements, there is a real opportunity to supplement the machine recommendations of Amazon with locally sourced recommendations from our library community (e.g., our librarians regularly compile reading recommendations from our faculty, students, and staff). Placing these recommendations alongside the BookMeUp search results could broaden the appeal of the application.

Bringing a working group together is the next step in the development of BookMeUp, and as I mentioned there is some interest within the library in developing the service. What is most empowering about the BookMeUp app development process is the way that HTML5 and common web development techniques open the door for simple prototyping and building for the multiple platforms people are now using every day. The goal will be to answer questions like those from our elementary school library patron—to find "the cloud book in the spotlight"—whether or not a librarian or library collection is physically present.

Endnotes

1. "Librarianship Quote of the Day: Kids' Reader's Advisory Edition," LibrarianShipwreck, May 3, 2013, librarianshipwreck.wordpress.com/2013/05/03/librarianship-quote-of-the-day-kids-readers-advisory-edition.
2. Wayne Wiegand and Donald Davis, eds., *Encyclopedia of Library History* (New York: Taylor & Francis, 1994), p. 538.
3. Tammera M. Race, "Resource Discovery Tools: Supporting Serendipity," (2012), DLTS Faculty Publications, Paper 22, digitalcommons.wku.edu/dlts_fac_pub/22.
4. Ian H. Witten, Eibe Frank, and Mark A. Hall, *Data Mining: Practical Machine Learning Tools and Techniques* (London: Elsevier Science, 2011).

References

Makri, Stephann, and Ann Blandford. "Coming Across Information Serendipitously–Part 1: A Process Model." *Journal of Documentation* 68.5 (2012): 684–705.

Sun, Xu, Sarah Sharples, and Genovefa Kefalidou." User Requirements for an Interactive System to Stimulate Serendipity." *Contemporary Ergonomics and Human Factors* 2012 (2012): 369.

Watson, Elizabeth A. "Going Fishing: Serendipity in Library and Information Science." Unpublished Masters Thesis. University of North Carolina, Chapel Hill, NC (2008).

## CHAPTER 17

Stanford's SearchWorks: Mashup Discovery for Library Collections

Bess Sadler
Stanford University

SearchWorks (searchworks.stanford.edu) is Stanford University's library discovery portal, built with the open source Blacklight (project blacklight.org) software. SearchWorks provides access not only to books and MARC records, but increasingly also provides access to Stanford's digitized archival materials, photographs, sound recordings, and geospatial data. This mashup approach to the library's collections has given us opportunities to think about the best ways to present diverse data formats in a unified interface design with a consistent look and feel. We are also increasingly publishing APIs for our digital library collections and infrastructure, and we hope to become a source of data for mashups that others will create.

A Shift in Perspective

The history of mashup applications is one of shifting perspectives and user expectations. According to the Wikipedia article on the history of mashup applications (en.wikipedia.org/wiki/Mashup_%28web_ application_hybrid%29), in the Web 1.0 business model there was an expectation that a website would manage and control access to all of its own content. With the shift to Web 2.0 thinking, there is no longer an expectation that all data will be stored in a single system or an expectation that a single delivery mechanism is sufficient for many collections. Discovery and delivery interfaces increasingly want to include content from other systems via APIs, and they increasingly want to expose their own content via APIs for inclusion elsewhere. SearchWorks is an example of how that shift in perspective has played out in library discovery with tremendous success. By concentrating on establishing application-building patterns, instead of putting effort into monolithic systems, Stanford's digital library has been able to accommodate a wide range of content and make it available in a variety of contexts, something that would have been impossible in the Web 1.0 mindset.

Blacklight as an OPAC

Blacklight is an open source discovery application for collections of digital objects. Originally conceived as a next-generation online public access catalog (OPAC), it has been widely adopted by institutions wishing to improve discovery for content traditionally managed by an integrated library system (ILS). The ILS is primarily a tool for managing collection inventory and library business workflows, and although ILS vendors have usually packaged a user-facing search component (the OPAC) with ILS software, these have often failed to measure up to rapidly evolving user expectations for what web-based search applications should be like.

Online catalog systems have long been a source of frustration for librarians and patrons alike. This frustration is due in part to librarians' desire— and patrons' expectations—for their online catalog to keep pace with the rapid development seen in other web applications, in contrast to the slower progress of new library catalog features. The relatively slow development of new features for library catalogs is in part caused by most catalogs' close ties to ILSs that run all of a library's transactions. Upgrading an ILS is a difficult and expensive process that has the potential to disrupt workflows throughout the library and is undertaken only when absolutely necessary. This is a suitable pace of change for business and workflow operations but not for front-end systems used by patrons accustomed to the pace of development of services like Netflix (netflix.com), Facebook (facebook.com), Google (google.com), and Flickr (flickr.com), each of which rolls out new features every few months.

By indexing the contents of the ILS into web-scale open source search engines like Solr (lucene.apache.org/solr), libraries can define their own measures of relevancy and customize indexing procedures to match the needs of local collections and audiences. By providing a flexible front end for a Solr index, one that allows different behaviors for different kinds of objects, Blacklight allows for flexibility and new innovation possibilities. This flexibility will become ever more important as libraries grapple with increasingly diverse collections and ever higher user expectations for delivery and discovery of content.

Discovery for Digital Collections

Digital library content has often suffered from a lack of user-facing visibility. At Stanford University Library, which has invested heavily in the creation and curation of digital library content over the years, Blacklight has provided a generalizable approach to discovery. Just as de-coupling the discovery interface from the ILS provided new opportunities for innovation, de-coupling discovery from object management systems like Fedora Commons (fedora-commons.org) has breathed new life into digital library interfaces without requiring the re-engineering of already established back-end management and preservation systems. Blacklight provides an opportunity for unified discovery of content across collections as well as user interaction and development patterns that can be used for building tailored discovery applications for specific collections or content types.

Unified Discovery for Heterogeneous Content

SearchWorks is Stanford University Library's primary collection discovery interface. The Solr index that SearchWorks runs on contains not only the millions of MARC records indexed from our SirsiDynix ILS, but also content from our digital library, including digital collections we host for other institutions, and content that has been submitted via our self-deposit interface for preservation in our digital library.

In Figure 17.1, two digitized collections from Stanford University Library's special collections are visible. Because Blacklight provides the flexibility to define different behaviors for different kinds of objects, we were able to define behavior tailored to the needs of a digitized image collection. This included creating a collection-level view, which merged metadata from the MARC record with metadata from the digital library, and a "filmstrip" view of a collection, which allows a user to quickly preview the images visually.

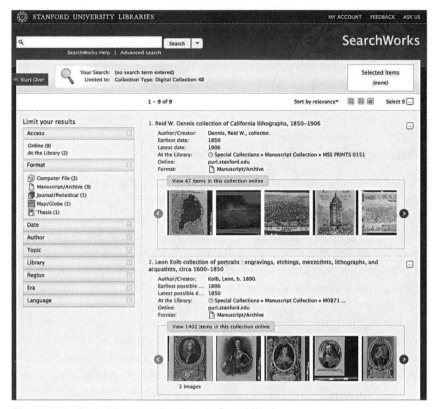

Figure 17.1 Digital image collections in SearchWorks

In Figure 17.2, the view of an individual image is shown. Note that a member of a collection maintains knowledge of its collection membership (RDF triples modeling each object's relationship to other objects is part of the metadata we store and can draw on for discovery), as seen in the left hand column where contextual information about the collection this image is part of is displayed.

Each object in our digital library also has a permanent URL (purl), as seen in Figure 17.3, and that purl has a machine-readable version, accessible via adding .xml to the end of the URL, for a full xml rendering of the public parts of a digital object, or .mods for an XML serialization of the MODS record for that object. Providing permanent, predictable URIs means that users of the collection can provide citations for publication, and that not only is our catalog a mashup

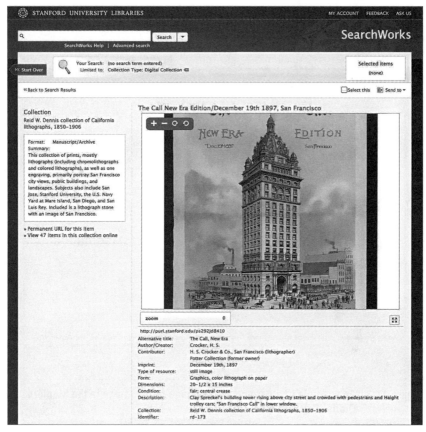

Figure 17.2 Image display page from SearchWorks

itself, but it is also a source of re-mixable data that allows others to include digital library content in their own mashup efforts.

User-Submitted Data

One rapidly growing source of data in our digital library is user-submitted research data. The Stanford Digital Repository (SDR) provides a permanent home for data publication by Stanford affiliated researchers (Figure 17.4). Depositing in SDR provides researchers with a permanent citation URL they can use in publications as well as a preservation strategy they can reference in their data management plan—a formal document that outlines how researchers will handle

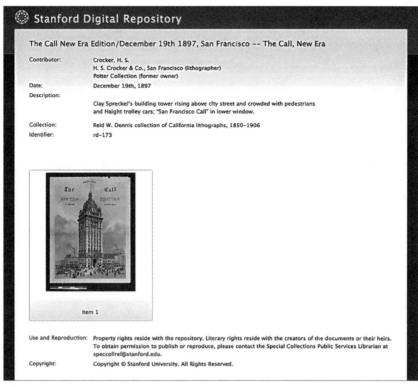

Stanford Digital Repository

The Call New Era Edition/December 19th 1897, San Francisco -- The Call, New Era

Contributor:	Crocker, H. S.
	H. S. Crocker & Co., San Francisco (lithographer)
	Potter Collection (former owner)
Date:	December 19th, 1897
Description:	
	Clay Spreckel's building tower rising above city street and crowded with pedestrians and Haight trolley cars; "San Francisco Call" in lower window.
Collection:	Reid W. Dennis collection of California lithographs, 1850–1906
Identifier:	rd–173

Item 1

Use and Reproduction:	Property rights reside with the repository. Literary rights reside with the creators of the documents or their heirs. To obtain permission to publish or reproduce, please contact the Special Collections Public Services Librarian at speccollref@stanford.edu.
Copyright:	Copyright © Stanford University. All Rights Reserved.

Figure 17.3   An example of a permanent URL page for an image in the Stanford Digital Repository

the data they collect during the research process and after the project is completed. Data management plans are increasingly required by research funders, including many federal government funding agencies. The presence of research data in our digital library has meant expanding SearchWorks to accommodate its presentation and discovery. Unlike digitized surrogates of physical library holdings, these objects never had a MARC record in the ILS. Instead, SDR uses the MODS standard, which has meant defining new MODS-based presentation logic in SearchWorks.

We further leveraged the modular nature of our digital library architecture by using this as an opportunity to encapsulate MODS logic in ruby gems, including one for general MODS parsing (github.com/sul-dlss/mods) that should be broadly useful to the library software community, one that contains local Stanford customizations

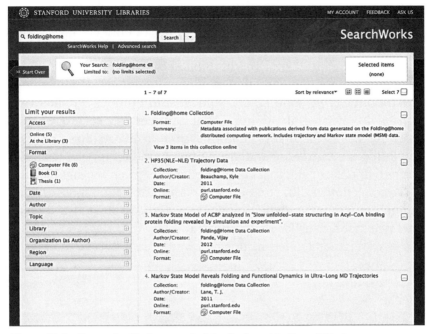

Figure 17.4   User submitted research data displayed in SearchWorks

(github.com/sul-dlss/stanford-mods), and one that contains display logic (github.com/sul-dlss/mods_display) so that presentation of MODS records is consistent and easy to add to any of our applications that needs to include that functionality.

New Views for Archival Collections

Part of the shift in perspective of the mashup mindset is letting go of the notion that a single interface will be able to accommodate the needs of every user and every collection. Instead, the Stanford Digital Library strategy is to adopt and build on workable patterns, applying them in new contexts as the need arises. While SearchWorks represents an opportunity to bring many diverse object types into a unified discovery solution, the application patterns established for SearchWorks have also allowed us to easily build sustainable discovery interfaces tailored for specific collections.

One recent example of the success of this strategy has been the interface for the Bassi-Veratti Collection (bv.stanford.edu), visible in Figure 17.5. The online collection is a multi-year collaboration of the Stanford University Libraries, the Biblioteca Comunale dell'Archiginnasio, Bologna, Italy, and the Istituto per i Beni Artistici, Culturali e Naturali della Regione Emilia-Romagna, to produce a digital version of the archive of the influential 18th-century scientist Laura Bassi. Bassi was the first woman to earn a professorship in physics at a European university and also to be offered an official teaching position at a European university. Particularly given the significance of the collection and the tremendous effort that went into its organization, description, and digitization, we wanted to create a discovery interface that did justice to the content.

We were greatly aided in this aim by the fact that we had well-established patterns already in place for the behaviors of digital

Figure 17.5 Bassi-Veratti Collection website

objects. Just like the images and data sets already referenced, each digital object has a purl and a MODS record. Because we had already invested in building MODS-based indexing and presentation behaviors for Blacklight, setting up a Blacklight instance that harvested only the Bassi-Veratti objects from the larger digital library and sorted them into collection-appropriate facets for discovery was much easier than it otherwise might have been.

We also benefited from participation in a larger community of open source software development. Blacklight has a variety of pluggable UI components developed by community members and contributed back to the project. One of these is the date slider visible in the left column in Figure 17.5, originally developed by the Johns Hopkins University Library. It allows users to narrow their search to a range of dates, while also providing visual feedback about how much of the collection is represented within a given slice of time. One can see at a glance that this collection spans the years 1591–1836 and that the bulk of the material is from the late 1700s and early 1800s.

The Bassi-Veratti archive also benefited from the increasingly rich world of geospatial mashup components. Using Google's geocoding API, we were able to transform place names into points on a map, allowing for geographical exploration of the content and allowing users to get a better sense of where the story told by this archive took place.

Finally, because sometimes the best tool is the one you're most familiar with, we also provided access to the complete archival finding aid, as seen in Figure 17.6. In the spirit of mashup, however, we provided access not only to an online display and a downloadable and printable PDF, but also to the actual EAD XML, in case researchers want to index the content themselves or run it through some other EAD presentation system.

Discovery for Space and Time

Near term development for our digital library will include expanding our infrastructure and software components to include more support for geospatial data. The geographic information system (GIS) is playing an increasingly important role in many academic fields, and GIS data are already well represented in our faculty-submitted content in SDR. The management of GIS data in libraries is also experiencing

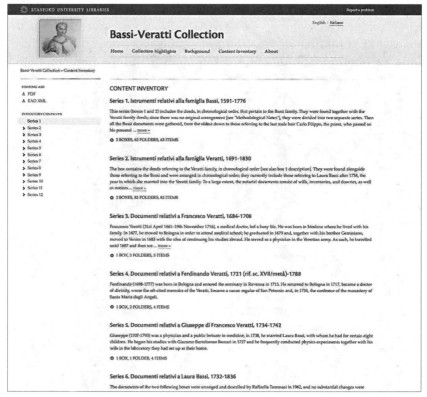

Figure 17.6   The archival finding aid to the Bassi-Veratti Collection

some exciting but challenging shifts in perspective, as GIS assets such as licensed data sets are exploding in popularity and requiring more sophisticated and systematized management strategies, such as those offered by a robust digital library infrastructure.

Current development efforts are focusing on data modeling for GIS content, attempting to encapsulate logic about ISO-19139, the GIS metadata standard we've chosen, the way we have MODS and MARC. A major part of our strategy for enabling management and discovery for GIS content is establishing predictable behavior patterns for each object and building discovery interfaces that can be assembled from re-usable components, as we have for other kinds of data. This will also provide us with the opportunity to enable more spatial discovery of non-GIS content, such as the map interface on the Bassi-Veratti website. Geolocating digitized historic maps and semi-automated place name entity extraction for full-text and archival collections are some of the opportunities we see on the horizon for improved spatial exploration of library collections.

Data Integration Challenges

The Stanford digital library has benefited greatly from embracing the mashup ethos, but combining data sources also comes with some inherent challenges. These are well recognized and widespread enough to have been detailed in the previously mentioned Wikipedia article on web application mashups, and include text data mismatch, abstraction level mismatch, and general data quality issues.

Text data mismatch can be understood as a problem with ambiguous naming. Text representations of personal names and place names are inherently ambiguous, since names in the real world are seldom unique, and names can shift over time (e.g., Istanbul was Constantinople, Jane Stanford was once Jane Lathrop). Data-driven applications, however, often assume the ability to gather sets of records together based on unambiguously shared characteristics. Libraries are well-versed in maintaining name authority records, but creating unambiguous name authorities is a challenging enough task for published authors of books; current name authority methods are unlikely to scale to the level needed to accommodate self-deposited data, journal articles, and persons of historical interest mentioned in archives. Instead, a shift in practice to recording both text representations and linked data URI representations in metadata, where possible, greatly increases the ease with which a given collection can be incorporated into mashup-style applications.

For example, as we establish cataloging practice for GIS data in library collections, Stanford University Library has started assigning entries from the GeoNames ontology (geonames.org), giving us much more value (e.g., the ability to co-locate records about the same place but that use a different place name, greatly improved mapping functionality) for a comparable level of cataloging effort. Similarly, by leveraging efforts like ORCID (orcid.org) and encouraging researchers to link their SDR deposits to their ORCID number, we hope to gain the ability to disambiguate authors with the same name as well as to make the data in our repository compatible with research aggregation services outside the library context.

Abstraction-level mismatch refers to the challenges inherent in combining full-text data records in the same discovery interface with metadata-only records. If naïve relevancy algorithms that simply look at word count matches are used, full-text records will overwhelm briefer records. One of the benefits of using a system like Solr is that we can tune our own definitions of relevancy. Combined with a robust suite of automated repeatable tests gleaned from staff and community feedback about how relevancy should behave, we are able to add more and more content to our discovery index without overwhelming and breaking search strategies that our users have come to count on.

Abstraction-level mismatch is also present in the challenge of how to represent collections of objects that should be discoverable both individually and within a collection context. A digitized letter from an archival collection, for example, might be discoverable and interesting on its own, but often much of the cataloging effort has occurred at a collection level, and archival content is also most valuable when it can be viewed in context. To represent objects at the collection level, we've incorporated behaviors such as the filmstrip view of image collections visible in Figure 17.1. To tie individual objects back to their collection context we've incorporated patterns like those seen in Figure 17.7; the breadcrumb links above the main image allow the user to quickly see what other letters were in the same folder as this one, and the button labeled "View this item in content inventory" will take the user to this object's location within the full context of the archival finding aid.

Finally, data quality issues are an ever-present challenge in any information system, but re-contextualizing and re-using metadata in new ways exposes previously hidden inconsistency. To address this we are attempting not only to remediate erroneous data when we find it, but also to put in place more automated data consistency procedures. Encapsulating expected behavior for MODS records in a suite of software tools, for example, allows us to quickly determine whether the records for a given collection match our expectations and improves our ability to achieve some measure of consistency across diverse sources of content.

The Future

Stanford University Library has reaped tremendous benefits from embracing a mashup mindset in its applications. In addition to allowing for more rapid innovation, it has challenged us to re-think

Figure 17.7 An individual document from the Bassi-Veratti archive, with links to its archival context in the breadcrumb links and via the "View this item in content inventory"

our cataloging and data quality processes to keep pace with desired new features. We have also benefited greatly from participation in larger communities of software development effort, in the form of specific collaborations like Project Blacklight and Project Hydra (projecthydra.org) as well as informal communities of practice like Code4Lib (code4lib.org).

Future efforts will include further investment in leveraging linked data vocabularies in our metadata practices, and as our body of linked data grows, discovering new ways of leveraging connections between objects to enable new forms of discovery and exploration. We are also investing in the creation of training curriculums and improved software documentation, so that the data and infrastructure we create will more easily be incorporated into the fabric of mashup applications elsewhere.

## CHAPTER 18

Libki and Koha: Leveraging Open Source Software for Single Sign-on Integration

Kyle M. Hall
ByWater Solutions

How does one go about getting two pieces of software to talk to each other? Pass them notes? Set them up on a blind date? It's unlikely that will work—at least not until our computers become self-aware.

If you are integrating two proprietary and/or closed source systems, you have a few options. If you are lucky, perhaps a protocol exists for those systems to speak to each other, and if you are really lucky, perhaps both systems already know how to speak the same language. Otherwise, be prepared to start writing checks! Likely, you'll need to pay one or both companies to get your systems to talk to each other, if they are even willing to work with and for you.

If your two systems are both free and open source software, you have another choice: You can do it yourself, or if not you, someone on your team or perhaps a freelance developer.

A good example of this type of integration can be found in the case of Koha v. Libki, which took place at the Crawford County Federated Library System in Pennsylvania.

Koha (koha-community.org) is the first free and open source software library automation package, or integrated library system (ILS). Libraries of varying types and sizes, volunteers, and support companies from around the world sponsor the development and growth of Koha. The name comes from the Māori term for a gift or donation.

Libki (libki.org) is is a free and open source kiosk management system, with a web-based administration system and a cross-platform client. Libki is ideally suited for use in locations where a controlled computing environment is paramount, such as public access systems, libraries, school computer laboratories, and more.

The pre 1.0 version of Libki did not have Session Initiation Protocol (SIP) support built in like it does today, so something more tricky, more clever, and more hackerish had to be devised to get it to communicate with Koha.

Crawford County in Pennsylvania has nine libraries, all sharing one Koha ILS server located in the most central location in the county, Meadville. Many of these libraries also use the Libki Kiosk Management System to time limit computer access, and these Libki servers are found on site at each library in the county.

The libraries want single sign-on between all these systems, yet no protocol that could accomplish this is supported between the two. So how do we accomplish this task? We start hacking.

Planning

The first task in this scenario is to decide which system is considered the primary source of information—in other words, from which system will the rest of the system receive information and update itself? In this case, the obvious choice is the Koha server, because not only do we have a single Koha server and many Libki servers, but because the data the Koha server stores far exceeds that of our Libki servers. Koha stores detailed information about all library patrons: names, addresses, birth dates, and so on. Libki, on the other hand, stores a very minimal amount of data such as usernames and passwords. Since the only pieces of information we need to transmit are usernames and passwords, this works very well.

Our next job is to locate how and where that information is stored in both systems, and also to locate the (hopefully singular) points in the software's source code where these values get modified.

In Koha, we can find this data in the MySQL database table "Borrowers" under the columns User ID and Password. The password is not stored in plain text, of course—that would be a terrible violation of security practices. Instead, if one examines the code for Koha 3.12 (the latest version at the time of this writing) or earlier, they will see that all passwords in Koha are hashed using md5 and then encoded in base64 by the aptly named function md5_base64, which is provided by the Perl library Digest::MD5.

In Libki < 1.0, the users are stored in the database table logins, using the columns Username and Password. As luck would have it, Libki also uses this same password storage scheme. If we had not been so lucky, we would still be able to accomplish our task, but it would have been slightly more difficult.

So, now that we know all about the data we are storing, we need to know where said data is created, updated, and deleted from within Koha. Those are the places where we need to set up triggers to update our Libki servers.

In the case of Koha, we have three subroutines dealing with this in the Members module of Koha: AddMember, ModMember, and DelMember respectively. In each of those subroutines, we add the following code:

```
if (C4::Context->preference('LibkiIntegration'))
{
  my $borrowernumber = $data{borrowernumber};
  C4::Libki::UpdateForLibki($borrowernumber);
}
```

This is just a fancy way of saying, "If we've enabled integration between Koha and Libki, and we are changing this user in some way, run the subroutine UpdateForLibki for this account."

So what is in the C4::Libki module, you may ask? Not much. Here is the source code for said module:

```
package C4::Libki;

# Copyright 2011 Kyle M Hall <kyle@kylehall.info>
#
# This file is part of Koha.
#
# Koha is free software; you can redistribute it
and/or modify it under the
# terms of the GNU General Public License as
published by the Free Software
# Foundation; either version 2 of the License,
or (at your option) any later
```

```perl
# version.
#
# Koha is distributed in the hope that it will
be useful, but WITHOUT ANY
# WARRANTY; without even the implied warranty of
MERCHANTABILITY or FITNESS FOR
# A PARTICULAR PURPOSE. See the GNU General
Public License for more details.
#
# You should have received a copy of the GNU
General Public License along
# with Koha; if not, write to the Free Software
Foundation, Inc.,
# 51 Franklin Street, Fifth Floor, Boston, MA
02110-1301 USA.

use strict;
use warnings;

use C4::Context;

use vars qw($VERSION @ISA @EXPORT);

BEGIN {
  # set the version for version checking
  $VERSION = 1.01;
  require Exporter;
  @ISA  = qw(Exporter);
  @EXPORT = qw(&UpdateForLibki);
}

sub UpdateForLibki {
  my ($borrowernumber) = @_;

  my $dbh = C4::Context->dbh;
    my $sql = "INSERT INTO libki_queue
(borrowernumber) VALUES (?)"
  my $sth =
   $dbh->prepare($sql);
  $sth->execute($borrowernumber);
```

```
}

1;
__END__
```

So to put it succinctly, UpdateForLibki simple puts the unique identifier into a new and special table we've created just for this task. Yes, we could have put this code directly into each of the previously mentioned subroutines, but doesn't it look so much prettier this way?

At this point, we have a list of all the accounts in Koha that need to be created, updated, or deleted in all of our respective Libki servers. The next task on our docket is to accomplish just that. How do we do this? With a daemon of course! The friendly, useful kind—not the fiery damn-you-to-eternal-pain-and-torture kind. For the uninitiated, a daemon is a computer program that runs as a background process, rather than being a program that you run and control interactively.

For example, at a restaurant, you could say your server is a program you interact with when you give that server your order. The server writes down your order and walks over to the kitchen window where he puts that order on one of those order wheels with the clips (and thus is revealed my deep understanding of restaurant nomenclature). The chef waits in the background, notices a new order is coming in, and begins preparing the food. In this example, our chef is much like a daemon, lurking in the background, waiting to spring into action.

Here is our daemon:

```perl
#!/usr/bin/perl

use strict;
use warnings;

use File::Basename;
use Fcntl qw(LOCK_EX LOCK_NB);

use C4::Context;

use constant SLEEP_INTERVAL => 15;
```

```perl
my $daemon = basename($0);
open(SELFLOCK, "<$0") or die("Couldn't open $0:
$!\n");
flock(SELFLOCK, LOCK_EX | LOCK_NB)
 or die("Aborting: another $daemon is already
running\n");

# Get ready to daemonize by redirecting our
output to syslog,
# requesting that logger prefix the lines with
our program name:
open(STDOUT, "|-", "logger -t $daemon")
 or die("Couldn't open logger output stream:
$!\n");
open(STDERR, ">&STDOUT") or die("Couldn't
redirect STDERR to STDOUT: $!\n");
$| = 1;   # Make output line-buffered so it will
be flushed to syslog faster

# Avoid the possibility of our working directory
resulting in keeping
# an otherwise unused filesystem in use
chdir('/');

# Double-fork to avoid leaving a zombie process
behind:
exit if (fork());
exit if (fork());

sleep 1 until getppid() == 1;

print "$daemon $$ successfully daemonized\n";

my $dbh = C4::Context->dbh;
my $sth;

while (1) {
  while (! $dbh->ping) {
    $dbh = C4::Context->dbh;
  }
```

```
   $sth = $dbh->prepare("SELECT * FROM libki_
queue");
   $sth->execute();
   while (my $r = $sth->fetchrow_hashref) {
     my $borrowernumber = $r->{'borrowernumber'};
     exec("koha2libki_update.php $borrowernumber &
");

     $dbh->do(
        "DELETE FROM libki_queue WHERE
borrowernumber = $borrowernumber"
       );
   }

   sleep(SLEEP_INTERVAL);
}
```

So what does all this fantastical nonsense accomplish? Every 15 seconds, it checks the table libkI_queue (our order wheel) to see if there are any user identifiers ("borrowernumber" in our case) in there. For each of these identifiers it finds, the daemon creates another process, which calls the script koha2libki_update.php to handle the real update for each of the Libki servers.

You may have noticed all our code examples so far have been written in Perl, but we are now executing a PHP script. Why, you may ask? That is because Koha is written in Perl, but the script we are calling was included with Libki, which is written in PHP.

Here is that script:

```
#!/usr/bin/php
<?php
# This file is part of Libki.
#
# Libki is free software: you can redistribute
it and/or modify
# it under the terms of the GNU General Public
License as published by
# the Free Software Foundation, either version 3
of the License, or
# (at your option) any later version.
```

```
#
# Libki is distributed in the hope that it will
be useful,
# but WITHOUT ANY WARRANTY; without even the
implied warranty of
# MERCHANTABILITY or FITNESS FOR A PARTICULAR
PURPOSE. See the
# GNU General Public License for more details.
#
# You should have received a copy of the GNU
General Public License
# along with Libki. If not, see <http://www.gnu.
org/licenses/>.

## Get borrowernumber from arguments
$borrowernumber = $argv[1];
if (empty($borrowernumber)) {
 die ("No borrowernumber given!\n");
}

## The libki ini file contains a section for
each of our Libki servers
$libki = parse_ini_file("/etc/libki/libki.ini",
$process_sections=true) or die("Unable to parse /
etc/libki/libki.ini\n");
## The koha ini file contains just data about
how to
## connect to our Koha server's database
$koha = parse_ini_file("/etc/libki/koha.ini");

## Open the Koha database
$kdbh = mysql_connect($koha["host"],
$koha["username"], $koha["password"]) or
die("Unable to connect to Koha MySQL Server\n");
mysql_select_db($koha["database"], $kdbh);

## Grab the userid and password of the user
based on the borrowernumber
$query = "SELECT userid, password FROM borrowers
WHERE borrowernumber = '$borrowernumber'";
```

```
$results = mysql_query($query, $kdbh);
$result = mysql_fetch_assoc($results);
$userid = $result['userid'];
$password = $result['password'];

foreach ($libki as $ini) {
  ## Open the LibKi database
  $ldbh = mysql_connect($ini["host"],
$ini["username"], $ini["password"]);
  mysql_select_db($ini["database"], $ldbh ;

 if ($userid) {
  ## Get default starting minutes from database
  $query = "SELECT value FROM settings WHERE
name = 'daily_minutes'";
  $results = mysql_query($query, $ldbh);
  $result = mysql_fetch_assoc($results);
  $daily_minutes = $result['value'];

  ## Check to see if this user is already in
libki
  $query = "SELECT COUNT(*) AS userExists FROM
logins WHERE username = '$userid'";
  $results = mysql_query($query, $ldbh);
  $result = mysql_fetch_assoc($results);
  $userExists = $result['userExists'];

  ## If the user doesn't already exist, create
the user in libki
  if (! $userExists) {
    $query = "INSERT INTO logins (username,
units, status, password) VALUES ('$userid',
'$daily_minutes', 'Logged out', '$password')";
    mysql_query($query, $ldbh);
  } else { ## Copy over the koha password
    $query = "UPDATE logins SET password =
'$password' WHERE username = '$userid'";
    mysql_query($query, $ldbh);
  }
```

```
  } else { # User no longer exists in Koha,
delete this user from Libki
    $query = "DELETE FROM logins WHERE username =
'$userid'";
    mysql_query($query, $ldbh);
  }
}
?>
```

What this script does, in layman's terms, is take a user identifier and look it up in our Koha database. If it finds it, it then calls out to each of the Libki server's databases and says "Hey you! Yeah, I'm talking to you! Does this user exist in your database?" The Libki database then replies with "Yeah! I got your user right here!" or "Heck no, we ain't got no user like that!" It's quite obvious that our Libki database did not go to an Ivy League school.

Once we know if the user exists or not, we can then tell the Libki database to update the existing user's password or to create the new user with the given username and password data, respectively.

To satisfy your curiosity, here is an example of what the libki.ini file would look like for a system with three libraries:

```
[LibraryA]
host = libki.libraryA.mylibrarysystem.org
username = libkiadmin
password = aPoorlyChosenPassword
database = libki

[LibraryB]
host = libki.libraryB.mylibrarysystem.org
username = libkiadmin
password = anotherNotSoGoodPassword
database = libki

[LibraryC]
host = libki.libraryC.mylibrarysystem.org
username = libkiadmin
password = theWorstPasswordYet
database = libki
```

Each Libki installation could have, in theory, a different username and database name, but why mess with success?

Conclusion

If you are a programmer, you may be saying "Wow, I could have done a way better job than this. What a mess!" To that I would reply "Cut me some slack! I was in a hurry! It works, doesn't it? Why do you have to kick me right in the self-esteem?"

Indeed, I'm sure there are many ways to improve and streamline this system, but it is merely an example of what can be accomplished when you leverage the power of free and open source software.

To reiterate our basic process, this is what we did:

1. Identify our data

   A. Identify our source data

   B. Identify our target data

2. Identify our relevant source code

   A. Identify data creation code

   B. Identify data modification code

   C. Identify data deletion code

3. Create a "shim" to communicate our source data to our targets

   A. Insert code to call shim for each data alteration

   B. Shim checks to see which action needs to be taken

   C. Shim implements said action

In our example (Figure 18.1), we were lucky in that both our source and target data were stored in MySQL databases. In the open source world, it is common for data to be stored in an open source DBMS such as MySQL or PostgresSQL. For other software where you cannot get direct access to the data, you may need to identify a service API you could call on instead. Remember, there's always more than one way to do it.

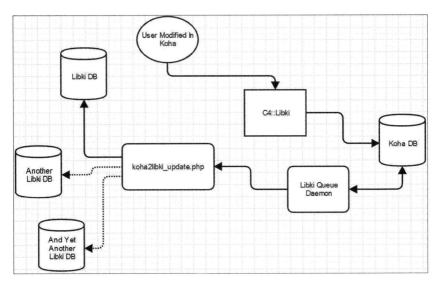

Figure 18.1   Data flow from Koha to Libki

I hope you've been informed and amused by my incoherent ramblings. And I hope my example illustrates how it's almost always possible to make two systems work together—if you put your mind to it!

## CHAPTER 19

Disassembling the ILS: Using MarcEdit and Koha to Leverage System APIs to Develop Custom Workflows

Terry Reese
The Ohio State University

The emergence of next-generation integrated library systems (ILS) has had a profound impact on how libraries think about and develop discovery services. These services have put new focus on the ILS, as system developers have slowly moved to provide access into their walled gardens through the development of APIs. As these barriers continue to be lowered, new techniques and systems have been developed to reshape how users search for and discover information within the library. While patrons and discovery service operations have surely benefited from the development of system APIs, technical and metadata services librarians have also begun to explore how these emerging API frameworks can be leveraged to create improved workflows and simplify metadata development and editing.

At many libraries, metadata creation and editing occurs in various environments. While most library staff create fewer original metadata records, the amount of bibliographic metadata processed by the average library continues to rise as libraries have moved to receiving more bibliographic data from their vendors, through metadata services, or through targeted metadata harvesting. For many of these operations, metadata specialists rely on tools like MarcEdit (marcedit. reeset.net) to simplify the process around batch metadata editing and development. Libraries often develop robust best practices around the editing of metadata prior to ingesting records into the ILS as this is the point at which they have the most flexibility and widest range of tools for editing bibliographic data. Once a record has been loaded into a library's ILS, the ability to edit and modify that metadata largely becomes limited by the functionality provided by the system. Traditionally, ILS vendors block the ability for specialized tools like MarcEdit to access and edit metadata directly within the system. As a result, metadata specialists seeking to edit large batches of records within their ILS would often have to resort to extracting these records from their systems for editing and reloading. While this process has worked for librarians for many years, the process can be complicated and introduces the possibility of overlay problems when reimporting data back into the library system.

However, just as the introduction of APIs has profoundly impacted how libraries think about and envision discovery services, the emergence of APIs with the capacity to read and write data back into a library's ILS is changing the way that technical services departments envision their workflows and best practices. As these interactive APIs develop and become a part of next generation systems, librarians and tool builders are actively beginning to investigate how these new APIs can transform and improve bibliographic workflows. This chapter will explore one such implementation: the development of an integration framework within MarcEdit specifically around the ability to interact with ILSs at the API level. The chapter will look at this implementation, utilizing the Koha ILS as an example of how these system-level APIs can be leveraged to improve metadata workflows.

MarcEdit

MarcEdit is a comprehensive metadata editing suite of tools designed to simplify the editing and automated manipulation of a wide range of library bibliographic data. I originally started working on what would become MarcEdit back in 1999 while learning how to copy catalog cartographic materials. At the time, only a handful of tools existed for users wanting to work with MARC data, and outside of a very well-developed Perl module, none of these tools provided a simple method for automating metadata editing on the desktop. So MarcEdit started as just a handful of libraries and interfaces that could be called and integrated into a number of Microsoft Windows scripting languages or be reused as a part of another application. MarcEdit didn't start to develop as a full-fledged application with a user interface until sometime in 2000, when, with the encouragement of some colleagues at Oregon State University Libraries, I decided to make the utility publically available to the library community.

Today, the tool supports a wide range of functionality, ranging from traditional bibliographic operations around the editing and translation of MARC data to the ability to translate metadata between a wide range of character sets, schemas, and formats. MarcEdit has been designed to simplify the process of working with large, hetero-geneous bibliographic datasets and includes access to a wealth of bibliographic services that support the merging, splitting, converting, validating, and querying of library data. For users interested in going beyond MarcEdit's built-in functionality, the application provides a robust set of APIs, accessible using either a set of COM (component object model) or .NET interfaces.

Since its initial release, the MarcEdit user community has steadily grown in size and scope. According to current logs, MarcEdit's active user community numbers in the tens of thousands, with international users making up close to a third of the community and growing. The program provides a number of different support mechanisms, including an active listserv (listserv.gmu.edu/cgi-bin/wa?A0=marcedit-l), a wiki (marcedit.reeset.net/wiki), and YouTube videos (goo.gl/ubNxvE).

Koha API

The Koha ILS (koha-community.org) represents the development of the first open source ILS. Developed during the period 1999–2000 by the Katipo Communications group for the Horowhenua Library Trust in New Zealand, the software is significant in that the devel-opment effort and success of the software opened the door for other large library community open source efforts. Today, Koha is sup-ported by a global development community, with both community and formal support options.

The Koha system is a full-featured library ILS system that provides support for both current and emerging standards. In fact, it is Koha's support for emerging standards that made the software ideal for investigating how new workflows could be designed around direct interactions with the system. While many library systems are only now moving to develop a comprehensive API for their ILS products, Koha has provided a lightweight read/write API into their system for some time.

The Koha API is separated into two distinct parts: discovery and record manipulation. They utilize different technologies to support interaction with the system. Discovery, the interface most often supported by ILS vendors, is provided primarily through the support of Z39.50. It should be noted that Koha does include the ability to support search/retrieval through a URL (SRU; loc.gov/standards/ sru/simple.html); MarcEdit has the ability to support it, but this functionality is not enabled by default. Interaction, or read/write, is supported through a robust HTTP-based API (wiki.koha-community. org/wiki/Koha_/svc/_HTTP_API) that supports the ability to create, edit, and set holdings on bibliographic records. Interactions through the API are mediated through a session cookie that is created prior to using the API and then passed as part of the HTTP request sent to the system. Unlike early API efforts, the Koha API doesn't rely on technologies like SOAP, but rather just passes data via HTTP through a series of HTTP POST and GET requests. Data packets are sent and received using MARC21XML, with data encoded into UTF-8.

It is also worth noting that, at the time of this writing, the Koha API is also different from other solutions being offered by library system vendors in that the API documentation is openly available. One of the largest constraints for tool builders in the library technology space is that library software vendors tend to not make their documentation or APIs available to anyone outside of their customer base. This policy can suppress integration efforts, in that a tool developer often must have a prior relationship with a specific vendor just to gain access to the documentation needed to understand the system. When considering integration work with MarcEdit, it is my intention eventually to support all the large ILS vendors, but whether that can happen will largely be up to the system vendors themselves as their integration information is hidden from view. Koha, on the other hand, provides a welcoming environment, and utilizing its open documentation and community support, I was able to use the Koha system as a proof of concept that I hope can be emulated by other library systems in the future.

Integrating MarcEdit Through the Koha API

The process of integrating MarcEdit with the Koha API required the development of two components. First was a common runtime library that would interact with the Koha API and encapsulate the interactions with the Koha system, allowing interaction within the application to be abstracted into a framework that could be used to support other ILS systems. The second part of the development would be using the abstracted framework within MarcEdit to enable users to interact with their ILS systems. One of the challenges of this approach is that unlike many of the APIs currently being developed by ILSs that move both discovery and read/write access to the HTTP level, the Koha API remained split between two different technology stacks: Z39.50 to support discovery and HTTP requests to support read/write operations.

Koha C# API Library

In order to support interaction with the Koha HTTP API in MarcEdit, the first thing that needed to be developed was an API library to abstract the calls made through the service. Since MarcEdit is written in C#, the library was developed using C# to simplify integration with the application. Because this library would serve as template for how MarcEdit would interact with other ILS systems, the following generic interfaces were defined by the program:

- Authorize: This function will perform the necessary interactions to authorize a user into a system. In Koha, this involves the creation of a secure session cookie that must be passed as part of subsequent requests:

```
public bool Authorize(string username, string
password)
    {
            Authentications objA = new
Authentications();
pusername = username;
ppassword = password;
bool is_authorized = false;
```

```
        try
        {
                is_authorized = objA.
Authorize(Host, username, password, out perror_
message, out cookieJar
        }
        catch
        {
                Error_Message = "Undefined
authorization error";
        return false;
        }

        return is_authorized;
}
```

- GetRecord: This function allows for the retrieval of specific records via a request string or id. Koha specifically supports the ability to return a single MARC21XML encoded record through this function, when passed with a record id.

```
        //data is retrieved in MARCXML
        public string GetRecord(string id)
        {
                string uri = Host + "/cgi-bin/
koha/svc/bib/" + id + "?userid=" + pusername +
"&password=" + ppassword;
                HttpWebRequest request =
(HttpWebRequest)HttpWebRequest.Create(uri);
                request.CookieContainer = cookieJar;

        try
        {
                HttpWebResponse response =
(HttpWebResponse)request.GetResponse();

                System.IO.StreamReader
reader = new System.IO.StreamReader(response.
GetResponseStream(), Encoding.UTF8);
```

```
                    string tmp = reader.
ReadToEnd();

                    reader.Close();
                    response.Close();
                    return tmp;
            }
            catch (WebException e)
            {
                if (e.Status ==
WebExceptionStatus.ProtocolError)
                {
                    Error_Message = e.Message;
                    return e.Message;
                }
                else
                {
                    Error_Message = e.Message;
                    return e.Message;
                }
            }

        }
```

- GetRecordId: This helper function was developed to simplify the processing of the internal XML record structure. In the case of the Koha API, this structure was simply MARC21XML.

```
        //pass in a marcxml record and return
        //the record id if present
        public string GetRecordId(string xml,
string field, string subfield)
            {

                string xpath = "";
                try
                {
```

```
                if (xml.
IndexOf("marc:collection") > -1)
                {
                        xpath = "/marc:collection/
marc:record/marc:datafield[@tag='" + field + "']";
                }
                else
                {
                        xpath = "/marc:record/
marc:datafield[@tag='" + field + "']";
                }

                System.Xml.XmlDocument objXML =
new System.Xml.XmlDocument();
                System.Xml.XmlNamespaceManager
ns = new System.Xml.XmlNamespaceManager(objXML.
NameTable);
                ns.AddNamespace("marc", "http://
www.loc.gov/MARC21/slim");

                System.Xml.XmlNode objNode;
                System.Xml.XmlNode objSubfield;
                objXML.LoadXml(xml);
                objNode = objXML.
SelectSingleNode(xpath, ns);
                objNode = objXML.
SelectSingleNode(xpath, ns);
                objSubfield = objNode.
SelectSingleNode("marc:subfield[@code='" +
subfield + "']", ns);
                return objSubfield.InnerText;

            }
            catch (System.Exception xe)
            {
                perror_message += xe.ToString();
                return "";
            }

        }
```

- CreateRecord: This generic function facilitates the creation of a MARC record.

```
public bool CreateRecord(string rec)
        {
                return UpdateRecord(rec, "");
        }
```

- UpdateRecord: This generic function facilitates the updating of both records and holdings data.

```
        //Data must be passed in MARCXML
        public bool UpdateRecord(string rec,
string id)
        {
                return UpdateRecord(rec, id, false);
        }

        public bool UpdateRecord(string rec,
string id, bool b_items)
        {
                string uri = "";

                if (id == "")
                {
                    //this is for new records
                    uri = Host + "/cgi-bin/koha/
svc/new_bib";
                }
                else
                {

                    //this is for updated records
                    uri = Host + "/cgi-bin/koha/
svc/bib/" + id;

                    //if the items bit is passed,
add
```

```
                    //the items element to the url
to
                    //indicate that item data
should be
                    //updated or added if present
in the
                    //record.
                    if (b_items == true)
                    {
                        uri += "?items=1";
                    }
                }

            HttpWebRequest request =
(HttpWebRequest)HttpWebRequest.Create(uri);
            request.CookieContainer = cookieJar;
            request.Method = "POST";
            request.ContentType = @"text/xml";
            System.IO.StreamWriter writer
= new System.IO.StreamWriter(request.
GetRequestStream(), System.Text.Encoding.UTF8);
            writer.Write(rec);
            writer.Flush();
            writer.Close();

            try
            {
                HttpWebResponse response =
(HttpWebResponse)request.GetResponse();

                System.IO.StreamReader
reader = new System.IO.StreamReader(response.
GetResponseStream(), Encoding.GetEncoding(1252));
                string tmp = reader.
ReadToEnd();

                reader.Close();
                response.Close();

                return true;
```

```
    } catch (WebException e ){
        Error_Message = e.Message;
        return false;
    }
}
```

- DeleteRecord: The Koha system doesn't currently provide an API for the deletion of records, but it is provided as part of the framework functions.

While Koha provides a simple and clean API, abstracting the API into a stand-alone library makes it simpler for other developers to integrate Koha interactions within their own applications. By referencing the library, which uses the snippets just listed, one can create a simple reference application using a handful of lines of code. For example, authentication can be reconstructed as:

```
string username = "[your username]";
string password = "[your password]";
objb = new koha_api.Bib_Actions();
objb.Host = "[your host]"; //i.e.: http://www.
kohacatalog.com

if (objb.Authorize(username, password) == true)
   {
        System.Windows.Forms.MessageBox.Show(objb.
Debug_Info + "\n" +

"Authorized");
   }
   else
   {
        System.Windows.Forms.MessageBox.Show(objb.
Error_Message);
   }
}
```

Once authorized, the C# library places all authorization in a session cookie that is then validated prior to calling an operation. This way, if a session expires while waiting to perform an operation, a new session can be transparently initiated and then used when making the request.

The C# library developed as part of this project has been placed onto GitHub (github.com/reeset/koha_api). All code in this repository has been placed into the public domain, utilizing the Creative Commons zero ("No Rights Reserved") license. The repository includes source code for both the C# library and a reference program that can be used to demonstrate specific functions of the library.

Integrating With MarcEdit

While the C# library provides an abstract method for interacting with the Koha API, it really functions only as a building block for developing a more finished solution. For users looking to utilize MarcEdit to interact directly with their Koha systems, a framework and interface still needed to be developed that would enable a user to easily configure MarcEdit to connect to their system and then work with their bibliographic data within the MarcEditor.

Developing a framework within MarcEdit to support multiple system APIs through an abstract set of libraries was a relatively straightforward process. By and large, MarcEdit already provides such a framework for loading compiled add-ins for use with the application. To support various system API interactions, this framework was merely extended to support these types of operations. This left the development of the use interface.

MarcEdit's workflow for configuring new functions and behaviors in the program is currently managed through its Preferences Center. Since this workflow would be well understood by current MarcEdit users, it made sense to place the configuration options in this section. Users looking to enable this functionality in MarcEdit simply need to open their Preferences and navigate to the ILS tab.

MarcEdit provides a number of different preferences that can be set depending on how the specific ILS performs operations around discovery and read/write operations. Because Koha uses two different technology stacks for the two operations, two sets of values need to be set. For the purpose of this example, I will be working from a sample set of data provided by ByWater Solutions (bywatersolutions. com), a company that provides Koha support services.

Figure 19.1 ILS integration preferences

In Figure 19.1, the following options have been defined:

- Select System: This list holds the current ILS systems that can be configured in MarcEdit.

- Host Name: This is your library ILS systems host name (e.g., http://koha.library.com).

- Username: This is the username with permissions necessary to read/write records in Koha.

- Password: This is the password for a username with read/write permissions in Koha. The password data is encrypted prior to storing the data.

- Use Z39.50 Settings: Systems that do not provide an HTTP-based discovery API must be configured to search through Z39.50.

- Enable ILS Options: This enables the Select System list so users can configure this option.

For a demo system located at marcedit.kohacatalog.com, a user would need to configure the following options (Figure 19.2):

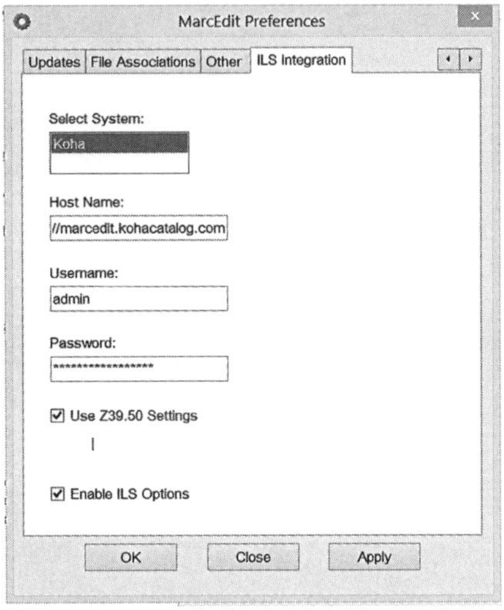

Figure 19.2 ILS integration properties

- Host: http://marcedit.kohacatalog.com

- Username: admin

- Password: [password]

- Use Z39.50 Options: Checked

- Enable ILS Options: Checked

When the user checks the Z39.50 Options, the next task is to set these values. For MarcEdit users, this configuration box (Figure 19.3) will look familiar because it is exactly the same as the configuration tool found in MarcEdit's Z39.50 client. On my demo system, the Z39.50 options for the server are the following:

- Host: marcedit.kohacatalog.com

- Database: biblios

- Port: 210

So, configuring this database for discovery using Z39.50 is accomplished by entering these values into the Preferences box (Figure 19.4). When completed, the ILS Integration Preferences should look something like Figure 19.5.

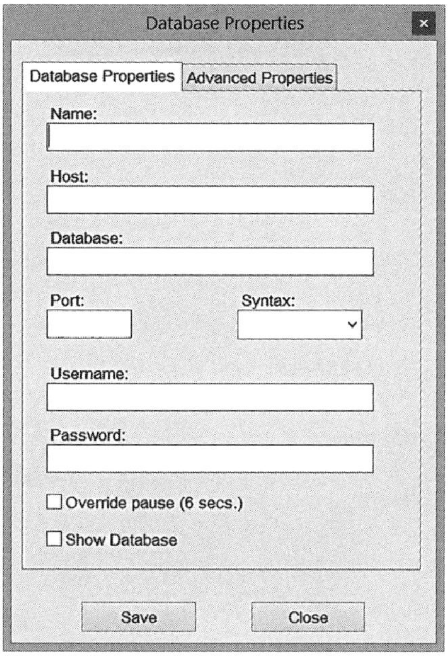

Figure 19.3   Z39.50 configuration

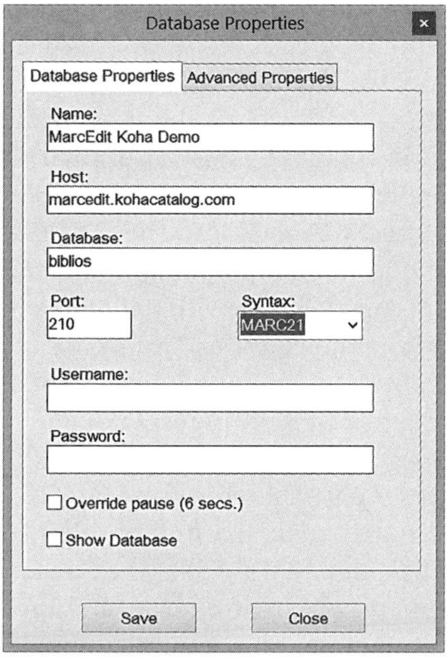

Figure 19.4   Z39.50 configuration options

Figure 19.5   Completed ILS integration settings

Koha and the MarcEditor

Once a user has enabled MarcEdit's ILS Integration framework and configured the resource, a new menu option will be enabled every time the user utilizes the MarcEditor (Figure 19.6).

Without ILS integration enabled, the most common workflow for MarcEdit users is to export the data out of their ILS system as a file and manipulate the data in a desktop application, before uploading and overlaying the records back into the ILS. The process requires users to move data between multiple systems and raises the possibility of an overlay error or issues with data extraction. What's more, this process is overly complicated, especially in cases when a user just wants to edit a handful of records utilizing one of MarcEdit's specialized bibliographic services. With the ILS integration option, records are sent directly from the ILS to the MarcEditor utilizing the API.

Users are able to import data into the MarcEditor by utilizing the Search Command under their ILS menu option. For this example, we'd use the Search Option found under the Koha menu (Figure 19.7).

For Koha, this initiates MarcEdit's Z39.50 Capture service (Figure 19.8). The MarcEdit Z39.50 capture service provides users with the option to do individual searches or batch queries against their ILS.

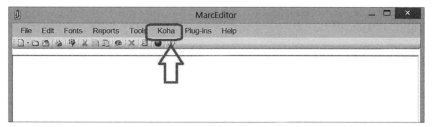

Figure 19.6   Koha ILS integration menu option in the MarcEditor

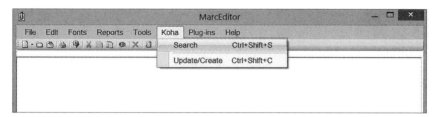

Figure 19.7   Search menu in MarcEditor

For batch queries, users would enter the file path that includes the terms to be searched rather than search term. Batch file format would be one query, per line. By default, MarcEdit's capture service predefines queries for title, author, ISBN, ISSN, subject, record number, and keyword, although users also have the option of constructing their own Z39.50 queries and utilizing the Raw search option in either single- or batch-query mode. Users also have the option to return data in UTF-8, even if the server doesn't support UTF-8 encoded data. To use this function, a user must know what character set the server will return when making a Z39.50 request. Using the demo server, a query on *Oregon* returns the records shown in Figure 19.9.

The capture service gives users the option to download records individually (select the record and right click) or download all the records found by a specific query. For the purposes of this demo, I'll download all the records. At this point, MarcEdit negotiates with the Koha web service to retrieve the records back from the Koha server and render them within the MarcEditor for editing. As mentioned earlier, the records that MarcEdit retrieves from the Koha web service are not in MARC, but rather are transferred in the MARC21XML

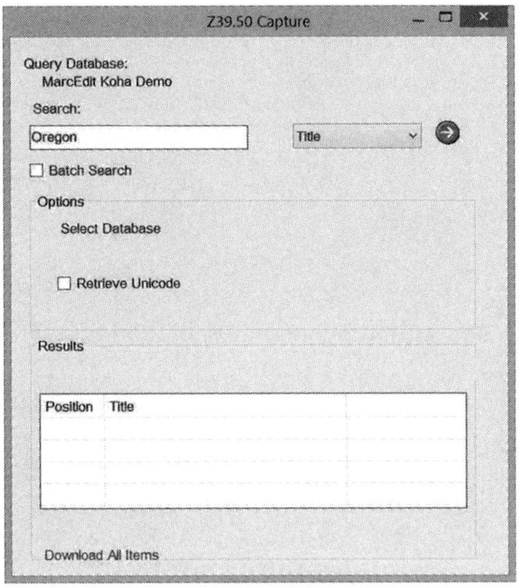

Figure 19.8 MarcEdit Z39.50 capture service

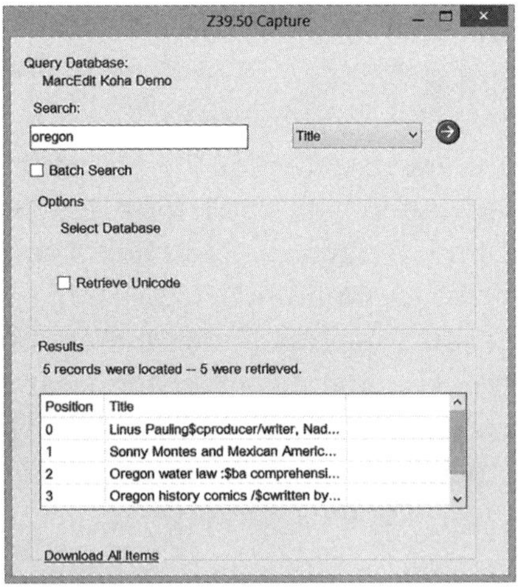

Figure 19.9 Z39.50 search response

format, which is much easier to work with, with data encoded in UTF-8. At this point in time, the Koha API doesn't provide an option to return multiple records using a single search string, so MarcEdit reads the response from the Z39.50 query and determines the internal record number from the defined MARC field/subfield combination (the default being: 999$c) in order to create the necessary request back into the Koha API to extract the requested record. In the case of the example, these requests utilize the "bib" API call, with MarcEdit enumerating through the results utilizing this API to retrieve the requested data. For example, if the results set included the record with an internal Koha identifier of 3, the API request (after authentication) would look like marcedit.kohacatalog.com/cgi-bin/koha/svc/bib/3, with the returned data packet from Koha being a MARC21XML record (Figure 19.10).

Users can continue to utilize the capture service to extract as many records from their Koha database as they would like to edit, and on each subsequent download, MarcEdit will simply append the new data to the existing data file for edit.

Once MarcEdit has enumerated through the records selected through the capture service, the MARC21XML records are then transformed into MarcEdit's mnemonic format and presented in the MarcEditor for edit. Once the data has been transformed and rendered in the MarcEditor, users are able to utilize any of the MarcEdit MARC editing tools to globally merge data, add/delete fields, move bibliographic metadata, generate automatic call numbers, and so on

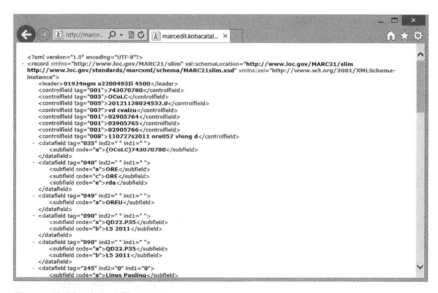

Figure 19.10   Koha API response

to update and enhance their data. For regular MarcEdit users, this workflow offers the ability to integrate MarcEdit's automated editing functionality with their ILS to create simplified workflows around common data editing tasks. What's more, users have the ability to edit any data that can be represented in a MARC field. In Koha, this includes the ability to modify existing holdings data or add new holdings information to a set of records.

Once a user has made the desired modifications, the records need to be re-imported back into the ILS. In the past, this process could be fraught with difficulty as many systems utilize specialized fields or command-line data to determine when data is to be overlaid and when an update represents a new record. However, utilizing the Koha API, these issues are largely mitigated, as MarcEdit utilizes a specific set of API instructions to denote new or updated records. What's more, MarcEdit is able to utilize the data found in the existing record to extract the internal Koha record number and utilize that information to construct an API request that will result in the update or creation of only that single record. This isolates potential data problems and simplifies the process of updating edited data for the user.

Initiating the update/record creation processes using the Koha API in MarcEdit is relatively straightforward. Just as users had to utilize the Search option found under the Koha menu entry to import their record data into MarcEdit, so, too, do users need to utilize the Update/Create option found under the Koha menu entry to utilize the Koha API to import the edited bibliographic data back into their ILS (Figure 19.11).

As noted previously, MarcEdit is able to extract data utilizing the API by extracting the internal Koha record identifier from the MARC data when utilizing the Z39.50 capture tool. Using the same process, MarcEdit pre-processes the data in the MarcEditor to determine if the data in the MarcEditor represents a new or existing record. This means that this process can be utilized for multiple workflows. Users looking to import new bibliographic record data into their Koha ILS after working with the data in MarcEdit could select the Update/ Create option to import new bibliographic data directly into their systems. MarcEdit determines which API to utilize when pushing data back to the ILS by looking for the presence of the internal Koha identifier. If that information isn't present, MarcEdit assumes that the bibliographic data represents a new record and passes the information to the Koha server utilizing the appropriate API. However, if a

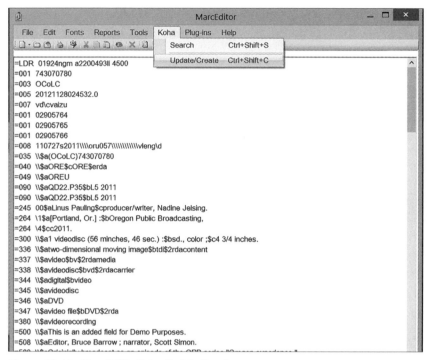

Figure 19.11   MarcEdit's Koha Update/Create menu

Koha record identifier is located, then MarcEdit will issue an update request, utilizing the Koha's update API request.

In both cases, MarcEdit performs a number of operations in the background to ensure that the Update/Create process can occur smoothly. The first of those operations is to test user credentials. MarcEdit will attempt to authorize the user through the Koha API to create a secure session cookie, which will be utilized throughout the transaction. If authentication succeeds, MarcEdit will then attempt to translate the data in the MarcEditor into the necessary MARC21XML package. If the conversion process is not successful, due to formatting or encoding errors, the application will stop the process and notify the user of the issue. If the conversion process succeeds, then the program will begin the Update/Create process. Because some users may utilize a different field/subfield combination to store the internal Koha record number, MarcEdit will ask the user the first time this

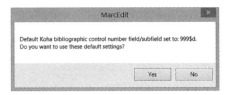

Figure 19.12 Confirmation of Koha control number

operation is run to confirm the location of the Koha record number in the bibliographic record (Figure 19.12).

Once the user has confirmed the location of the Koha control numbers, MarcEdit will store that information for subsequent transactions and use the user-provided data to complete the data transfer process. MarcEdit will then notify the user as each record is processed, culminating in a message notifying the user of completion and noting any errors that occurred during the transfer.

Conclusion

The availability of system APIs could provide librarians and library tool developers new and exciting opportunities to rethink how we interact with our existing systems. In the ILS space, the ability to easily extract, share, and update bibliographic data through a set of APIs will open up the possibilities for libraries and librarians to reimagine how they work with bibliographic data and the workflows in use to maintain that data. The MarcEdit/Koha integration provides a proof of concept for how tool developers can utilize these APIs to develop a sort of symbiotic relationship with a system, ultimately lowering barriers and expanding options for librarians. At the same time, the ability for libraries to take advantage of these new and exciting developments will be partially constrained by the systems that they work with. Koha is somewhat unique in the ILS space, in that its API is open for anyone to look at. In many instances this isn't the case, as API documentation is restricted to only a small number of a system's customers, potentially limiting their impact. Hopefully, more systems will follow the Koha model, providing a friendly and welcoming environment to tool builders, with documentation that is open to anyone.

Endnote

1. Joann Ransom, Chris Cormack, and Rosalie Blake, "How Hard Can It Be?: Developing in Open Source," *The Code4Lib Journal* no. 7 (June 26, 2009). journal.code4lib.org/articles/1638.

## CHAPTER 20

Mashing Up Information to Stay on Top of News

Celine Kelly
A&L Goodbody[1]

I've been the library manager with A&L Goodbody for 5 years. The firm is one of the largest corporate law firms in Ireland and has a reputation for providing legal advice of the highest quality in Ireland and internationally. Our primary office is in Dublin. Together with our office in Belfast, we advise clients on an "all Ireland" basis. The firm's lawyers advise on the most challenging and complex assignments for national and multinational corporations, financial institutions, and government. The firm's information service exists to meet the research needs of the firm's lawyers. Our information service and physical space is called the Knowledge Centre. Historically the Knowledge Centre has managed legal information only. This is the tale of how and why the Knowledge Centre started working with business and industry current awareness.

Current Awareness

When it comes to legal developments, lawyers do not want to be surprised. The Knowledge Centre has been deeply involved in the firm's legal news current awareness process for many years. We have put in place manual and automated systems to ensure that our lawyers know about any changes to the law as soon as possible. The Knowledge Centre works with a team of Professional Support Lawyers[2] to ensure that all lawyers in the firm are aware of any legal developments that will have an impact on our clients. Until recently, our current awareness services centered on legal news and legal developments.

We started to see that there was also a role for the Knowledge Centre team in the provision of business, industry, and client news updates. Informal feedback, and a growing number of ad hoc requests, told us that the firm's lawyers had an appetite for business information. Strategically this kind of service looked like a good move for the Knowledge Centre. The nature of the business in a law firm means that legal research is often delegated down to the more junior members of the team. A common problem for law firm libraries is that the heaviest users of the library are often those with the least political influence in the firm. I saw the provision of business and client updates as a way for the Knowledge Centre to communicate directly with the decision makers in the firm.

Information Overload

The phrase *information overload* conjures, for me, images of desk workers disappearing from view as an avalanche of papers flood around them. The reality refers to the constant and tremendous volume of mostly digital information that overwhelms the individual. As more and more streams of legal and business information came online, people reported that they felt less confident in navigating the myriad materials and sources now available to them.

The Knowledge Centre has the responsibility for conducting legal research and legal information literacy training and workshops for the lawyers. In the mid-2000s, to address information overload, we started to add information management sessions to the suite of training we offered. Some of these courses included using RSS readers to manage news streams and advanced Google searching to give our users a better set of tools to manage the information coming at them.

I'd been using RSS readers to manage much of my own content when I came across a presentation on SlideShare by Connie Crosby called "Media Monitoring and Current Awareness: New Tools."[3] As part of the presentation, Crosby suggested using Yahoo! Pipes to consolidate a selection of practice-specific RSS feeds into one data stream to allow the material to be output onto intranet practice-area pages. She described using Pipes to block or permit stories depending on whether they met certain criteria. To be useful, current awareness has to be relevant, so the idea of filtering news streams sounded like it could help us deliver bespoke updates to our lawyers. I had heard of Yahoo! Pipes but had only ever thought about them in a very superficial way. This was the first time I realized what they could do and how they might help us in the Knowledge Centre. Targeted news streams would be a valuable product to offer users. We had recently deployed SharePoint in the firm, and we would soon have an intranet that could display the aggregated news content on practice area pages. My interest had been piqued. So I set about familiarizing myself with Yahoo! Pipes.

Yahoo! Pipes

Yahoo! Pipes (pipes.yahoo.com) is an interactive feed aggregator and manipulator. It is a completely free service and is available to anyone with a Yahoo! ID. Pipes uses a completely graphical interface that allows the user to input a selection of RSS feeds from different sources, mash and mix up the information contained within the feeds, and then add a set of operators to that data and ultimately spit out one RSS feed of filtered and "relevant" information. There are many other things that you can do within Pipes but this is the key function that I've used the service for. The Pipes graphical interface means that no programming experience is needed, although a certain amount of time for experimentation and geeky patience are required to learn how to confidently create the pipes that execute your desired functions.

Varying amounts of time and energy are required to get familiar with new systems, and I found Yahoo! Pipes to be quite a challenge initially. There isn't a huge amount of official documentation on the site so the best way to become familiar with the process is to dive straight in and start experimenting and building pipes. Each pipe is built by dragging and dropping modules onto the canvas. The canvas is essentially the editing screen where each pipe is built and tested. Each module performs a specific function and can be connected to other modules. For example, the RSS feeds are added to the first module, while the next module might sort all stories in date order.

The early pipes that I created proved to me that Yahoo! Pipes was going to be a very useful tool. I started small, building pipes that simply combined a number of feeds. Then I added a label to each output story so an end user could see the source of the story. Finally I progressed to building in filters to block or permit stories based on specified data. When I had established that Pipes would do what I needed, I went about building my first template pipe. The template pipe was an Irish news-monitoring pipe that I would reuse as a starting point for all future similar pipes that I created. Any pipe can be cloned, which simply means that a copy is made of the original pipe. This copy can then be renamed and changed as required. My template contained all of the key modules I used, connected and ready to be put to work. The template also contained the RSS feeds for the main newspapers and online news sources in Ireland. Having my key sources collated and ready to go in a template meant that future current awareness pipes would be quicker to implement.

Key Modules for a Current Awareness Feed

Figure 20.1 shows the structure of a typical pipe used to monitor some press sources for mentions of a particular company. There are over 40 modules available from the Module Library. I've detailed the five modules that I couldn't be without when mashing up this kind of data:

1. *Fetch Feed:* Allows you to add the URLs of the news source RSS feeds. Absolutely indispensable!

2. *Filter:* Used to permit or block materials based on certain criteria, and ensures that only relevant articles get through to the end user. Filter provides a selection of different rules that can be applied to different parts of the content. Filtering is easy to manage if, for example, you are monitoring a company that has a very distinctive name. It is more of a challenge when the company name is made up of common words or if you only want to see certain types of stories associated with popular companies. In that case you may need to set further filters in an effort to retrieve only absolutely relevant news. One company I wanted to include had a distinctive name but was heavily involved in the sponsorship of sporting events. To block stories from the sports pages I needed to apply extra filters (see Figure 20.1). See also "More on Filtering" next in this chapter.

3. *Union:* Merges up to five different content streams into one, which allows the user to feed the new stream in to more modules.

4. *Sort:* Allows the user to set the order that stories appear in the final feed (e.g., newest first or in alphabetical order). It is hardly surprising that for current awareness feeds, reverse chronological order is the most useful.

5. *Unique:* Used to remove duplicate content. Many news sites offer different RSS feeds for various categories of stories so it is quite common that a story will appear in more than one feed from the same site. The user sets the element on which to filter, and the module removes the duplicates from the final feed.

Yahoo! Pipes offers a debugger on the editing screen. The debugger is an essential part of testing to ensure that a pipe is working as planned. Select a module and the debugger will show you how the data looks leaving that module. A module is selected when the user clicks on it and its header turns from blue to orange. If a pipe is not

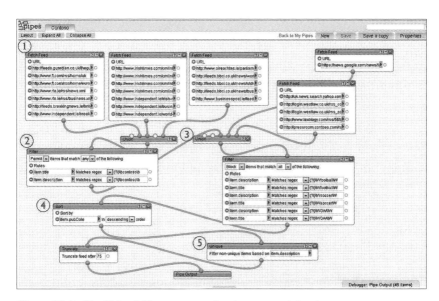

Figure 20.1   The Yahoo! Pipes canvas showing a complete pipe

behaving as expected the debugger is vital. Being able to examine the various stages of a pipe's output allows you to identify the root of any problems and confirm that your pipe is operating correctly.

More on Filtering

When creating a pipe to aggregate news, the key value of Pipes is filtering. End users only want to receive news stories that are relevant to them. There are five fields on which data can be filtered: author, description, link, publication date, and title (Figure 20.2). When building feeds to monitor industries, companies, or trends, I tend to set filters for both title and description. The title is the headline of the story; the description is the short summary of the news story or its first paragraph and normally does not include the full text of the article (Figure 20.3).

Once you have chosen on which field to apply the filter, you can then set the filter rule. Yahoo! Pipes offers eight rules by which the content can be permitted or blocked (Figure 20.4). The rules include matching a string of characters; occurring before or after a certain date; and being greater than, less than, or equal to a specified value.

Regex

Pipes contain a Regex module, which is described by the site as being "search-and-replace on steroids."[4] Regex, or regular expression, is a pattern describing a certain amount of text. Working with Regex is not intuitive for the uninitiated, and I found that if I hadn't thought about Regex for a couple of weeks I had to start from

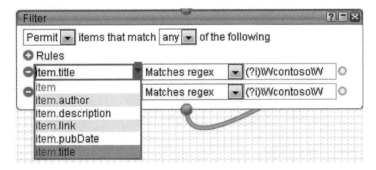

Figure 20.2   Filter module showing fields on which data filters can be applied

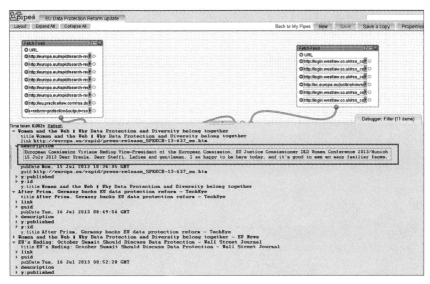

Figure 20.3   Debugger showing an item's description

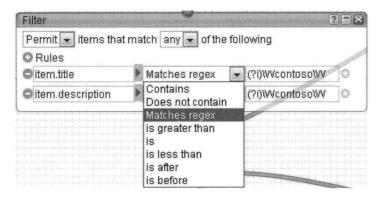

Figure 20.4   Rules by which content is filtered

scratch again. Many useful resources for Regex beginners are freely available online.[5]

I found the Regex module useful for applying source labels on the feed outputs. Users may value one source of information over another based on its coverage, accuracy, currency, or on some other aspect of its reputation. In these instances, users appreciate being able to quickly see where the information is coming from.

Using the Regex module I was able to apply source labels onto the feed output (Figure 20.5). A separate Regex module was required for each separate feed source. Once the labels were applied to each feed, I joined the feeds using the Union module and sorted them in reverse chronological order using a Sort module (see Figure 20.6).

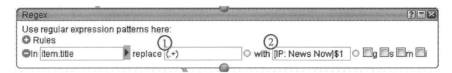

Figure 20.5 Regex module that appends the label *[IP:News Now]* to the titles of Outputted Stories

1. (.+)

The dot matches any character except line break characters. The dot is followed by "+", which means "one or more." So ".+" means "match one or more of any character at all."

2. $1

For every matched parenthesis in the regex, a numbered reference is created. That reference, preceded by a dollar sign, can be placed in the rule's value field. In our case, we only have one set of parenthesis, so we only have $1. The story title:

Fair Use Challenge Hampers Film's PR Campaign
In the recent blockbuster Hello, two character discuss fine art and wine on a bench in Central Park. One of the character's describes a recent visit to Tuscany by quoting...

```
where:
(.+) = Fair Use Challenge Hampers Film's PR
Campaign = $1
(.+) is replaced by [IP: News Now]$1
becomes:
```

> **[IP: News Now] Fair Use Challenge Hampers Film's PR Campaign**
> In the recent blockbuster Hello, two character discuss fine art and wine on a bench in
> Central Park. One of the character's describes a recent visit to Tuscany by quoting...

Once I had labels applied to each feed, I joined them using the Union module and sorted them in reverse chronological order using the Sort module (Figures 20.6 and 20.7).

Premium Content

Law firm libraries spend a significant portion of their budget each year on premium online legal information. These resources may contain primary authority (case law and legislation), secondary authority (books and journals), third-party precedents, know-how, legal updates, and business news. Many of these premium subscription sources permit the building of bespoke RSS feeds based on very specific and powerful searches. Used with IP authentication, these RSS

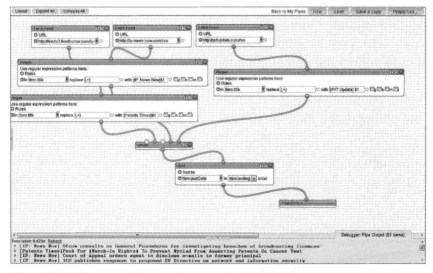

Figure 20.6   Regex modules used to append source labels

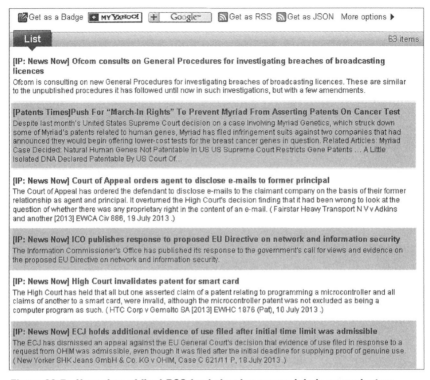

Figure 20.7 User view of final RSS feed showing source labels on each story

feeds can be input in to Yahoo! Pipes and serve to surface premium content to wider audience segments and ultimately squeeze more value out of existing subscriptions. This use of resources supports two of the key tenets of the 21st-century law librarian: to maximize what you currently have and to deliver more for less.

The Limitations and Compromises of Using Yahoo! Pipes

Yahoo! Pipes is a wonderful product that also is free. It allows powerful aggregation and filtering of data. However as a free, web-based application it has limitations. Following, I discuss some of the key considerations for its use in the corporate setting.

Information Scope

When filtering data for inclusion in the final pipe, it is important to remember that Yahoo! Pipes does not run full-text searches. Searches are limited to descriptions, titles, publication date, author, or link, depending on what parameters the user has set.

Newspapers may not route all news stories through to their RSS feeds. One paper told me that approximately 80 percent of stories were routed through at least one of their RSS feeds, so it is important to be aware that a proportion of stories may never be included in these feeds.

Broken and Changed Links

Yahoo! Pipes does not provide a mechanism to alert the user if a link has been "down" for a certain period of time. It is up to the user to monitor the pipes over time to ensure that all are working as expected. The more pipes you build, the more they will need to be monitored, so a workflow must be put in place to incorporate the checking and updating of active pipes.

If a source website changes its RSS URL, the user will need to update each and every instance where the feed has been used in Pipes. There is no way to centrally manage link updates, so this can be a laborious and time-consuming process.

Browser Compatibility

The Pipes website states "in order of preference we recommend: Firefox, IE8, IE7, WebKit, and Safari. Pipes is known not to work in Opera. Safari has minor issues. IE6 currently has troubles."[6] I now have a version of IE8 installed on one of my machines specifically for working in Pipes. In unsupported browsers the modules, connections, and canvas do not render properly and the debugger is unavailable.

The Longevity of Free Web Applications

The problem with using any free web application is that you simply don't know how long you have it for. The parent company can change the service significantly, start to charge for the service, or simply pull the plug (a la Google Reader). In a post on his Binary Law blog, Nick Holmes wrote: "It's a reminder that you rely on free platforms at your peril."[7] I've been using Pipes to assist with our current awareness services for a few years. We've built up a considerable collection of news streams that we use as part of our suite of current awareness systems, but we have no assurance that the service will continue to exist one year, or even one month, down the line. If these news streams were to disappear tomorrow we would need to find a replacement. I do feel that all would not be lost, though, and that we would have already proved to the business the value of delivering content in this way. Taking a "glass half full" approach I would, in this situation, look at Pipes as the proof of concept product, and I believe that it would go some way to support the business case for purchasing a premium service.

Data Storage and Private Pipes

I've used Yahoo! Pipes to create news feeds on particular industries and business types and to monitor specific legal developments. There is absolutely no sensitivity around the search terms chosen, the news sources being used, or the Pipes built. Yahoo! Pipes is a web application and all users' Pipes are stored on the Yahoo! Servers.

Completed pipes can be "published," which allows other Pipes users to search, see, and clone the pipe. An unpublished pipe can only be accessed if you know its unique URL. This means that the address can be shared by the pipe owner via email, but that if you don't share the URL the pipe effectively remains private and cannot be found by anyone other than you.

Support

There is no support service offered by Yahoo! The official user documentation for Pipes is quite light. There are, however, many useful online articles, blog posts, and books that offer practical advice on getting started, using the service, and troubleshooting. When problems do present themselves, it's worth checking Q&A forums such as Stack Overflow (stackoverflow.com), as it is unlikely you are the only person to have encountered a particular issue.

Resources

While there is no monetary cost involved in using the Pipes service, there will be a significant time investment. Building, testing, managing, updating, and troubleshooting a number of pipes can be time consuming.

After a few months of working with Pipes, we had created some useful news streams but they weren't getting the exposure I had hoped for. The reasons were twofold. First, I had planned that these feeds would live on our intranet. Practice-specific feeds would be placed on practice area homepages, industry update feeds would be placed on sector pages, and so on. We were moving to a SharePoint intranet and RSS feeds would be easily added to pages via WebParts. However, the intranet upgrade took longer than expected and so the feeds could not yet live on this platform. Second, lawyers tend to live in their email client. Written communication, document management, document filing, and calendaring is all done via the email client. Despite the ever-increasing number of mails coming into their inboxes, many lawyers still prefer to receive news and business updates this way.

I'm an avid podcast listener on my daily commute, and it so happened that while I was trying to solve the visibility problems stated previously, the company MailChimp was sponsoring some of my favorite podcasts. MailChimp is an email marketing and list managing service. It sounded like they might offer a way to turn my newly built and streamlined RSS feeds into branded email alerts.

MailChimp

MailChimp (mailchimp.com) is an online email marketing service that offers its users an easy way to design, implement, and manage email marketing campaigns. It enables users to create various types of newsletters and provides simple options for sharing them via email. Newsletter templates make designing an impressive professional-looking newsletter a piece of cake. MailChimp is a premium product but is available for free for users who have accounts of fewer than 2,000 subscribers.

One of the many campaign templates that MailChimp offers is an RSS-driven campaign.[8] RSS campaigns in MailChimp are driven by new content and are automatically triggered when the specified RSS feed is updated with new information. Using this type of campaign I could create emails in MailChimp, add my bespoke Yahoo! Pipes RSS feed as the source of new content, set the frequency of alerts, and—presto!—an automatically triggered email campaign. MailChimp will also provide open and click tracking, bounce management, list cleaning, and spam filter checks.

Creating the Campaign

MailChimp is a dream to use—just sign up and you're ready to start building campaigns. The site contains lots of documentation, tutorials, and how-to videos to guide the new user through the process of building campaigns. There are two key parts to any campaign: first, creating and building the list of subscribers, and, second, creating the emails.

The first step is creating the subscriber list. The list contains the subscriber details for each campaign and this is where you manage who receives the campaign. Subscribers can be added to lists by the campaign administrator or, if a sign-up form has been created, can self-register. Subscribers can easily unsubscribe from any campaign.

The second step is to develop the look and feel of the email. MailChimp offers pre-designed templates that are clean, simple, and flexible via its Campaign Builder (Figure 20.8). The template forms the framework of the email. The user can change the branding, color scheme, font, text, and content to ensure the final product fits within the library's brand. During this stage, the user defines how frequently subscribers will receive updates and at what time of day the emails will be dispatched. Once the design is completed the Yahoo! Pipes RSS feed is added as the source for new content. Once activated, the campaign dispatches updates to subscribers according to the frequency settings of the campaign (Figure 20.9).

MailChimp is a fantastic product that is simple to use. Its free-mium[9] business model means that it is available to anyone to use for free but that a premium account is required to access special features or for management of accounts with over 2,000 subscribers. As with any third-party service there will be limitations with how it interacts with the existing information workflows and information technology systems in place within the library or business.

End-User Development

It is becoming more common in the corporate environment for non-IT staff to develop solutions using existing software to better meet their needs. This concept is known as end-user development

Figure 20.8 The look and feel in the design step of the MailChimp
Campaign Builder

Figure 20.9 An example of an email generated via an RSS driven email campaign

(EUD). In EUD systems, the business managers and/or users, rather
than IT developers, assume the primary development role. Yahoo!
Pipes is a mashup web application that allows the user to combine
data from other web sources into new services. No programming is

involved in the construction of the mashup, so Pipes fits the description of EUD well.[10]

When end users exploit existing software and web applications to create innovative tools and services for their own use, there are both positive and negative implications for the business. Advantages often cited include:

- EUD reduces communication problems between users and the IT team, as the end user is the innovation driver.

- The end results are tailored specifically to the end users' needs.

- This way of working may help systems come to completion more quickly and reduce new system backlog as a wider group work on the implementation.

- The systems built may be very low cost or free.

Before considering rolling out any EUD projects, it is very important to be aware of the potential disadvantages, risks, and limitations. The systems, services, or applications used in EUD may not be supported by the IT team, so if something goes wrong the non-IT person is on his own. The decentralized nature of EUD may lead to duplication of effort or waste of resources. The work created may not be caught by existing document or knowledge management systems. There will often be issues over the quality and robustness of systems created by non-IT staff. Using free software or applications in EUD means that there are no legally binding commitments of quality or fitness of purpose from the provider, which means that the service can change without notice.

These limitations mean that EUD systems are not suitable for systems that are classed as business critical. This class of systems must have the security, support, and integrity that has been developed in-house by the IT department or that comes from the contractual commitments provided by third-party providers.

Final Thoughts

Working with Yahoo! Pipes and MailChimp to build and deliver current awareness tools has been a very positive experience. There were plenty of wrong turns and dead ends along the way, but with perseverance we were able to add useful tools to our suite of current awareness services. In the corporate environment, information professionals are often the ones to introduce new thinking around online information and communication. It is part of our job to be problem solvers, so it is no surprise that dabbling in and experimenting with tools to meet our needs and the needs of the business comes naturally. As long as the limitations of the tools and systems are understood, and they are used in an appropriate way, EUD systems can help plug information gaps, raise the profile of the library staff and service, and extend the skills of the information professional.

Endnotes

1. The views presented in this chapter are mine alone and do not necessarily reflect the views of my firm.
2. The Professional Support Lawyer (or PSL) provides know-how support to the firm's lawyers. In the most general terms, the firm's lawyers tend to be the PSLs' clients.
3. Connie Crosby, "Media Monitoring and Current Awareness: New Tools" (presentation for CALL/ACAB/MichAll 2010, May 10, 2010), www.slideshare.net/conniecrosby/media-monitoring-and-current-awareness-new-tools (accessed September 22, 2014).
4. Yahoo! "Regex Module," pipes.yahoo.com/pipes/docs?doc=operators#Regex (accessed September 22, 2014).
5. For example, "Regular Expression Basic Syntax Reference," www.regular-expressions.info/reference.html (accessed September 22, 2014).
6. Yahoo! "Pipes Troubleshooting," pipes.yahoo.com/pipes/docs?doc=troubleshooting#q7 (accessed September 22, 2014).
7. Nick Holmes, "Give Me My Life Back!" *Binary Law*, March 19, 2013, www.binarylaw.co.uk/2013/03/19/give-me-my-life-back (accessed September 22, 2014).
8. MailChimp, "Create an RSS Driven Campaign," July 16, 2013, kb.mailchimp.com/article/what-is-an-rss-to-email-campaign-and-how-to-i-set-one-up (accessed September 22, 2014).
9. Freemium describes the business model of a service that offers one version of the product for free and another, higher spec version, for a subscription or purchase fee.
10. Kwok-BunYue, "Experience on Mashup Development with End User Programming Environment," *Journal of Information Systems Education*, 21(1), 111–119.

## CHAPTER 21

A Mashup in One Week: The Process Behind Serendip-o-matic

Meghan Frazer
Knowlton School of Architecture

In July 2013, twelve scholars convened for One Week | One Tool (oneweekonetool.org), an open-source software development institute sponsored by the National Endowment for the Humanities at the Roy Rosenzweig Center for History and New Media (RRCHNM) at George Mason University. Our task was to conceive and develop a research tool in just one week. We built Serendip-o-matic (serendipomatic.org; Figure 21.1), a tool that connects a researcher's sources to digital materials located in libraries, museums, and archives around the world. By first examining a user's research interests and then identifying related content in locations such as the Digital Public Library of America (DPLA; dp.la), Europeana (europeana.eu), and Flickr Commons (flickr.com/commons), the serendipity engine helps users discover photographs, documents, maps, and other primary sources.

Serendip-o-matic leverages multiple APIs to return results from disparate platforms in a unified, engaging result set. Unlike a conventional web search tool, Serendip-o-matic extracts key terms from a given article or bibliography and returns related sources. The week-long institute provided an intensely focused collaborative environment in which our team crafted Serendip-o-matic to "re-create that moment when a friend recommends an amazing book, or a librarian suggests a new source."[1] The process we followed can be broken into

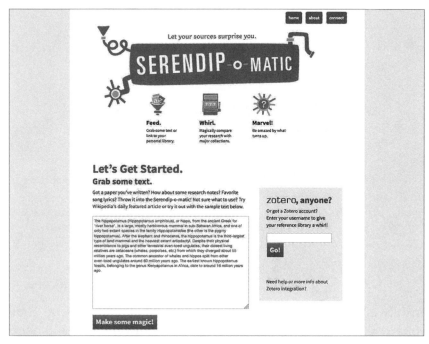

Figure 21.1 Serendip-o-matic

six general process steps, each of which contained its own unique challenges and lessons learned.[2]

Step 1: Set the Stage

To begin, RRCHNM issued an open call for applications and assembled a team with diverse skills. The team members possessed expertise in a wide range of subjects, including web development, historical scholarship, database administration, librarianship, human-computer interaction, and literature studies.[3] The team came equipped with the key competencies required to build a software application as well as individual strengths and interests that translated to our final project. Most importantly, RRCHNM selected participants capable of pitching in and working as a team. Team members showed a willingness to try new things and defer personal interests for the greater good of the project as a whole.

Next, lead facilitator Tom Scheinfeldt provided a general framework for the week before we began work. He emphasized the importance of the learning experience for the twelve assembled scholars. He encouraged the team members to learn from each other to "hitch our wagon" to another smart person in the room and figure out something new. As for the product, the goal was to build something that would be used. This meant that we needed to carefully define and target our audience. The organizers set a benchmark for success at the outset, in terms of both the event and the product.

Further, the RRCHNM mentors provided scaffolding in the areas of project management, software marketing, and open source development. While much of this advice was delivered on Monday, the salient points surfaced again and again throughout the week.

This initial step revolves around preparing the environment in which your team will work. Project leaders must not neglect to lay the groundwork for a project. Assemble a team with the appropriate skill set, but also recruit team members who bring an intellectual curiosity and willingness to try something new. Be sure to set clear expectations for the team. Provide background on what the team should accomplish.

In the following steps, the team identified what we wanted to build and we built it. Attention paid to preparation in Step 1 contributed to our success in the subsequent project stages.

Step 2: Identify Issues and Possible Solutions

At One Week | One Tool, our project team started work with unbridled brainstorming. In our case, we had not yet identified the desired tool, so we brainstormed both problems facing digital humanists and possible solutions. Ideas rang out from all the participants, and in some cases ideas sprang from other ideas. A whiteboard, a marker, and a scribe comprised our toolset. The team did not reject any ideas, instead filling the whiteboard with a giant word cloud (Figure 21.2). This free-form discussion aided in generating creative ideas.

The next part of this step called for more organized brainstorming. We organized our ideas in the following format: tool X solves problem Y for audience Z. Expressing the ideas in this way naturally eliminated some of the less practical ideas. The structure required the identification of an audience—essential if your goal is to build a tool that is

Figure 21.2 The whiteboard with a giant word cloud

used—and ensured that the team chose a solution based on a perceived need and not necessarily based on novelty. Here, our toolset
expanded to include multiple scribes and a shared Google document.

The team in the room and RRCHNM staff provided initial feedback
on each idea, but these slightly refined versions of the ideas were also
released to the public for feedback. Our team used an online voting
tool to elicit input from a wide audience of those interested in digital
humanities projects and, in 16 hours, received 271 votes and 39 comments from 102 users.[4]

Step 2 is all about idea generation. Start with a freeform brainstorming session and narrow from there. Be sure that the final suggested solutions address a need and have a defined audience. Get
feedback from stakeholders and potential users. In the next step, the
team utilizes that feedback.

Step 3: Pick a Solution Based on
Feasibility and Commitment

On the first day of One Week | One Tool, RRCHNM's Sheila Brennan
said, "Being willing to make concrete decisions is the only way you're

going to get through this week." While I was listening, I jotted down that one could replace "this week" with "any project." Projects frequently get stalled at decision points.

The team made its first high-stakes decision in Step 3. It was time to start looking critically at the ideas on the board. The team examined each idea from the previous evening and considered feasibility, the commitment of the people in the room, and the feedback from the humanities scholars who voted online. In developing an open source tool, the team needs to be on board, but community support is also essential. Open source tools flourish only through the support of the user community. The One Week | One Tool team exhibited true dedication to the end goal of our institute here, as team members stepped up and eliminated their personal projects from group consideration, based on lack of positive feedback in the online survey or on concern about the project's suitability for a one-week institute.

With the short schedule set in front of us, the feasibility issue was fundamental. Our team compared each suggested tool to the skill set in the room and the time constraint. We rejected several great ideas because we could not reasonably build them within our one-week window. After much discussion and several votes, we winnowed the list down to two choices.

While the team had discussed our own commitment to solutions, the voting brought this element to the forefront. Each team member cast multiple votes, allocated according to their level of commitment to each choice. After two rounds of this type of voting, we had our tool. At this early stage, the project description for our proposed tool read:

> A serendipitous discovery tool for researchers that takes information from your personal collection (such as a Zotero citation library [http://zotero.org] or a CSV file) and delivers content (from online libraries or collections like DPLA [http://dp.la] or Europeana [http://www.europeana.eu]) similar to it, which can then be visualized and manipulated.

In comparing this description to the final product, it is notable that the initial idea survived the development process almost completely intact. Taking the time to consider feasibility and commitment, both inside and outside the room, led us to select an achievable goal.

Clearly, most project teams do not constrain their work to one week. However, in our initial scaffolding conversations RRCHNM's Sharon Leon pointed out that a project with no end date is not a project. The danger of projects with infinite lifespans is all too familiar in libraries. Open source software leads us to believe that all things are feasible, because all things are changeable, given time. We often forget the last part of that sentence, and project timelines expand unchecked. Setting a hard deadline helps define a project and limits us to truly achievable goals.

Step 3 is the key decision point: What are we going to build? Process the feedback from stakeholders. Set a hard goal date for the completion of your project, and include that timeline in the team's evaluation of what is feasible. Weigh the project team's skill set against the proposed solutions. Gauge your team's commitment to a particular solution and, if applicable, the commitment of the community.

Step 4: Identify and Assign Tasks

At One Week | One Tool, Step 4 began after lunch on Day 2. One of our team members, Mia Ridge, suggested that before we assign tasks and sub-teams, we first establish a shared understanding of the tool. She led a discussion about the parts and functions of our proposed solutions and sketched a diagram on one of the whiteboards.[5] Three main functional areas emerged from the discussion: the input, the black box, and the results. I will address these areas in more detail in the discussion of the building step, but this crucial moment helped determine our success or failure.

Given the short timeline, it was tempting to plow forward with just our initial description of the idea. However, stopping and taking a collective breath ensured that everyone focused their efforts in the same direction. Throughout the project, we would revisit this diagram, and we all commenced work with the same vision in mind (Figure 21.3). Further, the definition of the tool and specific tasks emerged from this conversation. We classified the tasks as falling under project management, outreach, or development, and assigned resources to each set of tasks.

The teams then assigned tasks as appropriate. Armed with the initial idea and the group's planning sketch, the design and development team assessed the skills in the room and opted to work in

Figure 21.3 Teams at work

Python, utilizing the Django framework. They also selected Isotope, a jQuery plug-in, to power the display of results and opted to use GitHub (github.com) in order to manage the code.[6] Under Mia Ridge's leadership, the development team set forth a plan for an effi- cient process, with short "standup" meetings and large blocks of time dedicated to focused work, and assigned developers to initial tasks in each of the functional areas.[7]

Jack Dougherty led the outreach team in dividing their tasks, which included developing a brand and promotional strategy, writ- ing support text, and serving as user advocates. The team continued utilizing Google Drive (drive.google.com) to manage the documenta- tion coming out of the entire project. Working with the team leaders, project managers Brian Croxall and I organized these assignments and tasks and attempted to set an achievable schedule for the week.

In one specific case, the team arrangement required some flexibility as a subset of tasks fell under two teams. Amy Papaelias, tasked with graphic design, needed to work closely with the development team to ensure the web design complied with the technical capabilities of the tool and vice versa. The design of the visual identity of the tool, however, was also clearly an outreach activity. So, she floated between teams as appropriate and both teams benefited from her input.

The dual goals of One Week | One Tool occasionally raised organizational conflicts. On one hand, participants aimed to learn new skills, which meant that some volunteered for tasks that stretched them beyond their comfort zones. On the other hand, we sought to build a working tool in one week, so other tasks were assigned to the team members with the most advanced skills set in that area.

In Step 4, the project team develops a shared understanding. Schedule a time specifically for the purpose of talking through the final goal. This will produce a lot of little tasks to complete, which can then be assigned to the most appropriate team member, according to the goals of the project.

Step 5: Build It and Test It

Let us pause for a moment here. In terms of time and complexity, the step that comes next—creating a tool and then testing it—is out of proportion with those we've already discussed. In the case of One Week | One Tool, we started developing at the end of Day 2 and began testing on Day 4. Work on both tasks continued simultaneously almost up to our release, at the end of day 5.

From a planning perspective, Step 5 is also the least likely to be overlooked. If you are aiming to build an application, then you need to build it. Perhaps less obvious, but no less true, is the fact that you need to test it. I do not mean in any way to minimize this step. However, paying attention to the earlier steps provides for a smoother process when the time comes to build.

During the building and testing phase, our developers coded pieces of the three functional areas: input, the black box, and the results screen. First, there's the input. Serendip-o-matic takes a chunk of text and parses it. After removing poor search terms like *the* or *an*, the algorithm looks at the frequency distribution of the words and selects up to 15. The code also attempts to identify proper names.

Once the search term set is identified, the APIs are queried in our second functional area, the black box, so called because it contains the program logic that is invisible to the end user. In its earliest versions, the discovery tool queried the DPLA and Europeana. However, during this building step, the development team recommended adding support for the Flickr API (flickr.com/services/api) in order to access the Flickr Commons. The images available in the Flickr

Commons would enhance the search results and expand the coverage of subject areas and geographic locations. Also, after the project began, it was clear that the addition of a third API would not knock the team off schedule.

In the Serendip-o-matic code, we set up a parallel infrastructure in order to query all the different APIs with the same search terms. We requested API keys from each of the APIs we intended to include and then coded request queries for each. Each API provides documentation to guide the construction of the query and each is different.[8] We mapped the fields we needed from the returned results into a common data structure that we could use for display without needing to handle each type of return result differently. The results are randomized so that items from all the different APIs are mixed together in the result set.

The third functional area of the code displays the results of the query to the user. This involves building the HTML framework and then adding the jQuery for the Isotope result display. There is also still some Python handling in this stage to make sure that results display consistently, such as resizing variable-sized or too-large images returned from the APIs.

While the development team coded furiously, the outreach team tackled other crucial building tasks. They crafted the promotional and release strategies. They served as user advocates and collaborated with design and development on elements of the user experience and the brand. Naming the tool proved far more arduous than anyone expected. Dougherty noted:

> If you lock a bunch of very talented scholars, designers, librarians, and programmers into a room and ask them to come up with catchy names for an innovative software product (and half or more have advanced degrees in literary studies), then you are very likely to spend about five hours considering over 120 nominations.[9]

Everyone felt the importance of the naming decision. It needed to drive our visual identity as well as reflect the whimsical feeling the team wanted for the tool. The team finally landed on a name—Serendip-o-matic—intended to evoke the automation or mechanization of surprise. We also spent time crafting the tagline—"Let your sources surprise you"—to succinctly communicate the tool's unique function. Our designer had even less time in her "building" step because of this delay, but managed to create our visual identity in the time remaining.

The project managers largely served as facilitators during Step 5, supporting the team members and filling in on tasks as needed. We also consulted with the team leaders to determine when a meeting was necessary to bring everyone up to speed or when a meeting should be cancelled because everyone needed time to focus on their work. We needed to strike a balance between discussion and construction.

Step 5 is the thing. It is the bulk of what the team has convened to accomplish. Coders, designers, and promoters need to collaborate closely, but there should be sufficient time allocated for each to focus on their individual tasks. Evaluate the addition and subtraction of features against the initial vision and the project schedule. After building the tool, the final step is to release and promote it widely.

Step 6: Release, Promote, Repeat

As One Week | One Tool ended, we released Serendip-o-matic to the world. The outreach team orchestrated a live broadcast of a Google Hangout in which the project managers interviewed community stakeholders as well as the project team.[10] We also released an open GitHub repository with our source code. The open code, paired with our extensible design, will allow additional developers to contribute to the project. In fact, just one day following the release of the tool, Tim Sherratt added functionality for Trove, a discovery tool focused on Australia and Australians.[11]

The One Week | One Tool team utilized Twitter (twitter.com) extensively throughout the process to communicate with our target user community, and after the release we received lots of feedback, from reviews to bug reports.[12] Serendip-o-matic development continues, although much more slowly as team members have returned to their daily routines. The team's primary challenges lie in the maintenance and continual improvement of the tool as well as implementing the scaffolding needed for other developers and institutions to contribute further.

In Step 6, the solution goes live. Communicate with stakeholders and ask for feedback. Think about how to continue improving the tool. Reflect on the process. Then start again with the next release.

Conclusions

Serendip-o-matic invites serendipity to the research process. One Week | One Tool invites us to think about the open source software development process from a planning perspective.

This process clearly worked within the set timeframe allocated in this institute. However, more research is needed to determine if the one-week time frame can be imposed on more traditional library development projects, with sustainable results. As I write this chapter, I am embarking on a new project at my home institution that will follow these six steps. I do not have one single week of dedicated time from twelve people, but instead one hour a week from four people for as long as we need (my first job, of course, is to set a hard deadline). I am curious if we can replicate the results in a more traditional environment.

In the meantime, Serendip-o-matic continues to connect collections to researchers, teachers, students, and librarians. Give it a try—let your sources surprise you with Serendip-o-matic.

*** *

Author's Note: As with any project, each team member comes away with his or her own unique experience. If you are interested in reading more about the trials and tribulations of building Serendip-o-matic, I recommend visiting the One Week | One Tool Zotero group (zotero.org/groups/oneweekonetool2013) or reading the blog entries cited below. Special thanks to Jack Dougherty, Rebecca Sutton Koeser, Amanda Visconti, and Joshua Tucker, who provided feedback on this chapter. To see more photos from One Week | One Tool, visit flickr.com/groups/2280986@N23.

Endnotes

1. "One Week | One Tool Team Launches Serendip-o-matic," *Roy Rosenzweig Center for History and New Media Blog Archive*, August 2, 2013, chnm.gmu.edu/news/one-week-one-tool-team-launches-serendip-o-matic.
2. In previous writings on Serendip-o-matic and One Week | One Tool (such as "The Process Is the Thing: Lessons from Serendip-o-matic Dh+lib," *Dh+lib* (blog), September 4, 2013, acrl.ala.org/dh/2013/09/04/the-process-is-the-thing-lessons-from-serendip-o-matic), I identified only five of these steps. However, the organizers of One Week | One Tool ensured our success by taking specific action before

and at the beginning of our institute, and it is important to consider this first step separately from the rest of the work.

3. One Week | One Tool team: Brian Croxall, Digital Humanities Strategist and Lecturer of English, Emory University; Jack Dougherty, Associate Professor of Educational Studies, Trinity College; Meghan Frazer, Digital Resources Curator, Knowlton School of Architecture, The Ohio State University; Scott Kleinman, Professor of English, California State University, Northridge; Rebecca Sutton Koeser, Software Engineer, Emory University; Ray Palin, Librarian and Teacher, Sunapee Middle High School, Sunapee, NH; Amy Papaelias, Assistant Professor of Art, SUNY New Paltz; Mia Ridge, PhD Candidate in Digital Humanities, Open University, U.K., Chair of the U.K.'s Museums Computer Group; Eli Rose, Computer Science/Creative Writing Major, Oberlin College; Amanda Visconti, PhD candidate, University of Maryland English Department; Scott Williams, Collections Database Administrator, Penn Museum; Amrys Williams, Visiting Assistant Professor, Department of History, Wesleyan University.

4. We used IdeaScale for this purpose, which allows for voting and comments, but does require users to create or link an account to provide feedback (oneweekone tool.ideascale.com).

5. Mia Ridge, "Open Objects: And so It Begins: Day Two of OWOT," Open Objects (blog), July 31, 2013, openobjects.blogspot.com/2013/07/and-so-it-begins-day-two-of-owot.html.

6. For more information on libraries used, please see the Serendip-o-matic GitHub repository (github.com/chnm/serendipomatic).

7. Ridge, "Open Objects: And so It Begins: Day Two of OWOT."

8. "Digital Public Library of America API," accessed September 22, 2014, dp.la/info/developers/codex; "Europeana API: Introduction," accessed September 22, 2014, www.europeana.eu/portal/api-introduction.html; "Flickr Services API Documentation," accessed September 22, 2014, www.flickr.com/services/api.

9. Jack Dougherty, "Metaphorical Learning Moments at One Week One Tool, Day 3," Jack Dougherty (blog), August 1, 2013, commons.trincoll.edu/jackdougherty/2013/08/01/owot-3.

10. The archived broadcast is available at oneweekonetool.org.

11. "About Trove," *Trove*, accessed September 22, 2014, trove.nla.gov.au/general/about.

12. The project team and those in the community following the project tweeted using #owot and as of September 2014, the tweets are still available at twitter.com/search?q=%23owot&src=hash.

Websites

The websites here are listed in alphabetical order by chapter. All of these links can be found online at mashups.web2learning.net where they will be kept up-to-date.

Chapter 1

CloudWork, cloudwork.com
Diigo, diigo.com
Dropbox, dropbox.com
elastic.io, elastic.io
Evernote, evernote.com
Feedly, feedly.com
Google Calendar, calendar.google.com
Google Drive, drive.google.com
Google News alert for *library OR libraries*, news.google.co.uk/news/
    feeds?hl=en&gl=uk&q=library+OR+libraries&um=1&ie=UTF-
    8&output=rss
IFTTT, ifttt.com
IFTTT Channels, ifttt.com/channels
IFTTT Recipes, ifttt.com/recipes
LinkedIn, linkedin.com
Pocket, getpocket.com
SlideShare, slideshare.net
We Wired Web, wewiredweb.com
Zapier, zapier.com

Chapter 2

ArcGIS, arcgis.com
Esri, esri.com

Facebook, facebook.com

GeoCommons, geocommons.com

Google Drive, drive.google.com

Google Earth, earth.google.com

Google Earth API, developers.google.com/earth

Google Earth API Developer's Guide, developers.google.com/
earth/documentation

Google Earth Plug-in, google.com/earth/explore/products/
plugin.html

Google Maps, maps.google.com

Google Maps API, developers.google.com/maps

KML Interactive Sampler, kml-samples.googlecode.com/svn/trunk/
interactive/index.html

MangoMap, mangomap.com

OpenStreetMap, openstreetmap.org

Scribble Maps, scribblemaps.com

SIMILE Exhibit, simile-widgets.org/exhibit

SIMILE Widgets: Getting Started, simile-widgets.org/wiki/
Getting_Started

Sonoma County Timeline, library.sonoma.edu/regional/
timeline.php

Story Maps, storymaps.arcgis.com

Story Maps – Apps, storymaps.arcgis.com/en/app-list

Twitter, twitter.com

Web-Source.net HTML Codes, web-source.net/html_codes_chart.
htm

ZeeMaps, zeemaps.com

Chapter 3

Freebase, freebase.com

Google Groups – OpenRefine, groups.google.com/forum/?from
groups#!forum/openrefine

Google Refine 2.0 – Introduction (1 of 3) [video], youtube.com/
watch?v=B70J_H_zAWM

Gource, code.google.com/p/gource

Jorum, jorum.ac.uk

OER Visualisation Project: Fin (day 40.5), mashe.hawksey.info/2012/
02/oer-visualisation-project-fin-day-40-5

Open Archives Initiative Protocol for Metadata Harvesting,
openarchives.org/OAI/openarchivesprotocol.html#

Open Archives Initiative Protocol for Metadata Harvesting –
ListIdentifiers, openarchives.org/OAI/openarchivesprotocol.
html#ListIdentifiers

OpenDOAR (Directory of Open Access Repositories), opendoar.org

OpenDOAR – Jorum Open, opendoar.org/id/1834/

OpenRefine, openrefine.org

OpenRefine Wiki, github.com/OpenRefine/OpenRefine/wiki

OpenRefine Wiki – Google Refine Expression Language (GREL),
github.com/OpenRefine/OpenRefine/wiki/Google-refine-
expression-language

OpenRefine Wiki– GREL Other Functions, github.com/OpenRefine/
OpenRefine/wiki/GREL-Other-Functions#jsoup-html-
parsing-functions

OpenRefine(ing) and Visualizing Library Data [video],
youtube.com/watch?v=v4HQM6qk6kM

Chapter 4

Amazon, amazon.com

Google, google.com

Google Books, books.google.com

Google Scholar, scholar.google.com

HathiTrust Digital Library, hathitrust.org

Internet Archive, archive.org

LibX, libx.org

Umlaut, github.com/team-umlaut/umlaut

Chapter 5

CVS (Concurrent Versions System), cvs.nongnu.org

Drupal, drupal.org

Drupal API, api.drupal.org

Drupal – Calendar , drupal.org/project/calendar

Drupal – Date, drupal.org/project/date

DRUPAL4LIB List Archives, listserv.uic.edu/archives/drupal
4lib.html

Evanced Events, evancedsolutions.com/support/events

Chapter 6

Chapter 7

Using the Google Spreadsheets Data API to Build a Recommended Reading List – Code Words, alatechsource.org/blog/2012/05/using-the-google-spreadsheets-data-api-to-build-a-recommended-reading-list-code-words.h

WCC Library History Guide, library.whatcom.ctc.edu/guide/home/history

WCC Library Philosophy Guide, library.whatcom.ctc.edu/guide/home/philosophy

WCC Library Sustainability Guide, library.whatcom.ctc.edu/guide/home/sustainability

WordPress, wordpress.org

WordPress Plugin Directory – CSS & JavaScript Toolbox, wordpress.org/plugins/css-JavaScript-toolbox

WorldCat Search API, oclc.org/developer/services/worldcat-search-api

Chapter 8

@UBTestbot Twitterbot Pipe, pipes.yahoo.com/ubtestbot/ubtestbot_twitterbot_oct2013

GitHub, github.com

IFTTT, ifttt.com

IFTTT – Informal Experiment in Replying to Search Queries Directed at Library Databases via Twitter, ifttt.com/recipes/122007

pipe2py, github.com/ggaughan/pipe2py

pipes engine, pipes-engine.appspot.com

Yahoo! Pipes, pipes.yahoo.com

Chapter 9

AIDS posters, goo.gl/cHWBdR

Batch Geocoding, doogal.co.uk/BatchGeocoding.php

Geospatial Engagement and Community Outreach event, Geospatial in the Cultural Heritage Domain, geco.blogs.edina.ac.uk/events/geospatial-in-the-cultural-heritage-domain-past-present-and-future

Google Drive, drive.google.com

Google Fusion Tables, tables.googlelabs.com

Google Maps, maps.google.com

Google Maps Engine, mapsengine.google.com

The Guardian Datablog, theguardian.com/news/datablog

The Guardian Datablog – The Poverty and Deprivation Map of London, guardian.co.uk/uk/datablog/interactive/2012/apr/12/ poverty-deprivation-london-map

Items on loan to other exhibitions, goo.gl/LyMKm5

MapAList, mapalist.com

Medical Officer of Health Reports at the Wellcome Library, goo.gl/Ez3Tfl

OldSF map, oldsf.org

Putting Medical Officer of Health Reports on the Map, blog.wellcomelibrary.org/2011/03/putting-medical-officer- of-health-reports-on-the-map

Wellcome Library, wellcomelibrary.org

Chapter 10

Active Shelves – Extending the Book at Oslo Public Library [video], vimeo.com/68687814

Bibliographic Ontology Specification, bibliontology.com

Bokanbefalinger, anbefalinger.deichman.no

Bokelskere.no, bokelskere.no

Bokkilden, bokkilden.no

Core FRBR Concepts in RDF, vocab.org/frbr/core.html

Digital Development Team at Oslo Public Library, github. com/digibib

Dublin Core Metadata Terms, dublincore.org/ documents/2012/06/14/dcmi-terms/?v=terms

FaBiO, purl.org/spar/fabio

FOAF (Friend of a Friend) project, foaf-project.org

GeoNames Ontology, geonames.org/ontology/documentation.html

Goodreads, goodreads.com

Lexvo, lexvo.org

MARC2RDF, github.com/digibib/MARC2RDF

NoveList, ebscohost.com/novelist

REST API for Deichman's RDF's store, github.com/digibib/data. deichman.api or github.com/digibib/data.deichman.api/blob/ master/README.md

RFIDGEEK, github.com/digibib/rfidgeek
SKOS, w3.org/2004/02/skos
Virtuoso Universal Server, virtuoso.openlinksw.com

Chapter 11

Chrome DevTools, developers.google.com/chrome-developer-tools
Google Apps Script, developers.google.com/apps-script
Google Docs Power You Didn't Know About, appsumo.com/google-docs-unleashed
Google Drive, drive.google.com
Mashed Library – Menu Suggestions, mashedlibrary.com/wiki-content/cookbook/menu_suggestions
Mashed Library – Wiki, mashedlibrary.com/groups/wiki
Overview of Google Apps Script, developers.google.com/apps-script/overview
Wikipedia, wikipedia.org
Wikipedia Current Awareness Service, goo.gl/ZsmjRY
XPath, developer.mozilla.org/en/docs/Xpath

Chapter 12

Exploring the Trail of Tears, geography.wisc.edu/faculty/roth/interactive/TrailofTears_DemoVersion.swf
FusionCharts, fusioncharts.com
Gapminder – Health and Wealth of Nations, goo.gl/wpMr69
Google Maps, maps.google.com
Google Maps JavaScript API, developers.google.com/maps/documentation/javascript
PubMed, ncbi.nlm.nih.gov/pubmed
VICOLEX, abuchel.apmaths.uwo.ca/~obuchel/maps/VICOLEX.php

Chapter 13

Facebook, facebook.com
Flickr, flickr.com
Fusion Tables Layer Wizard, fusion-tables-api-samples.googlecode.com/svn/trunk/FusionTablesLayerWizard/src/index.html

Government of Ontario – Carpool Lots, ontario.ca/driving-and-roads/carpool-lots

Google Fusion Tables, tables.googlelabs.com

Google Images, images.google.com

Google Maps, maps.google.com

GRASS GIS, grass.osgeo.org

Instagram, instagram.com

Michael Geist [blog], michaelgeist.ca

Pinterest, pinterest.com

Scholars GeoPortal, geo2.scholarsportal.info

Shape Escape, shpescape.com

Chapter 14

Computer Availability Map Code, coastal.edu/library/maps/availability/zipfiles/availabilityfiles.zip

Kimbel Library Computer Availability Map, coastal.edu/library/maps/availability

LabMaps, labstats.com/Products/LabMaps

LibQUAL+, libqual.org

Chapter 15

CONTENTdm, contentdm.org

Dropbox, dropbox.com

DSpace, dspace.org

Flickr, flickr.com

Google Drive, drive.google.com

Google Maps, maps.google.com

Houston Public Library Houston Area Digital Archives, digital.houstonlibrary.org

Houston Public Library Houston Area Digital Archives – Timeline, digital.houstonlibrary.org/timeline/index.html

Houston Public Library Houston Area Digital Archives – When Camelot Came to Houston, digital.houstonlibrary.org/timeline/kennedy.html

Omeka, omeka.org

Photobucket, photobucket.com

Shared Shelf, artstor.org/shared-shelf/s-html/shared-shelf-home. shtml

TimelineJS, timeline.knightlab.com

Twitter, twitter.com

Vimeo, vimeo.com

Chapter 16

Amazon Product Advertising API, affiliate-program.amazon.com/ gp/advertising/api/detail/main.html

Amazon.com Product Advertising API License Agreement, affiliate-program.amazon.com/gp/advertising/api/detail/agreement.html

BookMeUp @ the Library, lib.montana.edu/beta/bookme

BookMeUp @ the Library – Where, lib.montana.edu/beta/bookme/ index?view=where

CSS Media Queries, goo.gl/AEhbke

Device APIs Articles, hacks.mozilla.org/category/device-apis

Device APIs Requirements, w3.org/TR/dap-api-reqs

Geolocation API Specification, w3.org/TR/geolocation-API

GitHub – Jason Clark, github.com/jasonclark

HTML5 Geolocation, w3schools.com/html/html5_geolocation.asp

HTML5 Please, html5please.com

HTML5 Rocks, html5rocks.com

Leverage Browser Caching, goo.gl/of5Crs

mapFAST, oclc.org/research/activities/mapfast.html?urlm=159681

Open Library Covers API, openlibrary.org/dev/docs/api/covers

WorldCat Search API, oclc.org/developer/documentation/worldcat-search-api/using-api

Chapter 17

Bassi-Veratti Collection, bv.stanford.edu

Blacklight, projectblacklight.org

Code4Lib, code4lib.org

Facebook, facebook.com

Fedora Commons, fedora-commons.org

Flickr, flickr.com

GeoNames, geonames.org

Google, google.com

Hydra, projecthydra.org

Mashup (Web Application Hybrid), en.wikipedia.org/wiki/
  Mashup_%28web_application_hybrid%29

MODS Display, github.com/sul-dlss/mods_display

MODS Parsing Gem, github.com/sul-dlss/mods

Netflix, netflix.com

ORCID, orcid.org

SearchWorks, searchworks.stanford.edu

Solr, lucene.apache.org/solr

Stanford Specific Parsings of MODS Metadata, github.com/sul-dlss/
  stanford-mods

Chapter 18

Koha Library Software, koha-community.org

Libki, libki.org

Chapter 19

ByWater Solutions, bywatersolutions.com

Koha Library Software, koha-community.org

Koha API, github.com/reeset/koha_api

Koha/svc/HTTP API, wiki.koha-community.org/wiki/Koha_/svc/_
  HTTP_API

MarcEdit, marcedit.reeset.net

MarcEdit/Koha Demo, marcedit.kohacatalog.com

MARCEDIT-L List, listserv.gmu.edu/cgi-bin/wa?A0=marcedit-l

MarcEdit User Wiki, marcedit.reeset.net/wiki

MarcEdit: Using the MARC SQL Explorer [video], goo.gl/ubNxvE

SRU – Search/Retrieval via URL, loc.gov/standards/sru/simple.html

Chapter 20

MailChimp, mailchimp.com

Stack Overflow, stackoverflow.com

Yahoo! Pipes, pipes.yahoo.com

Chapter 21

Digital Public Library of America, dp.la
Europeana, europeana.eu
Flickr – App Garden, flickr.com/services/api
Flickr – Commons, flickr.com/commons
Flickr – One Week | One Tool, flickr.com/groups/2280986@N23
GitHub, github.com
Google Drive, drive.google.com
One Week | One Tool, oneweekonetool.org
OneWeekOneTool2013, zotero.org/groups/oneweekonetool2013
Serendip-o-matic, serendipomatic.org
Twitter, twitter.com
Zotero, zotero.org

Glossary

A

AJAX. Asynchronous JavaScript and XML. Programming language comprised of JavaScript and XML; used for creating dynamic web applications.

Apache. An open source web server.

API. Application Programming Interface. Spells out how to formulate a query for the data from a web service.

applications/apps. Small, dedicated software programs that are focused on singular tasks. Mobile apps run specifically on mobile devices such as phone and tablets.

Atom. A way of delivering website updates in XML.

B

bookmarklet. A JavaScript function or set of functions saved to the browser as bookmarks or favorites.

C

caching. The practice of storing files locally or placing a timestamp on a file to dictate if or when the file should be downloaded; improves performance by limiting the use of bandwidth to move files across the network (as in browser caching).

CMS. Content Management System.

CSS. Cascading Style Sheets.

CSV. Comma Separated Values. A text file where each value is separated by a comma.

CVS. Concurrent Versions System. A open source system used to keep track of file revisions for projects that are worked on my multiple authors.

D

DSL. Domain-Specific Language.

Dublin Core. A metadata schema made up of 15 elements that offer expanded cataloging information that was created out of a cooperative venture involving academic institutions.

E

EXML Extended XML.

F

FRBR. Functional Requirements for Bibliographic Records. A conceptual entity-relationship model developed by the International Federation of Library Associations and Institutions that relates user tasks of retrieval and access in online library catalogues and bibliographic databases from a user's perspective.

G

Geocoding. Taking an address (typically a street address, city name, or ZIP code/postcode) and converting it to map coordinates.

Git. An open source system used to keep track of file revisions for projects that are worked on by multiple authors.

H

hashtag. A keyword or phrase, usually preceded by a hash, pound, or number sign (#), used to indentify the top of a post, link, or other web content.

HTML. Hypertext Markup Language. A programming language used to format and display information to be read as webpages in a web browser.

HTTP. Hypertext Transfer Protocol.

I

iCal. A file format that allows users to send meeting requests and tasks via email or by sharing files with an .ics extension.

ILS. Integrated Library System.

J

JavaScript. An object-oriented computer programming language commonly used to create interactive effects within web browsers.

JSON. JavaScript Object Notation. A text-based, human-readable format use for representing simple data structures and arrays. Many web services make their data available in JSON format.

L

LAMP. Linux, Apache, MySQL, PHP.

link resolver. A tool that gets the user from a citation in a licensed database that does not include full text to an appropriate full-text copy licensed by the institution on a different vendor platform.

Linux. An open source operating system.

M

MARC. Standards for the representation and communication of bibliographic and related information in machine-readable form.

mashup. A web application that uses content from more than one source to create a single new service displayed in a single graphical interface; originally comes from pop music, where people seamlessly combine music from one song with the vocal track from another, thereby mashing them together to create something new.

media queries. Provides a means to check for device display widths, heights, and resolutions. The values returned enable you to create a different layout or "look and feel" for your app (e.g., based on the size of a screen).

MeSH. Medical Subject Headings.

metadata. Data that describes data.

MODS. Metadata Object Description Schema.

MySQL. Open-source relational database management system.

O

OAI-PMH. Open Archives Initiative Protocol for Metadata Harvesting. A protocol used to harvest (or collect) the metadata descriptions of the records in an archive so that services can be built using metadata from many archives.

OPAC. Online Public Access Catalog.

OpenURL. A standardized format of Uniform Resource Locator (URL) intended to enable internet users to more easily find a copy of a resource that they are allowed to access. Although OpenURL can be used with any kind of resource on the internet, it is most heavily used by libraries to help connect patrons to subscription content.

P

Perl. Open source programming language used for web development.

PHP. Open source programming language used for web development.

plug-in. A small program to add additional functionality to an application.

PostgresSQL. An open-source object-relational database management system.

PURL. Permanent URL or persistent links.

R

RDF. Resource Description Framework. A means to model information on the web by assigning resources unique identifiers (generally by use of a *uniform resource identifier*) and describing the relationships between that resource and other resources via a structure known as triples.

Regex. Regular Expression. A set of characters used in searching for varying forms of strings.

REST: Representational State Transfer.

RFID. Radio-Frequency Identification. The wireless non-contact use of radio-frequency electromagnetic fields to transfer data for the purposes of automatically identifying and tracking tags attached to objects.

RSS. Really Simple Syndication. A way of delivering website updates in XML.

Ruby. A dynamic, open source object-oriented programming language.

Ruby on Rails. An open source web framework.

S

screen scrape. Information intended exclusively for human consumption extracted from a webpage and sent as input to a computer program. This method can be used to gather information from sites that do no provide readily available APIs to their data.

SIP. Session Initiation Protocol.

SOAP. Originally stood for Simple Object Access Protocol, a definition that is no longer used, relies on international standards and protocols and has been adopted primarily in the enterprise world. SOAP uses HTTP as the transport protocol for exchanging information, but it requires that both the requests sent by the service consumer and the answers returned by the service provider be wrapped in an XML envelope.

Solr. An open source enterprise search platform from the Apache Lucene project.

SPARQL. SPARQL Protocol and RDF Query Language. An RDF query language able to retrieve and manipulate data stored in RDF format.

SQL. Structured Query Language.

SRU. Search/Retrieve via URL. Standard search protocol for internet search queries, utilizing Contextual Query Language (CQL).

SRW. Search and Retrieve Web Service. Provides a SOAP interface to queries to augment the URL interface provided by its companion protocol SRU.

T

TOS. Terms of Service.
Tweet. A message sent via Twitter.

U

URI. Uniform Resource Identifier. A string of letters, numbers, and symbols used to identify or name a resource on the internet. A URL is an example of a URI.
URL. Uniform Resource Locator. The address of a page on the internet.
URL encoding. Also known as percent encoding, a technique used to convert special characters in a URL to a valid format. For example, the space between words in compound terms like *solar energy* should be encoded as %20 ("solar%20energy").

W

web service. A technology that enables information and communication exchange between different applications. Web services are based on a conceptual model that has a service provider, which is an application that makes certain information available or that provides the capability to perform certain operations, and a service consumer, which will make use of the information or the services.
widget. A snippet of code that allows for embedding content from a web service onto your website.

X

XML. Extensible Markup Language. A markup language for expressing and transporting structured data; as its name implies, it is extensible in that users can define their own elements.

XPath. XML Path Language. A query language for selecting nodes from an XML document.

Z

Z39.50: An established client-server protocol for searching and retrieving information.

About the Contributors

Scott Bacon is the Web Services and Emerging Technologies Librarian at Coastal Carolina University's Kimbel Library. He is the primary developer and administrator of the library website, web applications, digital collections, and mobile interfaces. He also identifies, assesses, and implements emerging technologies that increase and enhance access to library resources and services, such as discovery services, database-driven applications, and content management systems. He lives in Surfside Beach with his wife and two sons.

Aside from being a map lover and trivia enthusiast, **Francine Berish** is a Reference and Instructional Librarian at George Brown College in Toronto. Before pursuing librarianship, Francine specialized in Urban Systems and Geographic Information Systems at McGill University. Her current research delves into the intersection of these fields, focusing on geospatial data applications and access. Francine is a self-described information pusher and lover of the Canadian outdoors. She can be reached at francine.berish@gmail.com.

Olga Buchel has a PhD in Library and Information Science from the Faculty of Information and Media Studies, Western University. Currently she works as a data analyst/visualization designer at Counting Opinions (SQUIRE) Ltd., a company that provides evidence-based support for library management. She is also an adjunct assistant professor at Western University. She teaches Geospatial Data. Her research centers on map-based visualizations of document collections and the ways these visualizations can support higher-order cognitive activities such as decision making, sensemaking, visual analytics, Big Data, knowledge discovery, and serendipitous discoveries. In the past she worked at the Alexandria Digital Library at the University of California, which was the forerunner of Google Maps.

Jason Clark is an associate professor and Head of Digital Access and Web Services at Montana State University Library where he builds digital library applications and sets digital content strategies. He writes and presents on a broad range of topics including mobile design and development, web services and APIs, metadata and digitization, search engine optimization, interface design, and application development. When he doesn't have metadata on the brain, Jason likes to hike the mountains of Montana with his wife, Jennifer, their daughter, Piper, and their dog, Oakley. You can find Jason online by following him on Twitter at twitter.com/jaclark, catching up with him on Facebook at facebook.com/jasclark, or checking out his occasional thoughts and code samples on his site at jasonclark.info.

Eva Dodsworth is the Geospatial Data Services Librarian at the University of Waterloo library, where she specializes in teaching GIS and map-related content to the university community. Her interests include historical cartographic research and teaching geoweb applications and historical GIS. Eva is also a part-time online instructor for a number of library schools and continuing education organizations, where she teaches the use of GIS technology in libraries. Eva has published *Getting Started With GIS: A LITA Guide* (2012, Neal-Schuman) and is currently co-authoring a book on historical cartographic material.

Meghan Frazer is the Manager of Member and User Services for Ohio-LINK. She served as co-project manager for Serendip-o-matic while employed as the Digital Resources Curator for the Knowlton School of Architecture at The Ohio State University. Her professional interests include user experience design, open source software development in libraries, and digital collection management. She can reached via email at meghanfrazer11@gmail.com or on Twitter at @meghanfrazer.

Gary Green graduated in 1994 from Manchester Metropolitan University with a degree in information and library management. He currently works for Surrey County Council Public Libraries, where as Technical Librarian he supports development of the catalogue, EDI, and web and social media services. He is a founder member of Voices for the Library, a national advocacy campaign for public libraries and the staff who work in them. He can be reached at ggstopflat@gmail.com.

Kyle M. Hall received his MS in Information Technology from Edinboro University (PA). He has been fulfilling the IT needs of librarians for over a decade at the Crawford County Federated Library System as an IT specialist and Koha developer. His work has not only included enhancing Koha itself but also authorship of the Koha Offline Circulation tool and the maintenance of the Koha Virtual Appliance. He is also the sole author of Libki.

Sean Hannan is a Senior Web Developer at The Sheridan Libraries, Johns Hopkins University. He is responsible for library websites and discovery systems as well as helping them make sense to folks. A programmer since the age of 7 and library enthusiast since Dr. Seuss, Sean holds an IT degree from the Rochester Institute of Technology and a library degree from the University of British Columbia. He can be reached at shannan@jhu.edu.

Martin Hawksey has extensive experience supporting innovation in teaching and learning within further and higher education. His interests cover multiple aspects of open education and digital scholarship, his knowledge of social networks and analytics being applied in a number of varying contexts. In 2012, Martin produced a number of data visualization recipes for the Jisc UKOER Programme. Martin maintains the MASHe blog (mashe.hawksey.info). He can be reached at m.hawksey@gmail.com.

Celine Kelly is the Knowledge Services Manager with A&L Goodbody solicitors, one of the top Irish corporate law firms. Celine manages the firm's Knowledge Centre and legal research service to ensure the firm's lawyers have access to the right information when they need it. Celine has a particular interest in the changing nature of legal information in the digital environment and in how these changes can be applied for the benefit of the firm and clients. She can be reached at clkelly@algoodbody.com.

Bianca Kramer holds a PhD in neurobiology and works at Utrecht University Library as subject specialist in Life Sciences and Medicine. She is involved in developing elearning, teaching information literacy, and consulting on search strategies for systematic reviews and meta-analyses. She has set up in-house training programs for Web 2.0 and social media. She can be reached at b.m.r.kramer@uu.nl.

Stefan Langer is the Web Developer at Worthington Libraries. He has worked in library technology for nearly 10 years. He developed and maintains the Evanced Events Importer Drupal module. He can be reached at slanger@worthingtonlibraries.org.

Rowena McKernan is a community college librarian in Washington state and has been busy advocating for increased use of open source technologies for libraries. She loves developing websites with WordPress and was thrilled to be able to build the Whatcom Community College Library's subject guides on that platform. She also works to increase the use of open educational resources in higher education through her work for the Open Course Library project (opencourselibrary.org) and can be found most quarters teaching Information Literacy skills wide variety of students.

Natalie Pollecutt works in Digital Services at the Wellcome Library in London. She has been experimenting on the web since she first started working in libraries 15 years ago. Natalie likes to discover new ways of exploring library data and sharing her findings. She can be reached at n.pollecutt@wellcome.ac.uk.

Terry Reese is the Head of Digital Initiatives at The Ohio State University. He had many roles during his library career, working as a cataloger, developer, and project planner. He is responsible for the development and support of MarcEdit, a popular metadata editing tool, used by metadata specialists around the globe. Terry publishes and speaks often on topics related to metadata, discovery, and digital libraries.

Asgeir Rekkavik is a librarian at Oslo Public Library. He has a degree in Library and Information Science, with supplementary education in such diverse fields as history, literature science, mathematics, physics, and astronomy. He has a particular interest in linked data, ontology modeling, and the semantic web. He can be reached at asgeir.rekkavik@ kul.oslo.kommune.no.

Kara Reuter is the Digital Library Manager at Worthington Libraries. She has developed and managed digital libraries for young people and adults in school, academic, and public library settings for more than 10 years. She can be reached at kreuter@worthingtonlibraries.org.

Jonathan Rochkind is a software engineer with an MLIS working at Johns Hopkins University. He has made significant contributions to library-centered open source projects including Blacklight, Xerxes, and Umlaut. He believes libraries are important as civic information agencies whose interests are aligned with those of their users. He can be reached via his blog at bibwild.wordpress.com.

Bess Sadler is the Manager for Application Development in the Digital Library Systems and Services group at Stanford University Library. She is one of the co-founders of Project Blacklight (project blacklight.org). She has spent over a decade working on digital libraries and related digital humanities projects, with a particular focus on enabling better discovery and navigation for digital collections. Bess also contributed to a chapter in the first edition of *Library Mashups* and is pleased with how far we've come since those early days of mashup practice in libraries.

Michael P. Sauers is currently the Technology Innovation Librarian for the Nebraska Library Commission in Lincoln, Nebraska, and has been training librarians in technology for more than 15 years. He can be found online at travelinlibrarian.info.

Jeanette Claire Sewell is a Cataloging and Metadata Librarian at the Houston Public Library. She is never short of creative ideas and enjoys blogging and presenting about her various projects for the library. When not dreaming about books to add to her personal collection, Jeanette spends her time crafting, updating her Tumblr sites, and petting cats. Follow her on twitter @clairesayswhat. She can be reached at jeanette.sewell@houstontx.gov.

Sarah Simpkin is a GIS and Geography Librarian at the University of Ottawa. She holds an Honours BSc in Physical Geography, GIS, and Biology from the University of Toronto, and she completed her

MLIS at Western University in 2012. Sarah is a founding member of SimCoLab, a hackerspace in Barrie, Ontario, and enjoys working on art and electronics projects in her spare time. She can be reached at sarah.simpkin@uottawa.ca.

Anne-Lena Westrum is a Project Manager at Oslo Public Library. She has a degree in Computer Science and Interaction Design, with supplementary education in project management. She is currently coordinating the Digital Development Team for the new main library in Oslo. She can be reached at anne-lena.westrum@kul.oslo. kommune.no.

About the Editor

Nicole C. Engard is the vice president of education at ByWater Solutions. Her primary role at ByWater Solutions is to educate librarians about open source software with a focus on the Koha ILS. In addition to her daily responsibilities, Nicole keeps the library community up to date on web technologies via her website "What I Learned Today ..." (www.web2learning.net) and volunteers as a community moderator on opensource.com. In 2007, Nicole was named one of *Library Journal*'s Movers & Shakers. She is the editor of *Library Mashups* (2009, Information Today, Inc.) and the author of *Practical Open Source Software for Libraries* (2010, Chandos Inc.). She also worked on the second edition of *The Accidental Systems Librarian* with Rachel Singer Gordon (2012, Information Today, Inc.). Nicole lives in Austin, TX, with her two shelties, Coda and Beau.

Index

More Great Books From Information Today, Inc.

Educational Technology for the Global Village

Worldwide Innovation and Best Practices

Edited by Les Lloyd and Gabriel I. Barreneche

Editors Les Lloyd and Gabriel Barreneche present an eye-opening look at projects that are innovating with technology to improve education and, indeed, the very quality of people's lives around the world. From collaborative learning communities and social networks to Web 2.0 tools, MOOCs, and mobiles, a dozen case studies demonstrate tech initiatives that teach students to think and act globally while helping to close the education gap between developed and developing nations. The book describes how students and institutions can reuse "obsolete" technology in places where it will be "new" and the impacts of such efforts on communities abroad. If you are interested in service-learning, internationalization, or study abroad—or if you are just looking for a way to keep your organization's old technology out of landfills—*Educational Technology for the Global Village* is sure to inform and inspire you.

216 pp/softbound/ISBN 978-1-57387-481-6/$39.50
ebook also available

The Accidental Data Scientist

Big Data Applications and Opportunities for Librarians and Information Professionals

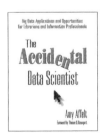

By Amy L. Affelt
Foreword by Thomas H. Davenport

Harvard Business Review recently tagged the data scientist—described as "a high-ranking professional with the training and curiosity to make discoveries in the world of big data"—with having the "sexiest job of the 21st century." Librarians and information professionals have always worked with data in order to meet the information needs of their constituents. Thus, "Big Data" is not a new concept for them, although it is spawning new approaches along with a language all its own. In *The Accidental Data Scientist*, Amy Affelt shows information professionals how to leverage their skills and training to master emerging tools, techniques, and vocabulary; create mission-critical Big Data research deliverables; and discover rewarding new career opportunities by embracing their inner data scientist.

224 pp/softbound/ISBN 978-1-57387-511-0/$39.50
ebook also available

The Cybrarian's Web 2

An A–Z Guide to Free Social Media Tools, Apps, and Other Resources

By Cheryl Ann Peltier-Davis

Volume 2 of Cheryl Peltier-Davis's popular guide presents 61 more free tech tools and shows how they can be successfully applied in libraries and information centers. Written for info pros who want to innovate, improve, and create new library services, Volume 2 combines real-world examples with practical insights and out-of-the-box thinking. You'll discover an array of great web resources and mobile apps supporting the latest trends in cloud storage, crowdfunding, ebooks, makerspaces, MOOCs, news aggregation, self-publishing, visualization, social bookmarking, video conferencing, wearable technology, and more—all tailored to the needs of libraries and the communities they serve.

480 pp/softbound/ISBN 978-1-57387-512-7/$49.50
ebook also available

Buying and Selling Information

A Guide for Information Professionals and Salespeople to Build Mutual Success

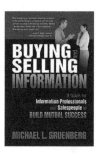

By Michael L. Gruenberg

Both sides of the negotiating table are represented in this practical and much-needed guide by Michael Gruenberg, a veteran of the electronic information field. With more than 30 years selling information to a wide variety of libraries, Gruenberg's time-tested tips, techniques, and strategies will be welcomed by information professionals and sales professionals alike. The author's personal stories are geared to helping librarians and salespeople understand what the "other guy" is grappling with in order to achieve the best possible outcome for everyone. The insights and knowledge presented in *Buying and Selling Information* shed light on the importance of relationships, some harsh realities of the business world, and the "music" of the sales experience.

224 pp/softbound/ISBN 978-1-57387-478-6/$49.50
ebook also available